*MINNESOTA SYMPOSIA ON*
*CHILD PSYCHOLOGY, VOLUME 5*

# MINNESOTA SYMPOSIA ON CHILD PSYCHOLOGY
## *Volume 5*

JOHN P. HILL, EDITOR

THE UNIVERSITY OF MINNESOTA PRESS • MINNEAPOLIS

*Library of Congress Catalog Card Number: 67-30520*
*ISBN 0-8166-0614-5*


PUBLISHED IN GREAT BRITAIN, INDIA, AND PAKISTAN BY THE OXFORD
UNIVERSITY PRESS, LONDON, BOMBAY, AND KARACHI, AND IN CANADA BY
THE COPP CLARK PUBLISHING CO. LIMITED, TORONTO

# Preface

THE PAPERS in this volume are based upon the 1970 Minnesota Symposium on Child Psychology, the fifth in the series which began in 1966. With the publication of this book, twenty-nine papers from forty-five contributors representing twenty-two universities, federal research agencies, and private research institutes will have been made available to readers in child psychology and related fields. Departments of anthropology, education, human development, pediatrics, psychiatry, psychology, social relations, and sociology, and institutes and laboratories of child psychology, child development, human development, and human learning have been represented.

In fourteen programs of research, populations of children have been studied who are other than white, urban, American, and living in intact families: in five, various social classes are contrasted; in three, institutionalized children are the subjects of study; in five, the special population consists of emotionally disturbed or mentally retarded children; in two, cross-national comparisons are involved; and, in three, the subjects are nonhuman offspring and their parents. Seven of the twenty-nine papers span two or more periods of the life cycle; five focus upon infancy; five upon early childhood; eight upon middle childhood; and two each on adolescence and adulthood. When it comes to methodology, three crosscutting variables apply: longitudinal versus cross-sectional, experimental versus differential, and field versus laboratory. Twelve of the programs are longitudinal; fifteen are experimental; and nine consist in field studies.

Substantive trends are more difficult to characterize. With some double and a rare triple classification or two permitted, seven of the papers have featured perceptual development and eight cognitive development; twelve have dealt with problems of learning, early experience, and behavior modification; and eighteen are classifiable within the broad domain of personality, social influence, and social development. In six of the twenty-nine papers research is reported which is either applied or has immediate practical applications. But this does not tell much of the story. Original, programmatic work in the social and personality development areas has seemed to be increasingly difficult to locate over this five-year period; with the exception of work on behavior modification, the same generalization would hold for the kind of work on children's learning which brought behavior theory and the developmental psychology establishment together for the first time in the 1950's. Commensurately, programmatic work in perceptual and cognitive development is more easily located. Whatever the substantive trends, a look backward over the twenty-nine articles is testimony to the heterogeneity and heterodoxy that has been claimed for child psychology in these prefatory remarks over the years. Good programmatic research is going on in many areas of inquiry, and it is being carried out in a variety of ways with many different populations of children. Our invitational policy has been to represent this diversity within the important constraint that an able investigator be at that point in his program of research where an integrative review would be helpful to him and useful to others. That this volume is typical of the series is suggested by the topics covered — cross-modal perception, hypnotizability, infant testing, aggression, models for parent and child behavior, and space perception — but is best seen by reading the papers themselves.

The proposition that the effectiveness of an exploratory method is due to the way it samples the properties of a stimulus does not sound very revolutionary until its implications for long entrenched modality-specific views of information gathering are considered. Jacqueline Goodnow offers such a consideration in her contribution to this volume. One of the developmental guises of the modality-specific view is that a given modality is more effective than another at a given stage of development (e.g., Piaget's sensorimotor period). In another developmental manifestation, preference for a given modality (often vision) in information gathering is held to be associated with maturity. By cutting across modalities, the stimulus sampling conception frees the investigator from restrictive assumptions in which difficulties in information gathering are attributed to a particular receptor or cortical area. Extent and order of stimulus sampling, for example, both affect the degree to which the subject will be informed about the properties of the stimulus which are critical to the task at hand. Thus, two or more inspections of a given stimulus may yield different information whether the inspections occur within one mode or are cross-modal. Goodnow reports on the empirical studies which were inspired by a general non–modality-specific framework and which have contributed to the development of her stimulus sampling view.

For over a decade, Hilgard and his colleagues at Stanford have pursued a program of research on hypnosis and hypnotizability. It has led to the view that the hypnotic state is better conceived as dissociative than regressive; correlates of hypnotizability in young adults do not suggest the *childishness* implied by the concept of regression. Instead the hypnotizable young adult seems to be *childlike*, capable of an imaginative involvement in a variety of experiences, among them an aesthetic interest in nature and an interest in creative expression. Hilgard's and others' cross-sectional studies suggest that susceptibility to hypnosis increases through childhood, peaks during preadolescence, and declines during adolescence and adulthood. It is hypothesized that the increasing reality-orientation necessitated by the transition to conventional adult roles diminishes susceptibility to hypnosis because it so often conflicts with childlike characteristics. Highly hypnotizable adult subjects are those whose childlike characteristics have not been left behind in late adolescence. The necessary longitudinal evidence it would take to confirm such a hypothesis is not available nor is there much known about those experiences or characteristics which would predispose to the persistence of childlike characteristics. Indeed, Hilgard and his group have only recently turned to the developmental study of hypnosis. Some of their early findings are discussed below. Among the more intriguing factors so far implicated in the development of hypnotizability are cross-sex identification, parental reliance on punishment as a control technique, and the greater similarity among monozygotic than dizygotic twins in response to hypnotic suggestion.

The practical uses to which intelligence tests have been put in the schools has sustained the effort in their development over the past half century. Infant tests, by and large, have not shared in this sustenance since it has seemed clear for some time that their predictive value was low. That very homogeneous samples were involved in such evaluations of "stability" or "constancy" has not been widely appreciated nor has the capacity of certain of the tests to discriminate between normal and retarded individuals. If these considerations are taken into account, simplistic and nativistic notions of constancy are dismissed, and the recent resurgence of theoretical interest in infancy and in cognitive development is acknowledged, a renewed interest in infant testing is predictable. There are signs of such interest in both practitioners and scientists and thus the newly released revision of the Bayley Scales of Infant Development is a timely one. Recent investigations employing these scales and their predecessors are discussed in the paper by Hunt and Bayley. The studies, in general, represent an item-analysis approach to the predictive value of the test rather than the search for a unitary intellectual predictor (i.e., the IQ score) which characterized earlier investigations. That data in thus far suggest that such an approach has promise but, as the authors point out, longitudinal data from heterogeneous samples of the population are requisite to more definitive findings. We may look forward to such data for the first five years of life, at least, since the revised Bayley Scales have been included in a nationwide longitudinal study, the Collaborative Perinatal Project. A preliminary finding mentioned here — namely, that test items have been found to discriminate at eight months between infants judged neurologically impaired and those normal at birth — is an enticing promise of things to come.

In 1969, Patterson, Littman, and Bricker published a monograph on assertive behavior in preschool children. The analysis was a "dyadic" one to the extent that aggressive responses were considered as a function of the consequences provided for aggression by *particular* victims of it. The operational meaning of dyadic is extended in several ways in the paper presented here by Patterson and Cobb. The locale for this field study is the home, the dyads are intrafamilial, and aggressive responses are analyzed in terms of certain aggressor and victim behaviors which precede and follow them. The major dependent variable in this molecular analysis is rate of aggressive behavior over time within a given setting. The task is to account for the major components of variance in the intra-subject distribution of fluctuations in aggressive behavior. Certain immediately preceding or following events may increase the probability that an aggressive response will occur (facilitating stimuli) and others may decrease it (inhibitory stimuli). The analysis is not, however, a traditional behavior theory or operant analysis. Facilitating stimuli are not the same as reinforcing stimuli; events called positive reinforcers may function as decelerators in ongoing interaction. The emphasis then, is on the analysis of sequences in short-term interaction. The observational data presented identify those stimuli which serve as inhibitors and facilitators of aggressive responses and confirm certain aspects of a coercion theory of aggression. The effectiveness of the analysis suggests that the question of whether or not behavior theory can handle naturalistic data can be put to empirical test. And, finally, insofar as inhibiting and facilitating stimuli are shown to differ with reference to the presence and absence of certain family members, a means of adding some empirical substance to the bare bones of role theory is also implied.

Bringing order to or out of the hundreds of studies of parental attitudes and practice is no easy task. The literature is a massive and inchoate one, owing to a cancerous empiricism and to most investigators' greater systematic interest in the consequences of parental behavior for children than in the behaviors themselves. When the focus has been squarely upon parental behavior, few have done the doing and the thinking that might make pattern vision possible. There are only a few names one can add to those of Baldwin and his colleagues who did the early classic studies in the dimensionalization of parental behavior at the Fels Research Institute in the 1940's. Among them would be Earl S. Schaefer, whose circumplex model for maternal behavior is the major contemporary attempt to order the parental behavior domain. Schaefer discusses the nature of that model in this volume, placing it in the context of the development of hierarchical and configurational models in general. In such a context, the factor-analytic method becomes an instrument helpful in the generation of models for the comprehension of a behavioral domain and not a tool for digging through to Underlying Reality. The factor-analytic evidence which supported the efficacy of a two-dimensional, circular model is reviewed and that which now suggests the great efficacy of a three-dimensional, spherical model is brought together for the first time. Doubtless, the conceptual content of this new model will change. What seems crucial for bringing order to the area is the form of the analysis: "By systematically reducing more abstract personality dimensions or traits to more concrete, specific, observable behaviors, the ambiguity of personality language can be significantly reduced. The configurational approach also defines a concept through the entire network of relationships in which it is embedded. The meaning of a concept can be clearly communicated by the specific behavior items that are used to define it as well as by neighboring concepts, by polar opposite concepts, and by concepts that are 90° removed in a spatial plot."

The program of research on the development of space perception at Clark University reported on here by Wapner, Cirillo, and Baker is noteworthy for several reasons. It is one of the longest programs of research reported in this series. The investigations which compose it have covered more of the life-span than do most. And, perhaps most important of all, the researches have benefited from and contributed to the genesis of a distinctive and influential perspective, the organismic-developmental point of view. Of all the psychologies which bear on developmental phenomena, it is this one which takes most seriously an ecological point of view — organism and environment are seen as part of a system; phenomena most psychologists are inclined to attribute to either organismic or environmental change are here viewed as transactions between the two. Although such views have been advanced many times in psychology, there are few examples of their empirical utility. The work on the development of objective and egocentric localization reported here is an important exception. Furthermore, the work on ontogenesis has been informed by the accompanying study of adult space perception and by various comparative investigations as well. The latter have been helpful because development is defined in terms of formal structural properties of a system and not in terms of age — another characteristic of the organismic-developmental approach to which many developmentalists aspire but few achieve.

In past prefaces to the volumes of this series, contributors have in some places been acknowledged in such a way as to exclude co-authors who did not participate in the presentation of their papers. This inadvertent slight is, I hope, remedied by its mention here; certainly neither this volume nor any of the others would have been possible without the knowledge, effort, wit, and cooperation of *all* of the contributors listed on the jacket and in the table of contents. Two other kinds of contributors have extended their role in the series to cover a fifth symposium. The Public Health Service (through National Institute of Child Health and Human Development Grant HD-01765) and the Graduate School of the University of Minnesota (through its research funds) joined with the Institute of Child Development to finance the meeting. The editorial and

# PREFACE

production staffs of the University of Minnesota Press invested their many skills to make a book of the papers presented.

The writing of this preface not only completes this volume but is among the last tasks of my five-year term as organizer and editor of the symposia. Coincidentally, between the time the fifth symposium was held and this writing, my association with the Institute of Child Development also has come to an end. Since the symposia, from their inception, have been a program of the Institute as a whole, many colleagues and students helped to make arrangements and provide editorial consultation. My thanks for their help with the symposia is but part of a more general appreciation for all that I have learned from them, of respect for their competence, and of gratitude for their encouragement and support. Professor Anne D. Pick is one of these colleagues, and I am pleased that it is she who now has the primary responsibility for the Minnesota Symposia on Child Psychology.

JOHN P. HILL

*Ithaca, New York*
*May 1971*

# Table of Contents

*MINNESOTA SYMPOSIA ON*
*CHILD PSYCHOLOGY, VOLUME 5*

◈ JACQUELINE J. GOODNOW ◈

# The Role of Modalities in Perceptual and Cognitive Development

IT SEEMS only fair that authors, rather than readers, should have the task of showing how a series of studies fit together. In the set I shall review, the central problem is apparently simple. I shall describe it in terms of objects, but the problem would apply to any stimulus event or situation. Faced with an object, an individual may explore it in a variety of ways. He may look at it, feel it, taste it, shake it, name it, ask someone about it, or wonder what it reminds him of. In the same vein, he may be presented with an object or event in a variety of forms: in the flesh or as a picture, a diagram, a set of sounds, a name either heard or seen. For these several forms and sources of information, two kinds of questions may be asked: First, *Which way* does an individual gather his information? What underlies the choice? Does it vary, for example, with age or culture? If so, how and why? Second, *Does it matter* which way? Perhaps it is true, as von Hornbostel argued, that it matters little how you know you have fallen into a pigsty (Gibson, 1966, p. 54). On the other hand, a number of theories are built

NOTE: It is a pleasure to acknowledge the large degree of help I have received, of several kinds and from several sources. Herbert and Anne Pick, upon whose work I have drawn freely, have been especially generous in exchanging ideas and in lending stimulus material. James and Eleanor Gibson, Lila Braine, Dick Walk, Neil O'Connor, and Hans-Lucas Teuber will, I hope, recognize the extent to which I have learned and borrowed from them. Less obvious, but also large, is the extent to which I have learned and benefited from a number of very good students and helpers: Stuart Appelle, Barbara Baum, Philip Davidson, Phyllis Evans, Sharon Larsen, Caroline Lebowitz, Ellen McGrath, Marcia Minichiello, and Barbara Weiner.

Almost all the research reported in this paper, along with the paper's preparation, was supported by the National Institute of Child Health and Human Development, in the form of Research Career Development Award I-K03-HD36971 and research grant I-RI-HD03105.

around the concept that the nature of information is affected by the way you gather it, that what you know is affected by the way you learned it. If that concept is true, what features of the gathering affect what aspects of the information?

I shall present some data on both these questions, with an emphasis on the second, after making some general points. The first is that both questions are about equivalence, the equivalence of different forms and sources of information. The difference lies only in the way equivalence is measured: by frequency of use, by relative accuracy, by consequences. The second general point is that such equivalence problems may be studied with a variety of techniques and situations (Pick, Pick, & Klein, 1967). One has to make a choice about where to start. My own choice stemmed from a sense of discomfort with some assumptions about the nature of exploratory behavior and its development:

*a. Assumptions about modality as a critical aspect of method.* An object may be explored in a large variety of ways, and on any two inspections an individual may have difficulty recognizing that he is dealing with one and the same object. The problem is to account for why he has difficulty on some occasions and not on others. The solution is most often sought by looking for aspects critical to the method of inspection.

At this point, the literature presents a choice. We may regard modality as a critical aspect, calling some inspections "visual," some "tactual," and some "kinesthetic," some comparisons "intramodal" and others "crossmodal." Phenomenally, this way of grouping exploratory behaviors seems to have a strong appeal. It also seems reasonable phenomenally to regard the sources as separate, and to think of particular modalities as uniquely necessary for particular achievements — we find it a little strange that children who are greatly restricted in motor movement may learn easily, that children who are deaf or speak only dialect may think clearly, or that blind children may develop accurate concepts of space.

The alternative is to find some way of describing exploratory behavior that cuts across modalities. The critical aspect may be, for example, something to do with the nature of the scanning (Gibson, 1966; Zinchenko & Lomov, 1960), the extent to which the information becomes available at once or serially (Lashley, 1951; Teuber, 1960), or the degree to which attention is "centered" (Abravanel, 1968; Piaget, 1961).

In the course of reading about exploratory behavior, I found the nonmodality approach by far the more attractive of the two. In fact, it was

4

difficult to see what modalities had to do, in any direct sense, with most exploratory behavior. At best, I felt, modalities might be a rough approximation of the really critical aspects of method, or might coincide occasionally with them. In this view, incidentally, I was much encouraged by a paper by Herbert Pick (1970), who stressed the importance of "systems" in development that might coincide with modalities but would not necessarily do so. Nonmodality views, however, seemed to be out of step with a large part of the literature. Moreover, they did not help account for some kinds of task behavior. If, for example, information is not modality-specific, how could one account for the difficulties children have when asked to integrate information from different sensory sources? I had no answer to that question, and decided that some firsthand knowledge of the problem was needed. Translated into action, that decision took the form of a set of studies on the way individuals match objects or patterns that are experienced through different modalities.

*b. Assumptions about superiority and developmental order.* Along with the assumption that modalities are important and separate, psychologists often assume that one modality is superior to another, and that in the course of development control shifts from the poorer to the better. To use a single word, I shall call these "dominance" relationships, partly because they seem analogous to the dominance relationships we think exist between two hands.

The assumption of a hierarchy seems especially strong when psychologists write about solutions achieved by the use of one's hands. To interact directly and physically with the material is usually regarded as an impoverished and, at best, inelegant way of solving a problem. Duncker (1945) expresses this attitude succinctly by calling solutions achieved in this way solutions "from below" rather than "from above." In the developmental area, we show the same kind of bias: We tend to assign the use of manipulative exploration to the earliest "unthinking" ages. Piaget, for example, divides an early sensorimotor period from a concrete-operational period. Bruner, in his first approach to the problem, described a progression of "enactive," "iconic," and "symbolic" stages (Bruner, 1964). Zaporozhets (1965) sees the child as progressing from a stage of dependence on "practical" motor activity to a stage where he can manage by visual analysis alone.

The bias appears even in our experimental work. It is as if manipulative behavior or sensorimotor behavior were important only for babies and for

5

human engineering, a fit topic for study only when words are not available. This slights an important area of human activity, a slight based more on our failure to observe than on the realities of the situation. We know now, for example, that an infant is learning a great deal in the first year of life both by ear and by visual observation, as well as by motor action. In general, we appear to confuse an observed order of some kind with a necessary order. Our theories contain a cultural bias toward the value of solutions achieved with "no hands" and a well-turned phrase.

Nonhierarchical models do exist. Piaget, for example, avoids any hierarchy of words and images by insisting that children develop increasing skill in the use of both, skill that reflects the growth of underlying operations (see Robertson & Youniss, 1969). Bruner, in his later analyses of exploratory behavior, sees a whole variety of such behaviors — looking, handling, sucking — as showing common developmental changes (Bruner, 1969a, 1969b). Such nonhierarchical models are not as common in the literature as hierarchical models, and they are hard to fit with data showing that sometimes the exploratory use of one sensory source is more accurate, more effective, or more sophisticated than the use of another. I decided, again, that I needed some first hand knowledge of tasks where performance might be hindered or helped by the use of particular methods. That decision meant a set of studies comparing performance with and without the use of manipulative activity. This set will be discussed after the set dealing with the way an individual compares or matches objects experienced by way of different sensory sources.

## Matching Within and Across Modalities

To explore relations among different sources of information, experimenters often set the task of interrelating information from two sources. The subject may be required to match, to transfer training, or to resolve conflict. Of these three techniques, I chose matching, partly because of some interesting studies already reported, and partly because the task has a fairly central place in discussions of how best to describe methods of information-gathering. In its simplest terms, the issue may be stated: If modalities are not the critical aspect of method, how do you account for difficulties in matching across modalities? And how do you account for difficulties' often being more pronounced with younger than with older subjects?

We need first a sense of the data to be accounted for. Most of it has been very well covered by the Picks and their associates (Pick & Pick, 1970; Pick et al., 1967), so I need now only summarize the main points:

a. Age changes occur in the ease with which children can match across modalities — can match, for example, an object seen to an object felt (Birch & Lefford, 1963), or a visual series to an auditory series (Birch & Belmont, 1965).

b. The relative difficulty of various matches is not consistent from study to study. Sometimes, for example, cross-modal matching is more difficult than intramodal matching (Caviness, 1964). Sometimes the reverse is true (Muehl & Kremenak, 1966; Rudel & Teuber, 1964), and sometimes no differences occur (Hermelin & O'Connor, 1961). Sometimes the direction of the match (e.g., going from eye to hand as opposed to going from hand to eye) makes a difference (Rudel & Teuber, 1964); sometimes it does not (Caviness, 1964).

c. Even within a study, some stimuli can be matched more easily than others. Circles, for example, can be matched across eye and hand at an earlier age that most other shapes (Birch & Lefford, 1963; Piaget & Inhelder, 1956). And diameter can be matched across eye and hand at an earlier age than length can be (Abravanel, 1968).

An explanation in terms of modalities, or modality-specific information, will not cover this range of data. If the only phenomenon involved is the modality-specific nature of information, you cannot account for any direction in matching or for the varying difficulty of intramodal and cross-modal matching, points made forcefully by Teuber (1960) and by Rudel and Teuber (1964).

What other explanation is possible? Suppose the real phenomenon were the extent to which overlap occurred in the stimulus properties perceived on two inspections. On one inspection of an object or event, you perceive it as having certain properties, properties 1, 2, and 3. On another occasion, you perceive it as having properties 3, 4, and 5. If the common property 3 is more important to you than the nonoverlapping properties, you will call the two occasions "the same thing." And if the experimenter agrees with you, you will be "correct." The situation will be very different, however, if you or the experimenter regards the common presence of property 3 as an insufficient basis for saying "the same." It would also be different if you perceived properties 1, 2, and 3 on one occasion, and properties 4 and 5 on another.

7

Modalities could be one of many conditions that might bring about differential sampling. The eye and the hand, for example, might each consistently sample certain properties, but not the same properties. In such a case, cross-modal matching would tend to be less accurate than intramodal matching. And children might be especially prone to differential sampling. One can, in fact, ring a number of changes on the idea of differential sampling. The question is whether the idea has any fit to the data.

A study by Anne and Herbert Pick (1966) suggests that the idea is not impossible. Using the Cornell letter-like forms (Gibson, Gibson, Pick, & Osser, 1962), the Picks found that children's judgments by hand appeared to be different from those obtained earlier by eye. A change in line curvature, for example, was discriminated later by hand than by eye, but a change in orientation was picked up at an earlier age by hand.

A difference in sensitivity to orientation struck me as a particularly interesting form of differential sampling. One might, for example, begin to speculate that the help given by methods such as tracing in the discrimination of letters like b and d might lie in drawing attention to an aspect of the letters more salient to the hand than to the eye. For this reason, and because sharing an office with Lila Ghent Braine had convinced me that orientation was a puzzling and important property of form, I decided to use a follow-up of the Pick and Pick (1966) study as my first plunge into work on matching.

The follow-up can be briefly described (Goodnow, 1969b). The task was a match-to-sample task, in which the child was given on each trial a standard and two variations on the standard (e.g., a change in line curvature and a change in orientation). All told, the variations were in size, left-right position, up-down position, curvature of line, and number of lines. Each child worked with only one standard through a series of ten trials. On each trial, he chose one of the two variations as the more like the standard.

The task yielded a large difference between eye and hand; the main effect was that when children judged by hand, but not by eye, a change in orientation gave rise to a strong sense of difference from the standard. A change in curvature yielded the opposite result: a strong sense of difference judged by eye but not by hand. This effect held for a couple of age groups — kindergarten and second grade — and was not simply a matter of failing to discriminate. Children would say, for example, that they knew a change in orientation was "just the same figure turned around" but none-

8

theless it felt very different. To our surprise, however, the result did not hold for all stimuli. With the third standard we tried (mostly as a routine check on generality), a change in orientation did not yield a sharp sense of difference from the standard.

The solution turned out to lie in the fact that not all parts of a shape explored by hand are equal. One part tends to become a critical or organizing feature, to become what Lila Ghent Braine has called a "focal" part (Ghent, 1961), and some changes in orientation yield little or no change in the focal part. Suppose, for example, the standard is like the letter *t*, and the top crossing of lines becomes focal. A left-right reversal does not change this part, and the new figure will feel similar to the standard. If the direction of the bottom hook becomes focal, however, a left-right reversal will feel quite different from the standard.

At this point, we have the beginnings of an alternative to describing exploratory methods in terms of modalities. The use of eye or hand may be significant because each may sample different properties of the stimulus. It may be possible to go even further: inspection by eye or hand may sample different stimulus properties in a particular way — that is, they may select different parts of a figure as "focal." Ellen McGrath and I are currently making a little headway with that problem. We are exploring to determine whether the eye may be especially sensitive to vertical lines and the hand to loops. We are only nibbling, however, at the harder questions: What makes one part "focal"? How does a child detect change in a focal part? and How do you account for the effect of a focal part on the child's judgment? In Lila Ghent Braine's analysis of focal parts in visual judgments, there is a provocative hypothesis for some of these questions. The effect of the focal part is related to the presence of a vertical scanning process, an internal order of processing parts of the stimulus. The available data on haptic judgments are nowhere so fine, perhaps partly because the figures normally used are complex. They often give rise to some children's choosing one part as focal whereas others choose a different part. We need simpler figures and more work on the scanning process, both overt scanning and internal scanning.

The more immediate problem, however, is the nature of matching. All that I had shown so far was the presence of differential sampling by eye and by hand. I had not shown that differential sampling was in fact responsible for difficulties in cross-modal matching, and there was no evidence that would allow me to extend the idea of differential sampling to

9

age changes in the difficulty of matching. Since the variations in matching behavior were what I had set out to account for, I needed a more direct test before I could tell how useful the idea of differential sampling might be.

For that test, I decided to work with a different task. Birch and Belmont (1965) had observed striking age changes on a task of matching auditory to visual series. The child hears a series of taps, (.. ..) and is asked to choose a visual equivalent from such alternatives as (.. ...), (. ...), and (.. ..). Performance, Birch and Belmont (1965) reported, was at chance level in kindergarten and did not rise to significantly above chance level until age 7 (second grade). In addition, performance within age groups was correlated with difficulties in reading, itself a task that might be called cross-modal matching. If I could understand the age changes on the Birch and Belmont (1965) task, I should be in a better position to understand what underlies cross-modal matching judgments.

As it turned out, we needed a couple of variations on the Birch and Belmont (1965) task to uncover what was happening (Goodnow, in press a). In one variation, children simply tapped out a series they had just heard; in another, they wrote out what they thought a tapped message would look like; and in a third, they tapped out the equivalent of a visual series that was always available. The last task is from work by Stambak (1951, 1962). It was administered with a great deal of help from Sharon Naecker, now Sharon Larsen, who had also worked on the "focal part" problem.

The major results, in terms of cross-modal matching, come from the second and third tasks. Briefly, the main differences among age groups are two: (a) the recognition that a visual interval and an auditory interval are "the same" and can be substituted for each other; and (b) the recognition that this is the only substitution required. To illustrate, among the kindergarten children who wrote out the visual equivalent of a tapped series, the most common response was to represent the auditory interval by a pause in writing. For (.. ..), for example, they wrote two dots, paused, and then wrote the further two dots, giving a final (....). Stambak (1962) reports that her youngest Ss (first grade) showed a similar tendency: they did not give a longer time interval between taps for the visual series (. .) than they did for the series (. .), but instead traded only space for space, spreading their taps out across the table.

In contrast to the kindergarten children, first- and second-graders recognized and used the substitution of space for time, but, for a while, they also tended to add a number of flourishes. When they wrote out a tapped series, for example, a number of first-graders tried to incorporate "high" or "low" properties they heard in the series, and many of them used variations in size as well as visual spaces to show that a series was divided into segments. The series an adult or a fourth-grader represents as (. ...) may be represented as (O ...) by a first-grader, or even as (O$^{ooo}$). A similar decline in "flourishes" occurs with Stambak's task. Children at the beginning of second grade were likely to give a tapped-out translation that contained intervals in both space and time. They would give a clear pause in time between segments, but they also spread their taps out across the space of the table, often from end to end. By the end of the second grade, the taps were either all on one spot, with only time intervals between segments, or else the spacing was far less generous. Like children who learn that only some of the vowel sounds they can make are needed by their society, these children have begun to learn that only some of the matchings they can make are likely to be the ones needed.

The simple procedures of asking children to repeat, or to translate a series of stimuli, either auditory, tactual, or visual, yielded responses that were both charming and provocative. There is obviously a great deal to be learned about the child's perception of intervals and about the properties he considers important for the equivalence of two series. Marcia Minichiello and I, for instance, have played with the simple request that the child repeat a series tapped out by the experimenter, and there are signs of some interesting progressions. The youngest children we tested (around age four or five) were predominantly interested in reproducing the act of tapping without regard to intervals. One four-year-old, for example, would not tap unless he could tap under the table as we had tapped, the location being apparently the property he regarded as critical in doing "the same thing." Attention to intervals was far more marked after the age of five, and seemed to precede attention to the total number of taps. That statement is provisional, however. Most of the series from the Birch and Belmont (1965) task contain fewer intervals than they contain taps, and one clearly needs to develop new series with more deliberate control over the number of segments, the number of units, and the rhythmic structure of a series. It is my impression, for example, that children are more likely to attend to intervals, and to substitute one type of interval for another, when a structure is highly rhythmic or redundant (e.g., .. .. ..), and it

11

would be interesting to know both whether this impression is true and, if so, why.

With the auditory-visual problem, I was in danger of leaving the general matching problem and concentrating on the way children broke series into segments or "chunks." Actually, the two problems are closely related, and I should like to give one example of interrelationship. In an unsystematic manner, I asked children how they remembered a tapped-out series. The result was a progression in the type of coding that seems to parallel the changes in writing out a visual equivalent. The youngest children, the ones who remembered well but gave no visual spaces, remembered the series "like a song" — they "heard it in their head." It was not until first grade that children began reporting the use of numbers. These were initially reported in "sung" fashion, with no break in number. For example, (.. . ..) was "sung" as (1 2 3, pause, 4 5). The report (1 2 3, pause, 1 2) came later, and represents a major change in coding. The complete switch to number ("a 3 and then a 2") did not appear until the end of second grade, and was still rare at that point, even with children whose IQ's were a minimum of 120. Elyse Lehman is currently gathering more systematic material on these changes; it would be fascinating to determine the relation of coding to the ability to remember and to the type of equivalence used in translating auditory into visual series and vice versa.

#### THE ROLE OF MEMORY IN CROSS-MODAL MATCHING

By this time, I had begun to feel that differential sampling was an important source of difficulty in cross-modal matching. Either the child did not attend to the same properties on two inspections; or he attended to them, and did so accurately, but lacked a rule that would convert one into the other, or both into the same form. The lack of a rule appeared to be a promising way of explaining why some cross-modal matches were more difficult than others, and why children might have more difficulty than adults. I shall return to this conceptual explanation later. Much as I liked its implications, there seemed to be some areas in the data on matching that would not be easy to account for in these terms. One of these was the data on directional effects — sometimes cross-modal matching is more accurate when the first object is inspected by eye rather than by hand (Rudel & Teuber, 1964), and sometimes there is no effect (Caviness, 1964). The other awkward area was the varying difficulty of "intramodal" matches by hand and by eye — sometimes the two were very far apart in accuracy

(Rudel & Teuber, 1964), and sometimes they were quite close together (Caviness, 1964).

I did not look forward to having to check for differential sampling in each of these studies, and I had been carrying around the idea that memory was somehow involved in matching. In some studies, a subject is asked to inspect one object, then to inspect another, and to say whether the two are the same or not. In others, a subject is asked to pick out a match for the first object from a set of five alternatives (Cashdan, 1968; Rudel & Teuber, 1964), a procedure that may involve a considerable demand on memory. Demands on memory were, I thought, another possible way of grouping exploratory methods, but I had no grasp of how memory demands might affect the matching process or how they might be linked to the modality properties of a method.

A study by Posner (1967) provided a lever for this problem. Posner asked his subjects to reproduce a distance they either saw or felt, and found that reproductions of distances felt were more vulnerable to time delay than were reproductions of distances seen. Now a time delay before reproduction could be like an increase in the number of comparison objects; both may make it harder for the individual to remember the first event. With this equivalence recognized, I went back to studies on matching and sorted out the studies that compared two events (one standard and one comparison) from the studies that compared more than two events (e.g., one standard and the $S$ required to find its match from among five comparison objects). With this sorting, some of the variability in matching began to show a pattern. To check the pattern I went on, with the help of Barbara Baum, to a deliberate variation of the number of comparison objects. We used 1, 3, or 5 comparison objects after a standard first inspected by eye or by hand. The stimuli were copies of Gibson's (1962) free-form solids.

The results are simple and clear-cut (Goodnow, in press b). When the standard is visual, and the comparisons are visual, mean errors do not vary with the number of comparison objects (with a maximum of 10 errors, the means are 1.5, 1.2, and 1.6 for 1, 3, and 5 comparison objects). When all inspections are by hand, the number of comparison objects makes a difference (the comparable means are 4.2, 4.5, and 6.8). Moreover, the direction of matching interacts with the number of comparison objects. Cross-modal matching shows no directional effect when there is only one comparison object (4.1 errors going from eye to hand, and 4.2

13

going from hand to eye). A strong directional effect occurs, however, when three comparison objects are used (3.8 for eye to hand, but 7.8 errors for hand to eye).

In general, these results tell us that a match starting from inspection by hand is easily thrown into error. The results were reassuring in the way that they helped to account for a lot of the variability in the literature. They are useful for designing any study on matching, and they may be even more useful if it turns out that the difference between one age and another is small when one comparison object is used, but large when more than one is used. The only cloud on the horizon is that I seem to be back into a modality-specific position after rejecting it in the earlier part of this paper. Here again, however, modality turns out to be a loose shorthand characterizing the true variable. Judging from some work with blind subjects by Joan Shagan (1970), the critical variable is not the modality per se but the degree of experience in working with a modality. Memory for events experienced by hand and arm movement appears fragile, not because it is intrinsically fragile, but because we are requiring our normally sighted subjects to use a way of gathering information with which they have had little experience.

We appear now to have two explanations of matching: one is memory; the other is stimulus overlap at the time of perception. Distinctions between perception and memory are often artificial, and matching appears to be a case in point. On all occasions, I suggest, the problem is one of overlap in stimulus properties at the moment of comparison. On the occasions we call "perceptual," the lack of overlap may occur because the stimulus properties attended to are clear, but are either not the same or not perceived as the same. On the occasions we call "memory," the lack of overlap occurs because some of the stimulus properties in the first event are no longer clearly or accurately grasped. On both kinds of occasion, modalities may make an indirect contribution to a lack of overlap — in the first case by way of differential stimulus sampling, in the second by way of varying familiarity of use and susceptibility to delay or interference.

## Performance with and without Manipulative Action

In an earlier part of this paper, I commented that often modalities are thought to make unique or special contributions to various achievements, and that often these contributions are considered to interact with age. Infants and preschoolers, for example, are thought to need particularly the

JACQUELINE J. GOODNOW

special contributions of sensorimotor activity or manipulative action. Again it seemed that a description of method in terms of modality was at best a rough approximation of the real phenomenon. By itself, for example, the presence or absence of manipulative action cannot account for the fact that allowing the subject to handle the stimuli sometimes has a helpful effect (e.g., Davidon, 1952), sometimes a negative effect (e.g., Huttenlocher, 1962), and sometimes no effect (e.g., Sigel, 1954).

I had had some prior experience with this kind of problem, and the experience had left me with a bias against the idea that the modality was critical, and against the idea that man naturally evolves from the use of a lower modality to the use of a higher one. My first direct encounter came when Tom Pettigrew and I were trying to explain why some adults — all Harvard or Radcliffe students — took so long (up to 90 trials) to realize that a machine was scheduled to pay off on an alternating basis: once on the left key, then once on the right (Goodnow & Pettigrew, 1956). On each trial, the S made a choice and pressed a key; the machine either paid off or did not. Eventually we realized that the problem lay in the way Ss gathered information about the machine's payoff. Ss who jumped back and forth between one key and the other were likely to be slow learners: they had to keep track both of what they did and what the machine did. Ss who pressed one key consistently learned far more quickly. So also, as Bruner, Wallach, and Galanter (1959) showed, did Ss who could watch a sequence of events without carrying out any action. The critical difference, then, was not between a motor act and no motor act, but between a motor act that varied and a motor act that was consistently present or absent.

My next encounter with the problem came in the course of trying to account for some cross-cultural data based on a group of Piagetian tasks. From two-choice studies to cross-cultural Piaget is a leap, and I shall make it quickly by saying that I had begun to feel a little stale on probability problems and had decided to read something quite different, a book on children's concepts of chance by Piaget and Inhelder (1951). The experience was, to say the least, disconcerting. The tasks I found fascinating, the concepts incomprehensible, even when I slowly translated large parts of the text into English. I decided two things were needed: I should have to read more of Piaget, and, to understand the concepts, I should have to give some of the tasks. Since my husband was working in Hong Kong for a couple of years, the tryout took the form of a cross-cultural study (Goodnow, 1962).

15

The Hong Kong study was a comparison of boys with a variety of backgrounds. Among these, the critical cut turned out to be schooling rather than nationality or class. And schooling interacted with the kind of task. For the three conservation tasks (weight, surface, and volume with displacement of water), it did not matter whether the boys were Chinese or European, went to Chinese schools, European schools, or no school. On a task of combinatorial reasoning, however, the boys with little or no schooling did very poorly. The task requires a child to make all the pairs possible out of six colors, after practice in making pairs with three and four colors.

How does one account for this mixture of results? My first hypothesis was that success on the conservation tasks might be relatively unrelated to intelligence. Instead, the judgment of "same" might be closely related to chronological age, as some perceptual constancies seem to be (Jenkin & Feallock, 1960). I was not at that time convinced of the logical quality in conservation judgments. I also had a constricted view of "intelligence," and thought it not unlikely that the performance differences reflected differences in an "intelligence" for which the combinatorial task was the truer test.

A follow-up study in the United States with Gloria Bethon (Goodnow & Bethon, 1966) disabused me on the role of simple chronological age. We went to some pains to keep "culture" constant by setting up pairs or triads of children with varying IQ's in the same school, and we found a large gap between "dull" and "average" boys of the same chronological age. More important, the gap was as large for the conservation tasks as it was for the combinatorial task. In other words, if we wished to talk about the intelligence of the unschooled Chinese boys, we would have to say that they were as intelligent as the schooled on three measures, but not on a fourth.

With the simplest hypothesis ruled out, I turned to a more complex one. Something in school experience gives rise to some kind of skill needed on the combinatorial task — but what these somethings were, I did not know. Fortunately, we were by this time in Rome for two years, and I had the luxury of time for reading. I looked at a large number of cross-cultural studies, took a closer look at the kinds of skill that Piagetian tasks involve (Goodnow, 1969c), and ended with a point of view, a hypothesis, and the two general questions I mentioned at the start of this paper.

The point of view sets aside questions of intelligence as an entity. It offers as an alternative the argument that poor performances occur on tasks requiring skills neither practiced nor valued by the culture. This working hypothesis comes from several people (e.g., Nissen, Machover, & Kinder, 1935; Price-Williams, 1962; Tax, 1965).

The specific hypothesis developed for the Hong Kong data was in two parts. First, success on the combinatorial task is defined by the experimenter as being able to solve the problem in a highly specific way — that is, when the child comes to pairs with six colors, he must think of a system before he touches the stimuli or moves them around. It is not enough for the child to come up with all fifteen pairs by trial and error. He is correct only if he can think through much of the problem "in his head." Second, the value of solving problems in this particular way, along with practice in the technique, is most likely to be stressed in school. The combinatorial task was probably a perfect mismatch. It came from a culture that values "pure reason," without the use of "props," and was given to a group with little exposure to these particular European rules. In contrast, the conservation tasks dealt with properties that were significant for an urban, trading culture, with or without school. The invariance of these properties had a functional value, and daily life supplied experiences from which an alert mind could abstract the principle of conservation.

Short of a return to an unschooled culture, this hypothesis was difficult to test. I contented myself (Goodnow, 1970) with seeing how far the hypothesis brought order to the Hong Kong data and to some data on "imaging" tasks reported by Vernon (1965) for boys who were schooled but predominantly schooled by words. And I began asking myself more seriously about relations between success on a problem and the use of a particular method of exploration. How far, for example, were these relations functional? And how far did they represent some kind of intellectual ritual?

To answer these questions, I turned again to a variety of tasks, all involving a contrast between two methods: look-only and look-and-handle. Most contrast studies involve a greater isolation of methods (e.g., look-only versus handle-only), and I have contributed my share to this type of design (Appelle & Goodnow, 1970). In the developmental literature, however, this is not the kind of contrast we usually have in mind when we talk about the significance of stimulus-handling for children. For this reason, the studies I shall report with children as subjects are all contrasts of look-only with look-and-handle.

17

The specific data are easily summarized:

a. Nursery school children are more likely to remember shapes they have seen-and-handled than shapes they have seen-only or handled-only (Zinchenko & Ruzskaya, in Zaporozhets, 1965). But the effect does not depend on the child's touching the actual contour of the shape. Touching a plastic globe that surrounds the object will work as well (Denner & Cashdan, 1967). In fact, the child does not need to do any touching. If the shape is enclosed in an eye-catching plastic globe, the child will remember as well when he looks-only as when he looks-and-handles (Weiner & Goodnow, 1970).

b. Five- and six-year-olds give more correct judgments on a conservation task when the initial equality of the two events is defined by their actions. More concretely, suppose some children place grapes in two beakers, on a one-for-me, one-for-you basis; other children are presented with two beakers already containing an equal number of grapes. For both groups, we proceed through the usual steps of a conservation task: leave beaker A as it stands, pour the contents of beaker B into a taller, thinner beaker C; and ask if A and C contain the same amount. Five-year-olds show more correct answers on the grapes task when they "construct" the initial equality, but show no transfer to a task where the amounts are liquids and they start with filled beakers. Six-year-olds are already at ceiling on the grapes task, but do show transfer to the liquids task (Minichiello & Goodnow, 1969).

c. Six-year-olds give more nonstandard uses for objects they may see-and-handle than for objects they see-only. The objects are a piece of Kleenex, a paperclip, and a screwdriver (Goodnow, 1969a). The standard use of an object is its usual function — a Kleenex, for example, is used to wipe or clean something. A nonstandard use is a departure from the usual function — a Kleenex's being used to draw on, make doll clothes with, or wrap loose teeth in. The difference between look-and-handle and look-only declines with age (Lebowitz, 1968; McAnany, personal communication). It also declines or disappears entirely if the object looked at is moved around by the experimenter, essentially presenting the child with new views of the object (McAnany, personal communication).

These three sets of data all cluster around the same points. First, they suggest that the motor action is not always necessary. There are other conditions, not calling for motor actions, that can have the same effect.

Second, the motor action or its substitute has an effect because it counteracts some particular aspect of a response. In other words, the contribution of a motor action is not unique; substitutions are possible. Neither is the nature of the contribution constant; it interacts with the kind of response the child is most likely to give.

"Interaction" explanations are usually unsatisfying unless they can be made in fairly concrete form, so I shall analyze the data from each task in turn. On the memory-for-objects task, the most likely response is to attend to the interesting or informative objects in the environment. In that case, a two-dimensional, static shape is not likely to be given much attention — it is not novel; it does not move; it has few associations and little meaning for the child. All these aspects contribute to there being little reason to look at this part of the environment rather than others. Requiring something to be done with the object and making the object eye-catching will both be beneficial, because both increase the likelihood that the object will be looked at.

The same kind of analysis can be used for the conservation task. The most likely response is to work from the object in the form in which it is usually given, or in its last state — that is, from the whole object, the whole set of grapes, or the whole amount of water in the beaker. This response is at odds with one of the main routes to the achievement of conservation, namely the ability and the readiness to perceive the whole as made up of units that do not change in number. This latter response is apparently present but weak among five- and six-year-olds. The one-and-one action serves as a reminder to them that the units remain the same, a reminder that lasts for the six-year-olds but not for the five-year-olds.

The uses-for-objects task is somewhat more complex, and also more provocative. The most likely response is to give uses that stay within the standard class. In kindergarten, this response is extremely likely, and in fact the difference between look-and-handle and look-only stems predominantly from a decline in the incidence of children who give only standard uses.

The likelihood of standard responses appears to be altered in several ways. It may be increased by a particular stimulus condition, in this case by presenting the stimulus object in a static visual form. I suspect it may be increased also by some response conditions. Verbal fluency or a great deal of experience with one type of use may make the child more likely to continue giving minor variations on the same theme. Girls, for example,

19

are more likely than boys to give only standard uses for Kleenex (or for a tin can). They know a multitude of objects that can be wiped and a multitude of small objects that can be placed in a tin can. If one is scoring for nonstandard uses, they often are undone by the sheer length of the inventory their experiences provide.

The likelihood of standard responses may also be decreased by changes in both stimulus and response conditions. In kindergarten, the changing feel or the changing look of the object may jolt the child off the standard track. At a later age, the actual stimulus change may not be needed, in part because the child can image changes in the stimulus, and in part because he has changed his standards for a correct response. This change in standards is conjectural and stems from my observing differences between kindergarten and fourth-grade children. The fourth-graders, but not the kindergartners, would sometimes say, "Oh, I said that before," referring not to exactly the same use but to the same kind of use. It is as if they have acquired standards that they use to define and reject a duplication of response.

For an age change to occur, both the goal of nonduplication and the skill to imagine stimulus variations may need to be present. One would expect, then, that in some persons and in some cultural groups, the age change may take place earlier than others. Where "repeating yourself" is either acceptable or has to be almost exact before being called "repeating," the difference between looking-and-handling and looking-only should last longer than in a climate that stresses coming up with something "really new" each time, with a shift in categories rather than only in instances. This kind of cultural effect on response may help account for the large difference McAnany found between two groups of children from the same neighborhood in San Salvador, one group attending a traditional school, the other a school more innovative in approach.

*Some Negative Contributions from Manipulative Action.* I have dealt mainly with the helpful aspects of manipulative action and with a particular kind of situation, one in which the stimulus presents an aspect not conducive to success and does not vary. The other side of the coin can easily be found, however. The machine that shifts its payoff from left to right key is one example. The subject needs to attend only to what the machine does, and he attends best when there is either no motor action or when his motor actions are always the same (i.e., contain no distracting information). He perceives least well what the machine is doing when he has to cope with variations in what the machine did, what he himself did, and what the consequences were for what he did. In this case, the motor actions lead attention away from the essentials and overload the subject with more information than he can cope with. Once again, however, the interfering effects of motor actions may not be unique to motor actions. The effect is probably the same as the interference sometimes produced by introducing material rewards into a learning situation.

*Comment and Summary.* Motor or manipulative actions, it now appears, have no blanket effect on performance. What they really do is to alter the likelihood that people will attend to particular parts of their environment or make particular responses. At the risk of overworking a useful idea, the presence of a motor act leads to a differential sampling of stimulus properties or to a differential sampling of responses. The changed sampling may be either helpful or harmful, may lead either toward or away from the response defined as correct.

## An Overall View

I began with a very broad question — the effect of one's method on the information one gathers — and chose the effect of modality as a specific form of the question. In part, the choice reflected general history: the receptor as a critical aspect of what one perceives or learns has been for some time a strong theme in psychology and neuropsychology. And in part, the choice reflected my own more recent experience as a developmentalist: a number of concepts about cultural and developmental changes in method seem to cluster around the role of modalities. Individuals are often viewed, for example, as slowly acquiring the ability to integrate information across modalities, or as varying in their dependence on vision and motor activity.

I began also with the hope of ending positively. I hoped to gain some alternative to a stress on modalities, some other way of looking at the behavior that modality theories did attempt to cover.

An alternative approach has been mentioned off and on in the course of describing the series of studies. In summary, the approach runs as follows:

a. A critical aspect to any exploratory method is the way it samples the properties of a stimulus, both the extent and the order of sampling. A sampling may be, for example, restricted or extensive; it may focus on property $A$ or property $B$, ignore property $C$ or property $D$. In terms of order, sampling may proceed in small or large steps, be orderly or disorganized,

21

consistent or inconsistent from trial to trial. From this point of view, the significance of modalities lies in there being one way in which two inspections of a stimulus can yield two different samplings of stimulus properties. Such differential sampling, however, need not be viewed as something intrinsic to the receptor or as basically different from the differential sampling that may occur from one occasion to another with one modality.

b. The equivalence of any two inspections of a stimulus depends on the degree of sampling overlap, on the extent of correspondence or isomorphism between the sets of properties sampled on the two occasions. The overlap may be direct (e.g., two inspections focus on the same corner of a shape) or indirect (e.g., one set of properties can be converted into another by some rule of correspondence or translation).

c. The accuracy or superiority of any particular method will depend on the extent to which it samples or highlights the properties that need to be attended to. In a sense, the problem is now one of overlap between the set of properties that is salient for the experimenter and the set that is salient for the subject. In the simplest case, one method may have the advantage simply because it is tuned in to the critical property right from the beginning. In others, the advantage may lie in allowing more rapid recognition of the need to re-sample, or an easier way of keeping track of several properties or several samplings.

This kind of approach is first of all more flexible than a straight modality approach. In addition, it opens up some interesting research problems, freeing us from restricting preconceptions. As examples, we may look briefly at research problems dealing with individual differences on matching tasks, with the advantages of particular methods, and with hierarchical or modality arrangements among modalities.

### INDIVIDUAL DIFFERENCES ON MATCHING TASKS

In this area, we no longer need to rely on hypotheses that put all the stress on a receptor mechanism or a cortical area. Instead, errors may be viewed as stemming from one or all of several parts to a task. The major difficulty for an individual may lie, for example, in the initial scanning (Zinchenko & Lomov, 1960), in the way he goes back and forth between the stimuli being compared (Gould, 1967), or in the way the initial event is coded or remembered (Hermelin & O'Connor, 1961; Posner, 1967).

For young children, all three areas may contribute to a high incidence of errors. On a particular task, they may have difficulty because they explore only part of a stimulus (Abravanel, 1968), because they jump erratically back and forth between one object and another (Lavrent'eva & Ruzskaya, 1962), or because they do not remember the first stimulus clearly (Blank, Weider, & Bridger, 1968). Where cross-modal matching is especially difficult, the trouble may lie in a spiraling of problems: any tendency to explore only some properties of the stimulus makes it less likely that the properties sampled on two inspections will overlap one another. Equally, the difficulty with cross-modal matching may lie in a tendency to use different forms of coding for different material. One has the feeling, for example, that young children are more likely to use number coding for a series of dots on a page than for a series of sounds (they have learned to count with visual material). Older children, however, give the impression of being more likely to use number codings for both kinds of stimuli. Finally, the young child may have particular difficulty with some cross-modal tasks (matching auditory to visual series, for instance) because he lacks the rules that convert one stimulus pattern into another, or knows the rules but cannot juggle them effectively.

Individuals with neurological damage, or with reading difficulties, may fruitfully be considered from the same viewpoint. Some forms of neurological damage, for instance, may have their primary effect on the way the initial stimulus is scanned (Luria, Karpov, & Yarbuss, 1966; Tyler, 1969). Others may leave the stimulus scanning unchanged, but affect memory for the initial event (Butters, Barton, & Brody, 1970). Similarly, some forms of reading difficulty may be associated with difficulties in remembering (Blank et al., 1968), whereas others may affect the way in which an individual scans back and forth between two events (Goodnow, 1969b).

In short, we are encouraged to break away from any analysis of matching tasks, either intramodal or cross-modal, that stresses single factors such as the modality used for inspection. We gain the possibility of a finer match between the quality of performance and some internal state of the individual.

### THE ADVANTAGES OF PARTICULAR METHODS

Once we set aside attachments to any particular method as superior (vision, touch, or sensorimotor activity), we can adopt a more flexible

23

position toward the benefits of any particular method or combination of methods. Suppose, for example, the question is one of whether two modalities are better than one as a way of presenting stimulus material. If the two methods highlight the same properties, the redundancy may be useful, or it may stand in the way of locating some critical property that is not usually sampled. If the two methods do not highlight the same properties, the combination may be useful, particularly if the critical property is more often sampled by the second method than by the first; or it may be harmful, loading the individual with more information than he can handle and leading him away from the critical property.

In effect, we move toward asking what specific aspects of exploratory method affect what specific aspects of judgment. This is not an easy question, and fortunately two of our students at George Washington are tackling problems of this type. Riki Koenigsberg is asking about the contributions of specific sensorimotor behaviors to the visual discrimination of letters such as *b* and *d*, and Philip Davidson is asking about the nature of learning in exploratory behavior, analyzing the way in which blind and sighted adolescents judge the curvature of an edge.

### HIERARCHICAL ARRANGEMENTS AMONG MODALITIES

Suppose we assume that behaviors are grouped or organized into "systems" of some kind. In one form or another, this assumption is always made in psychological theory, since otherwise we have to cope with an infinite number of specific behaviors, all acting independently and none affecting any other. Quite frankly, I do not know how to define a "system," and I admire Herbert Pick's courage in tackling this critical problem, searching for improvements and alternatives to the concept that behaviors are grouped around modalities and integrated across modalities (Pick, 1970).

My suggestions have to do with the kinds of interaction we think of as occurring between two systems, whether the systems are two hands, the eye and the hand, the eye and the mouth, or even two general methods of search displayed by one hand.

First of all, when we cease to assign one system to the bottom of the developmental heap, we gain a greater variety of behaviors with which to analyze development. Once we take "sensorimotor behavior" away from infants, for example, we acquire a gamut of sensorimotor tasks as indices of development up and down the age range. The work of Bruner and his associates (Bruner, 1969b), and of Davol and Hastings (1967) are examples of how one may put such tasks to work.

In addition, we become more ready to consider a variety of relations among different methods, relations other than dominance. A large part of development, for example, can be regarded as the growth of divisions of labor and interweavings of method rather than as the supplanting of one behavior by another. This kind of concept is well known in some parts of psychology. The information coming in to the two ears, for example, is regarded as chunked, interwoven, or held in place rather than information from one ear being "dominant" over another (e.g., Maccoby & Konrad, 1967). Within developmental studies, however, such concepts are relatively rare, a major exception being Bruner, who suggests that skill in interweaving and place-holding may be a general aspect of development that cuts across such diverse behaviors as the combined use of two hands, the combination of looking and sucking, and the construction of subordinate phrases or clauses (Bruner, 1969b).

Work by two students at George Washington provides some interesting examples of the process. One comes from work by Hana Bruml (1968), and is concerned with some old bimanual measures of hand dominance (e.g., winding a thread around a spool). These measures have not been easy to interpret or to relate to development, but a clear relation exists in terms of divisions of labor. As the child grows older, one hand takes over more of a stabilizing, supporting role, while the other moves. The progression may be seen even in a simple task like clapping hands. The kindergartner typically claps by bringing both hands together at the midline. The fourth-grader typically cups his left hand upward, and moves the right hand down toward the left.

The second example comes from work by Elyse Lehman, who has been interested in the way children treat redundant and irrelevant stimulus properties. When a child is required to match two objects on the basis of shape, for example, and the objects vary in both shape and texture, how do children of different ages respond to the irrelevant but attractive texture? The older child, Elyse Lehman finds, may manage by clever interweaving to have his cake and eat it, too. He explores for shape, announces his decision, and then feels the texture.

My last point is one that has nothing to do with exploratory methods that are physically expressed. One of the greatest handicaps to a stress on modalities, I believe, has been its tendency to carve up the literature on various ways of gathering information or establishing equivalence. The literature on cross-modal equivalence, for example, makes a number of the same points that are made in literature on the equivalence of words and pictures (Paivio, 1970), but the two literatures seldom meet. And both literatures are segregated from the literature on problem-solving, even though overlaps in stimulus properties and ways of converting one set of perceived properties into another are the heart of theories like Duncker's (1945). One may hope that, as we acquire more insight into the general properties of how information is gathered or generated, these unfortunate divisions by content will disappear.

## References

Abravanel, E. The development of intersensory patterning with regard to selected spatial dimensions. *Monographs of the Society for Research in Child Development*, 1968, 33 (2, Serial No. 118).

Appelle, S., & J. J. Goodnow. Haptic and visual judgments of proportion. *Journal of Experimental Psychology*, 1970, 84, 47–52.

Birch, H. G., & L. Belmont. Auditory-visual integration, intelligence, and reading ability in school children. *Perceptual and Motor Skills*, 1965, 20, 295–305.

Birch, H. G., & A. Lefford. Intersensory development in children. *Monographs of the Society for Research in Child Development*, 1963, 28 (5, Serial No. 89).

Blank, M., S. Weider, & W. Bridger. Verbal deficiencies in abstract thinking in early reading retardation. *American Journal of Orthopsychiatry*, 1968, 38, 823–834.

Bruml, H. The development of consistency in hand usage. Ph.D. thesis, George Washington University, 1968.

Bruner, J. S. The course of cognitive growth. *American Psychologist*, 1964, 19, 1–15.

————. Eye, hand, and mind, in D. Elkind & J. H. Flavell, eds., *Studies in cognitive development*, pp. 439–444. New York: Oxford University Press, 1969. (a)

————. *Processes of cognitive growth: Infancy*. Worcester, Mass.: Clark University Press (Heinz Werner Lecture Series, Vol. 3), 1969. (b)

————, M. A. Wallach, & E. H. Galanter. The identification of recurrent regularity. *American Journal of Psychology*, 1959, 72, 200–209.

Butters, N., M. Barton, & B. A. Brody. Role of the right parietal lobe in the mediation of cross-modal associations and reversible operations in space. *Cortex*, 1970, 6, 174–190.

Cashdan, S. Visual and haptic form discrimination under conditions of successive stimulation. *Journal of Experimental Psychology*, 1968, 76, 215–218.

Caviness, J. A. Visual and tactual perception of solid shape. Ph.D. thesis, Cornell University, 1964.

Davidon, R. S. The effects of symbols, shifts, and manipulation upon the number of concepts attained. *Journal of Experimental Psychology*, 1952, 44, 70–79.

Davol, S. H., & M. L. Hastings. Effects of sex, age, reading ability, socioeconomic level and display position of a measure of spatial relations in children. *Perceptual & Motor Skills*, 1967, 24, 375–387.

Denner, B., & S. Cashdan. Sensory processing and the recognition of forms in nursery-school children. *British Journal of Psychology*, 1967, 58, 101–104.

Duncker, K. On problem-solving. *Psychological Monographs*, 1945, 58 (Whole No. 270).

## JACQUELINE J. GOODNOW

Ghent, L. Form and its orientation: A child's eye view. *American Journal of Psychology*, 1961, 74, 177–190.

Gibson, E. J., J. J. Gibson, A. D. Pick, & H. Osser. A developmental study of the discrimination of letter-like forms. *Journal of Comparative and Physiological Psychology*, 1962, 55, 897–906.

Gibson, J. J. Observations on active touch. *Psychological Review*, 1962, 69, 477–491.

————. *The senses considered as perceptual systems*. New York: Houghton Mifflin, 1966.

Goodnow, J. J. A test of milieu differences with some of Piaget's tasks. *Psychological Monographs*, 1962, 76 (36, Serial No. 555).

————. Effects of active handling, illustrated by uses for objects. *Child Development*, 1969, 40, 201–212. (a)

————. Eye and hand: Differential sampling of form and orientation properties. *Neuropsychologia*, 1969, 7, 365–373. (b)

————. Problems in research on culture and thought, in D. Elkind & J. H. Flavell, eds., *Studies in Cognitive Development*, pp. 439–462. New York: Oxford University Press, 1969. (c)

————. Cultural variations in cognitive skills. *Cognitive Studies*, Vol. 1, pp. 242–257. New York: Brunner/Mazel, 1970.

————. Auditory-visual matching: Modality problem or translation problem? *Child Development*, in press. (a)

————. Eye and hand: Differential memory and its effect on matching. *Neuropsychologia*, in press. (b)

———— & G. Bethon. Piaget's tasks: The effects of schooling and intelligence. *Child Development*, 1966, 37, 573–582.

Goodnow, J. J., & T. F. Pettigrew. Some sources of difficulty in solving simple problems. *Journal of Experimental Psychology*, 1956, 51, 385–392.

Gould, J. D. Pattern recognition and eye-movement parameters. *Perception and Psychophysics*, 1967, 2, 397–407.

Hermelin, B., & N. O'Connor. Recognition of shape by sound and subnormal children. *British Journal of Psychology*, 1961, 52, 281–284.

Huttenlocher, J. Effects of manipulation of attributes on efficiency of concept formation. *Psychological Reports*, 1962, 10, 503–509.

Jenkin, N., & S. M. Feallock. Developmental and intellectual processes in size-distance judgment. *American Journal of Psychology*, 1960, 73, 268–273.

Lashley, K. S. The problem of serial order in behavior, in L. A. Jeffress, ed., *Cerebral mechanisms in behavior*, pp. 112–136. New York: Wiley, 1951.

Lavrent'eva, T. A., & A. G. Ruzskaya. Comparative analysis of touch and vision: Report V. Simultaneous intersensory comparison of form at a preschool age. *Soviet Psychology and Psychiatry*, 1962, 1, 28–31.

Lebowitz, C. Uses for objects seen and handled. B.A. honors thesis, George Washington University, 1968.

Luria, A. R., B. A. Karpov, & A. L. Yarbuss. Disturbances of active visual perception with lesions of the frontal lobes. *Cortex*, 1966, 2, 202–212.

Maccoby, E. E., & K. W. Konrad. The effect of preparatory set on selective listening: Developmental trends. *Monographs of the Society for Research in Child Development*, 1967, 32 (4, Serial No. 112).

Minichiello, M. D., & J. J. Goodnow. Effect of an "action" cue on conservation of amount. *Psychonomic Science*, 1969, 16, 200–201.

Muehl, S., & S. Kremenak. Ability to match information within and between auditory and visual sense modalities and subsequent reading achievement. *Journal of Educational Psychology*, 1966, 57, 230–239.

Nissen, H. W., S. Machover, & E. P. Kinder. A study of performance tests given to a group of native African Negro children. *British Journal of Psychology*, 1935, 25, 308–355.

Paivio, A. On the functional significance of imagery. *Psychological Bulletin*, 1970, 73, 385–392.

Piaget, J. *Les mécanismes perceptifs*. Paris: Presses Universitaires de France, 1961.

—— & B. Inhelder. *La genèse de l'idée de hasard chez l'enfant*. Paris: Presses Universitaires de France, 1951.

——. *The child's conception of space*. London: Routledge & Kegan Paul, 1956.

Pick, A. D., & H. L. Pick, Jr. A developmental study of tactual discrimination in blind and sighted children and adults. *Psychonomic Science*, 1966, 6, 367–368.

Pick, H. L., Jr. Systems of perceptual and perceptual-motor development, in J. P. Hill, ed., *Minnesota symposia in child psychology*, Vol. 4, pp. 199–219. Minneapolis: University of Minnesota Press, 1970.

—— & A. D. Pick. Sensory and perceptual development, in P. H. Mussen, ed., *Carmichael's manual of child psychology* (rev. ed.), pp. 773–847. New York: Wiley, 1970.

—— & R. E. Klein. Perceptual integration in children, in L. P. Lipsitt & C. C. Spiker, eds., *Advances in child development and behavior*, Vol. 3, pp. 192–223. New York: Academic Press, 1967.

Posner, M. I. Characteristics of visual and kinesthetic memory codes. *Journal of Experimental Psychology*, 1967, 75, 103–107.

Price-Williams, D. R. Abstract and concrete modes of classification in a primitive society. *British Journal of Educational Psychology*, 1962, 32, 50–61.

Robertson, A. de S., & J. Youniss. Anticipatory imagery in deaf and hearing children. *Child Development*, 1969, 40, 123–135.

Rudel, R., & H. L. Teuber. Crossmodal transfer of shape discrimination by children. *Neuropsychologia*, 1964, 2, 1–8.

Shagan, J. Kinesthetic memory in blind and sighted individuals. Ph.D. thesis, George Washington University, 1970.

Sigel, I. E. The dominance of meaning. *Journal of Genetic Psychology*, 1954, 85, 201–207.

Sokolov, E. N. A probabilistic model of perception. *Soviet Psychology and Psychiatry*, 1962, 1, 28–36.

Stambak, M. Le problème de rhythme dans le développement de l'enfant et dans les dyslexies de l'évolution. *Enfance*, 1951, 4, 480–502.

——. Trois épreuves de rhythme, in R. Zazzo, ed., *Psychologie de l'enfant et méthode génétique*, pp. 81–94. Neuchâtel: Delacaux & Niestle, 1962.

Tax, S. Group identity and educating the disadvantaged, in R. Corbin & M. Crosby, eds., *Language programs for the disadvantaged*, pp. 204–215. Champaign, Ill.: National Council of Teachers of English, 1965.

Teuber, H. L. Perception, in J. Field, H. W. Magoun, & V. E. Hall, eds., *Handbook of physiology*, Vol. 3, pp. 1595–1168. Washington, D.C.: American Physiological Society, 1960.

Tyler, H. R. Defective stimulus exploration in aphasic patients. *Neurology*, 1969, 19, 105–112.

Vernon, P. E. Environmental handicaps and intellectual development. *British Journal of Educational Psychology*, 1965, 35, 1–12, 117–126.

Weiner, B., & J. J. Goodnow. Motor activity: Effects on memory. *Developmental Psychology*, 1970, 2, 448.

Zaporozhets, A. V. The development of perception in the preschool child, in P. H. Mussen, ed., European research in child development, pp. 82–101. *Monographs of the Society for Research in Child Development*, 1965, 30 (2, Serial No. 100).

Zinchenko, V. P., & B. F. Lomov. The functions of hand and eye movements in the process of perception. *Problems of Psychology*, 1960, 1, 12–26.

# Hypnosis and Childlikeness

IT IS important to distinguish between *childlikeness* and *childishness*. The root meanings of the two words are the same, but their connotations are different. *Childlikeness* has come to be interpreted as the qualities of childhood which, when they continue into adult life, are highly regarded; *childishness,* by contrast, suggests the less pleasing and less admirable characteristics of childhood that, in the adult, are signs of immaturity. The ideal course of development is to leave childish qualities behind as one matures, but somehow to preserve the childlike qualities.

The thesis to be offered in this paper is that certain childlike qualities have been preserved in the hypnotizable adult. These qualities have their origins in childhood, but only if developmental circumstances have been appropriate will they be retained as the individual grows up. Childlike maturity for the adult does not mean a childish adult; a childish adult is emotionally immature, dependent, or neurotic, but a childlike adult functions at a mature adult level. The contrast may be expressed as that between the unchildish adult and the childlike adult.

First, consider the unchildish adult. The qualities of an unchildish adult are those that we associate with a strong ego, with a person who is able to adapt to the physical and social environment in a masterful way. He is skillful in the exercise of his trade or business or profession; he is socially adept at managing his relationships with other people, whether at home, in the office, or at social gatherings. He is independent, capable of planning, and does not feel bound by the pressures upon him from outside. He is generally thought to be a competent person; he possesses many of the qualities desirable and essential for civilized living. But these unchildish adult qualities are *not*, as such, the qualities characterizing high hypnotizability.

Now, the childlike adult. We do not contradict the qualities of the unchildish adult if we supplement them with some qualities of childlikeness. The childlike adult is zestful and enthusiastic, and capable of joyful abandon. He is not blasé or surfeited with knowledge, but full of curiosity about the unknown, with a sense of wonder about the world and people. Although capable of rational behavior, he enjoys fantasies that lie outside the realms of proved validity.

It may be that in our historical concern for "adjustment" as the criterion for mental health, we have paid too much attention to the unchildish adult characteristics as those to be sought and too little to desirable childlike qualities in the adult. We need not ask the adult to choose one set of values against the other, but to manifest an appropriate combination of both.

### THE HYPNOTIZABLE YOUNG ADULT

The hypothesis requires that I first establish the picture of the hypnotizable young adult as possessing some of the childlike qualities just described. Then I can turn to the development of these qualities in childhood and to the circumstances for their preservation.

Much of the evidence comes from a recent book by Josephine Hilgard, on the basis of an interview program carried out in the Stanford Laboratory of Hypnosis Research (J. R. Hilgard, 1970). In the course of developing the Stanford Hypnotic Susceptibility Scales, André Weitzenhoffer and I found it necessary to attempt to hypnotize a large number of college students, who composed the standardization sample, and with the aid of a number of associates we kept on testing later groups to supply subjects for the experiments going on in the Laboratory. Our staff of interviewers, under the guidance of Josephine Hilgard, took advantage of this ongoing measurement program to parallel it with an interview program, in which interviews were conducted in advance of hypnosis in order to detect those personality qualities associated with hypnotic susceptibility. The opportunity was a fruitful one, because susceptibility was measured after the first interview had been conducted; and a second interview after hypnosis guided the interviewer on the relevance of findings in the first.

The unifying theme in the hypnosis-related qualities deriving from the interviews has been described by Josephine Hilgard as the capacity for and enjoyment of *imaginative involvement* in a variety of experiences — not

30

just the same for everyone, but usually one or more areas of such involvement in the hypnotizable person. We may begin with imagery itself, as closely related to imagination.

*Imagery* for our purposes may be defined as the capacity to form vivid mental pictures in the absence of appropriate external stimuli; the problem is to relate imagery to hypnosis. The terms *hypnotic susceptibility* or *hypnotizability* here mean the extent to which, when given the opportunity, a person behaves in the manner characteristic of hypnotized individuals. Given twelve specific opportunities to behave like a hypnotized person in response to specific suggestions — after an attempted induction of hypnosis — some people yield no such responses at all, others give a few, and some do everything that might be expected of a highly hypnotized person. By simply counting up the number of items "passed" in this way, a hypnotic score is obtained that can then be correlated with other kinds of scores (E. R. Hilgard, 1965, 1968; Weitzenhoffer & Hilgard, 1959). An imagery score can be derived from a self-report of the vividness with which events can be experienced in various sensory modalities, according to a method early developed by Betts (1909). Table 1 shows a relation between self-reported imagery and hypnotic susceptibility. Results are from two samples, one from the University of Sydney in Australia, one from the Stanford Laboratory. Both yield small but significant correlations for the samples as a whole. Although in Sydney the correlation for female subjects was not significant, and in Stanford that for male subjects was not

Table 1. Correlation between Scores on Betts Imagery
Scale and Hypnotic Susceptibility[a]

| Group | University of Sydney | Stanford University |
|---|---|---|
| Males | | |
| Correlation | .58** | .17 |
| N | 53 | 65 |
| Females | | |
| Correlation | .20 | .32* |
| N | 42 | 55 |
| Total | | |
| Correlation | .39** | .26** |
| N | 95 | 120 |

[a] After J. R. Hilgard, *Personality and Hypnosis: A Study of Imaginative Involvement* (Chicago: University of Chicago Press, 1970), p. 95. © by the University of Chicago. All rights reserved.
* $p<.05$  ** $p<.01$

significant, these are merely the kinds of fluctuations found with low correlations, and tell us nothing important about continental differences in
response by sex. The data show that there is a relation between a life of
imagination and hypnotic susceptibility. If imagination and fantasy are
characteristics of childhood, then we have some *childlikeness* here.

Another possible childlike quality is an *aesthetic interest in nature*. This
differs from a scientific interest in nature. It is fine to be a student of
ecology or systematic biology, and to go on field trips in order to make a
study of nature appropriate to scientific knowledge on special topics. But
there is another way to view nature — to savor it, to love the sunset, to be
enraptured by the brook or the waterfall, to empathize with the soaring
bird — without worrying about the Latin names of the living things one
meets. It is this kind of absorption in nature that is related to hypnotizability, as shown in the top of Table 2. If we divide the hypnotic scores at
about their midpoint and the ratings of aesthetic involvement in nature at

Table 2. Correlations between Aesthetic Involvement in
Nature and Hypnotic Susceptibility and between
Creativity and Hypnotic Susceptibility

| Score | Low (0–5) | High (6–12) | Total |
|---|---|---|---|
| *Involvement in Nature*[a] | | | |
| High (5–7) .......... | 37 | 53 | 90 |
| Low (1–4) ........... | 56 | 38 | 94 |
| Total ............... | 93 | 91 | 184 |
| *Interest in Creative Activities*[b] | | | |
| High (5–7) .......... | 13 | 24 | 37 |
| Low (1–4) ........... | 82 | 67 | 149 |
| Total ............... | 95 | 91 | 186 |

[a] $\chi^2 = 6.27$; $p < .02$. Data from J. R. Hilgard (1970), p. 81.
[b] $\chi^2 = 4.70$; $p < .05$. Data from J. R. Hilgard (1970), p. 101.

about their midpoint, we derive a fourfold table that shows high involvement more often than not associated with high hypnotizability, and low
involvement more often than not associated with low hypnotizability. The
relationship is statistically significant by the chi-square test, as shown.

Another example would be an interest in *creative expression*. Some
people enjoy engaging in artistic, literary, or musical creation, giving
themselves the involvement which, in the extreme, leads to the feeling that
the art and the artist are one. This is also related to hypnotizability, as
shown in the bottom of Table 2. The interpretation is the same as before:

high interest in creative activities, high hypnotic susceptibility; low interest in creative activities, less likelihood of hypnotizability. A supporting study has been reported by Bowers and van der Meulen (1970). They show that highly susceptible hypnotic subjects score consistently higher than low susceptibles on nine measures of creativity.

There are many more imaginative involvements that show relationships similar to those that have been presented. These include involvement in reading (particularly science fiction and other imaginative literature), drama (both dramatic viewing and dramatic participation), religion (especially a deep personal religion rather than a more formalized religious commitment), particular athletics, and some features of adventuresomeness. These are discussed in detail in the book from which the material thus far presented has all come. I wish to call attention to just one of these, the kind of adventuresomeness that has led us to call some of our laboratory subjects "space travelers." They fall into two classes: the physical space traveler and the mental space traveler. The physical space travelers are those who enjoy being out in space, piloting an airplane or a glider, skiing, mountain climbing, exploring caves, skin diving. The mental space travelers, by contrast, get into space while sitting in a chair or being otherwise sedentary, through meditation, or drugs, or getting interested in ESP or astrology. The two types are quite different in the extreme, although occasionally they may both be found in the same person. What they have in common is an escape from the mundane, from the earthbound character of daily existence. They were first noted in an early sample of volunteers who came to the laboratory in response to an advertisement in the college paper that we would hypnotize anyone who appeared. Prospective candidates were lined up in front of the laboratory the following morning before the doors were opened. This proved to be a sample with higher mean hypnotic scores than in our usual samples, and the relation to "space interests" was striking, as shown in the accompanying tabulation ($\chi^2 =$ 25.6, $p<.001$; data from J. R. Hilgard [1970], p. 127):

| | Low to Moderately High (0–8) | High Hypnosis (9–12) | Total |
|---|---|---|---|
| Mental or physical "space travelers" ....... | 11 | 22 | 33 |
| No evident "space" interests ............. | 51 | 9 | 60 |
| Total .............. | 62 | 31 | 93 |

33

Note that two-thirds of the space travelers had scores of 9–12, higher than those classified as high in Table 2. And of those lacking in such interests only 9 of 60, about one in seven, scored that high, despite their interest in volunteering.

The adult fairylands described by our physical and mental space travelers may be located on the same dimensions as those of childhood, though of course they are adult versions. That is why I refer to childlikeness instead of childishness. This sample of data on involvements shows that the young adult who is hypnotizable has carried into his early adult years some of the attractive qualities of children. His ego has not thereby been weakened; it is the impression of those working with these subjects that their lives have been enriched and strengthened by their involvements.

Our interviewers felt a little uneasy about resting with statistical findings which allow so many individuals to be placed in the wrong quadrants of the fourfold tables, even though enough fall in the right places to lend overall significance. They suggested that we would understand hypnosis better by testing the inferences through studying a new group of highly susceptible subjects, who ought to show some of the characteristics in clearer form, and thus validate the earlier conclusions.

The subjects interviewed were very hypnotizable, that small percentage of the population which sometimes does not turn up at all in a sample of fifty or so. Although most of the findings of the larger samples were confirmed, there were some constructive supplements to the general picture. A summarization of interviews from 20 such subjects follows:

a. High involvements of the kind previously discussed, as expected, appeared in 19 of the 20 cases; usually there were several involvements reported by each subject.

b. Severe discipline leading to strict conformity demands by the parents was reported in 19 of 20 cases. This confirms an earlier discovered relation between punishment and hypnosis to be discussed below. (Because the one case not reporting involvements did report a strict discipline, he does not deviate entirely from the pattern of the statistical findings in the general sample.)

The severe discipline took several forms. Of the 20, 7 subjects reported severe physical punishment, beatings often lasting into the teen years; another 6 reported verbal beatings — being yelled at by parents enraged by the child's infractions. These assaultive types of discipline accounted together for 13 of the 20 cases, or about two-thirds. Another 6 subjects reported neither physical nor verbal punishments, but a strongly ordered home in which the parents held tight reins and the child was made to feel deeply guilty over rule violations. In only one of the cases could the home be described as undisciplined; this subject said that his mother sometimes yelled at him, but when she did he yelled right back, and by his own testimony he was not made to conform to family rules. In all of the cases there was agreement upon discipline between the father and the mother even though one of the parents may have done the actual disciplining. Usually the children believed that their parents had been right to punish them for what they had done.

c. These highly hypnotizable subjects tended to cast some doubt on the generalization from the earlier and larger samples that high susceptibility is more often associated with normality than with neuroticism. The very high subjects fell pretty well along the scale of adjustment, 7 subjects being rated as generally high in adjustment, 5 as average, and 8 as on the introvert-neurotic end of the scale. The less-well-adjusted ones give the impression that some subjects who become deeply engrossed in reading or a life of fantasy may not develop commensurate social skills, so that they remain somewhat isolated and ill at ease with their fellows without lessening their hypnotizability. The following case serves as an illustration of what was so typically found.

Bernice shows a high level of involvement in reading novels, watching movies, enjoying sensory experiences, and the aesthetic appreciation of nature. She is dramatic in her telling of stories to her parents and others. As to her reading, she says, "I usually get right in there — I get locked into it." In Dostoevsky's *Crime and Punishment*, she identified herself to some extent with almost every character. On the movie *Dr. Zhivago*: "When Lara was going to shoot, I really wanted her to; I hated him, I wanted him dead. I was Lara. The strength of the experience scared me." Bernice recalled with embarrassment her involvement in a Bradbury science fiction movie when she was in the eleventh grade. "I shrieked out in the movie, I was in it so far. I was embarrassed; you have to suppress these feelings."

Her interest in reading was supported since earliest childhood by both parents. "They're smart, but they didn't have a chance to go to college, and they wanted me to. Mother had me reading before I went to school. Father would bring books home from the library every other day for me to read. If they were hard ones we'd read them together."

How does she react to nature? "I go in the rain to the eucalyptus grove — exhilarating, so incredibly beautiful. I'm by myself; I appreciate the world; I'm in awe." She enjoys the Botanical Garden: "There are exquisite brilliant colors, special forms . . . They grow, they change . . . I watch them." A couple of weeks before she had sat all day on a hilltop, watching the hawks as they entered an updraft; she also admired the patterns of grasses in a dry wind; she enjoyed seeing the beetles and other bugs come walking by.

She dramatizes informally when telling stories to her friends. "I like to do things colorfully, so people will really get a good picture. I like to make them laugh." Her parents had always been good audiences: "My mother intensely enjoys the vicarious experiences of my life. Father likes to listen, too. He has said to mother, 'You always get to hear her stories first.'"

Discipline was unexpectedly strict in view of her warm relationship with her parents. Bernice was often slapped by her mother, at least until she was in junior high school. Mother would become angered and hysterical over some infraction. Bernice said, "I learned to duck as a reflex when she slapped me." Mother would raise her voice and disturb father, who would then order Bernice to stop whatever she was doing, thus taking mother's side. Bernice reported, "There was much isolation: 'Go to your room until you can be good.'"

How did she react to her mother's barrage of words, and to the isolation? "I could turn myself off to my mother and not hear it at all. I ignored all emotional unpleasantness. I blanked her out . . . I thought of nothing or I turned my thoughts to projects I was interested in." When sent to her room she thought of plans for the future, like going away to college: "It was all get-away stuff. The only way to handle it was not to be there psychologically."

Bernice described the experience of hypnosis as exhilarating — a word she had used in connection with her experiences of nature. She likes new experiences connected with the mind. "Hypnosis is pleasant, relaxing, timeless, a respite from the uptightness of the day." She spontaneously described the role of the hypnotist: "He's like a tour guide: he thinks up places to go, things to experience."

### THE HYPNOTIZABILITY OF CHILDREN AND ADULTS

We do not know very much about the hypnotizability of young infants; perhaps rocking an infant to sleep has something hypnotic about it, just as a lullaby may have. The kind of hypnosis that we can measure is heavily dependent upon words, and upon some fairly subtle distinctions in words — such as that between "let it happen" and "make it happen," a distinction that lies at the heart of the involuntary-voluntary dichotomy. In any case, the usual verbally induced hypnosis gets off to a slow start around the age of five or six, and climbs to a peak of responsiveness somewhere about nine or ten, as shown in Figure 1, which summarizes several investigations. After that, the responses to suggestions decline slowly. Some new data have been added from our laboratory, through the study of hypnotic susceptibility in the families of twins, a study presently to be discussed in another connection (Fig. 2). With more than twenty-five cases at each point except the last, the rise in early childhood is again shown, with a sharp decline in later adolescence and a gradual decline into middle life. These are, of course, cross-sectional curves; longitudinal curves may differ strikingly from these, as Schaie and Strother (1968) have shown for cognitive functions. We are planning some repeat testing which will permit us to do for hypnosis what they have done for cognition, but the data are not yet in.

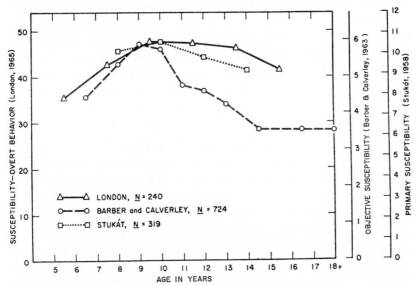

*Figure 1.* Changes in suggestibility with age. Barber and Calverley's and Stukát's (not involving hypnosis) suggestibility scales correlate highly with hypnotic performances. London did use hypnotic techniques. (Adapted from E. R. Hilgard, *Hypnotic Susceptibility* [New York: Harcourt, 1965], p. 288, by permission of Harcourt Brace Jovanovich, Inc.)

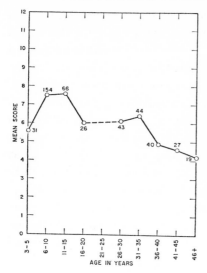

*Figure 2.* Changes in hypnotic susceptibility scores with age on SHSS, Form A,
for 277 children and 173 adults. The numbers at each point refer to the number of
cases averaged at that age; too few were
tested at ages 21–25 to provide a stable
mean. (Reprinted by permission from J.
R. Hilgard, *Personality and Hypnosis: A
Study of Imaginative Involvement* [Chi-
cago: University of Chicago Press, 1970],
p. 188. © 1970 by the University of Chicago. All rights reserved.)

How can we interpret the decline in hypnotic susceptibility with age?
My interpretation is this: Hypnosis reaches its height in the preadolescent
period because by that time language and experience have stimulated imagination and given it content, so that those characteristics described as
childlikeness have had a full opportunity to bloom. Presently, with the
conflictual self-awareness of adolescence, there comes a gradual separation from parental values as identity crises are faced, along with the actual
assumption of responsibility to become skilled, to face the need to earn a
living, to find a mate, and to establish a family. These reality-orientations
conflict with the free enjoyment of a life of fantasy and adventure, and for
many people this means a reduction in their hypnotizability. By the same
token, there are some who do not leave childlikeness behind; there are
many in the present generation who are unwilling to accept the usual transition to conventional adult responsibilities, and instead take to various
forms of personal fulfillment. One reason we need longitudinal studies is
to determine what fraction of the population loses hypnotic susceptibility,
and what fraction retains or even enhances it. The possibilities are several.
It may be that those who had little susceptibility to begin with had no experiences to enjoy or to serve as reinforcements; hence they might drop
even lower than they began. Others, moderately susceptible, might have
found the experiences satisfying, and, the times being what they are,
would find ways of enhancing their potentials. We have noted, for exam-

38

ple, a gradual increase in hypnotic scores over the last half dozen years among our Stanford students, and we have no reason to suspect that there have been changes in our standards of testing. The increasing emphasis on personal fulfillment, on consciousness expanding, on "doing your thing," may be associated with this.

A person may of course achieve satisfactions within reality orientations that are antithetical to hypnosis. The basic conflict would appear to be that between a highly responsible, vigilant, perhaps compulsive, orientation to environmental and social reality, on the one hand, and a free setting aside of reality occasionally in order to enjoy the moment for itself, as in the imaginative involvements already described. Those who hold on to the latter type of experience remain hypnotizable. Presumably adult life in general has tended to favor reality orientation, and hence, on the average, hypnotizability declines.

### THE FAMILY BACKGROUND: HERITABILITY OF HYPNOSIS

There are individual differences in hypnotic susceptibility at all ages, and despite the established personality correlates a great deal of the variance remains unaccounted for. Because we have been unable to achieve multiple correlations with known personality predictors beyond a value of about .50 (J. R. Hilgard, 1970, p. 243), some three-fourths of the variance remains unaccounted for. The possibility therefore exists that there may be some genetic correlates determining susceptibility — genotypical aspects not clearly expressed in phenotypical characteristics other than hypnosis itself. I have sometimes referred to this as a "diabetes theory." Diabetes is a disease with a known hereditary basis, but it cannot be inferred from personality tests even though it may have an influence on personality if it is long uncontrolled. It has to be detected by something specific, like sugar metabolism. Furthermore, the course of the disease is not inevitable; it can be controlled by insulin, and the amount of insulin required can sometimes be changed through psychotherapy. My argument is that hypnosis may be something like this; perhaps there is some innate capacity for dissociation that is only well brought out under the hypnotic manipulation; even a sizable hereditary correlate would not of course prevent experience from modifying the actually observed hypnotic performance.

One reason for suspecting some persistent hereditary relationship is the relatively high correlation of hypnotic susceptibility items among themselves despite their low correlations with other personality measures. The scores are highly persistent over time as determined by retest reliabilities. Few, if any, personality measures show either the internal consistency or the retest reliabilities of these hypnotic scores. A hint of a neural basis for hypnotizability comes in the positive correlation between the resting EEG-alpha duration, outside hypnosis, and the ability to exhibit hypnotic behavior (London, Hart, & Leibovitz, 1968; Nowlis & Rhead, 1968). Because resting alpha is associated with meditative experiences, it is plausibly related to hypnotic involvement. There is at present no direct evidence for genetic correlates here, but the possibility is opened up.

In any case, it seemed desirable to explore the possibility of genetic correlates through a twin study. We have made such a study, and have reported preliminary results (Morgan, Hilgard, & Davert, 1970). A twin sample was made available through the cooperation of the National Organization of Mothers of Twins Clubs, Inc. These mothers recognize that their children are of scientific interest, and are encouraged to cooperate with investigators. We invited the members of eight California chapters to participate in our project, the invitation calling for the whole family to be hypnotized: mother, father, twins, and non-twins. A team of hypnotists administered the scales in individual 45-minute sessions. The whole family was tested largely on one occasion, with the greatest of care taken to have the twins simultaneously tested in separate rooms, so that any communications between the pair would be avoided, and any experimenter bias controlled. The tested twins averaged 10.5 years of age.

Not everyone in the 80 participating families cooperated, so that we hypnotized 137 parents of the possible 157 (3 being one-parent families), and 240 of the 262 children of hypnotizable age. The details are presented in Morgan et al. (1970), so only the major results will be given here. The intraclass correlations for pairs of brothers and sisters are given in Table 3. The only significant correlation is that for monozygotic twins a highly significant $r = .63$. This significant correlation appeared in both the San Francisco and Los Angeles areas; none of the other correlations is significant.

The classification according to monozygotic or dizygotic for same-sex pairs depended upon parental accounts, and is thus subject to some error of classification, perhaps on the order of 20 per cent (Smith, 1965). Still, the effect of misclassification should dilute the MZ pairs with DZ ones, and should add some MZ pairs to the DZ ones, attenuating the differences. It is obvious from the data that we have two distinct populations of twins.

Table 3. Intraclass Correlations of Hypnotic Susceptibility
Scores of Twin and Non-Twin Pairs of Children[a]

| Subjects | Number of Pairs | Intraclass Correlation (r) |
|---|---|---|
| Monozygotic twins .............. | 35 | .63*** |
| Dizygotic twins | | |
| Same-sexed ................. | 27 | .08 |
| Opposite-sexed .............. | 14 | .04 |
| Total ...................... | 41 | .07 |
| Sibling non-twin pairs | | |
| Same-sexed ................. | 16 | .22 |
| Opposite-sexed .............. | 12 | .01 |
| Total ...................... | 38 | .14 |

[a] Reprinted by permission of Greenwood Periodicals, Inc., from A. H. Morgan, E. R. Hilgard, & E. C. Davert, "The Heritability of Hypnotic Susceptibility of Twins: A Preliminary Report," *Behavior Genetics*, 1970, 1 (No. 3), 213–223.
*** $p < .001$

Because there are no sex differences in hypnotizability, the fact that same-sexed and opposite-sexed DZ twins correlated alike (and near to zero) indicates that misclassification is probably not seriously affecting the results. If one adopts the usual methods of determining an index of heritability (H), this derives from the intraclass correlations as follows (Vandenberg, 1966):

$$H = (R_{MZ} - R_{DZ})/(1 - R_{DZ}) = .56/.93 = .60$$

A nearly equivalent, though computationally slightly different value, is obtained from variance estimates, in this case yielding an index value of $H = .64$. Accepting this conventional measure uncritically, we would say that about three-fifths of the intrafamilial variance in hypnotic susceptibility is correlated with heredity. This is the same order of magnitude as the highest values Gottesman (1963, 1969) has found in his studies of the hereditary correlates of personality test scores of traits such as anxiety or social introversion.

It is important to remember that one does not disprove a hereditary correlate by proving an environmental one, and vice versa. There is no contradiction between having at once hereditary and environmental antecedents; the hereditary-environmental interaction is what usually turns out to be most interesting, if it can be unraveled. At the present stage of our knowledge, we seldom can do this with any precision. I shall therefore accept the heritability calculation as indicating a possible hereditary correlate, and go on to see what further evidence can be found for either hereditary or environmental relationships.

I would predict from the failure of correlations for either dizygotic twin pairs or sibling non-twin pairs that there would be an absence of correlation with parental hypnotizability. This is what is found (Table 4). There are three significant correlations, of which two are with the father — a correlation of .35 with the scores of male children, and a correlation of .33 with twin pairs. The single significant midparent correlation, that with male children, is evidently created primarily by the father because the mother correlates only .04 with these boys.

Table 4. Correlations of Hypnotic Susceptibility Scores of Parents and Children[a]

| Children | With Father | | With Mother | | With Midparent[b] | |
|---|---|---|---|---|---|---|
| | N | r | N | r | N | r |
| Mean of tested children in family .... | 52 | .17 | 67 | .15 | 52 | .16 |
| Mean of male children in family ..... | 45 | .35* | 55 | .04 | 45 | .36* |
| Mean of female children in family ... | 33 | −.02 | 46 | .05 | 33 | .08 |
| Mean of twin pairs | | | | | | |
| Monozygotic pairs .............. | 21 | .38 | 24 | .22 | 21 | .36 |
| Dizygotic pairs ................ | 21 | .27 | 30 | −.17 | 21 | .12 |
| Total ....................... | 42 | .33* | 54 | .07 | 42 | .26 |

[a] Reprinted by permission of Greenwood Periodicals, Inc., from A. H. Morgan, E. R. Hilgard, & E. C. Davert, "The Heritability of Hypnotic Susceptibility of Twins: A Preliminary Report," *Behavior Genetics*, 1970, 1 (No. 3), 213–223.
[b] Average of father and mother.
* $p < .05$

The unique father-son correlation is difficult to explain on any simple hereditary basis: on a genetic basis, a son should resemble the father and mother equally in a non–sex-linked trait; if the trait is sex-linked, he should be more likely to resemble the mother. If we examine an identification basis (that is, an environmental correlate), we might expect the son to resemble the father through some sort of emulation. But hypnosis itself is not indulged in enough to be the basis for imitation; what must be emulated are some of the traits related to hypnotizability. We devised a test for this conjecture. As part of the twin-family study we had the parents fill out personality questionnaires, rating their children on eleven characteristics selected in part on the basis of results from the interview study. Then, for each of the characteristics the parents indicated whether or not the child was more like father or mother, indistinguishably like both, or like neither. It is possible to derive a "resemblance score" for the number of these traits

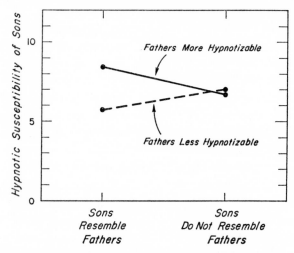

*Figure 3.* Resemblance of sons to fathers in hypnotizability as related to their resemblances in personality. (From Morgan, Hilgard, & Davert, 1970.) (Reprinted by permission of Greenwood Periodicals, Inc., from A. H. Morgan, E. R. Hilgard, & E. C. Davert, "The Heritability of Hypnotic Susceptibility of Twins: A Preliminary Report," *Behavior Genetics*, 1970, 1 [No. 3], 213–223.)

in which a boy resembles his father, or for any other child-parent combination. This was done for sons and fathers, with the result shown in Figure 3.

Note that if a son resembles a highly hypnotizable father he tends to be more hypnotizable himself; if he resembles a less hypnotizable father he tends to be less hypnotizable. If, on the other hand, sons do *not* resemble their fathers according to the personality ratings, their hypnotizability is *not* differentiated by the fact that the father is high or low in hypnotizability. The interactions are statistically significant, and the scores of those resembling high and low fathers differ significantly by a *t*- test. If accepted, the results of this analysis would argue that some portion of hypnotic susceptibility is *not* directly inherited, but is inherited socially, through identification with a hypnotizable or nonhypnotizable father. The difficulty with this analysis is that it does not hold for other parent-child relationships; but there may of course be something unique in the relationship between a father and his son.

In any case, we cannot rest with a demonstration that monozygotic twins correlate significantly in hypnosis. The matter is much more complex than this.

## PARENTAL INFLUENCES IN CHILDHOOD

Children who develop the kinds of imaginative involvements that are associated with hypnotic susceptibility commonly do so through parents who have similar involvements. This turned up time after time in the interviews with students, and led to the conjecture that one reason some children retain their hypnotic abilities into young adult life and others do not is that the presence of a supporting adult helps keep the involvements (and hence hypnotizability) alive. The relationships are complex, however, and difficult to show through parent-child correlations.

The one environmental imposition upon the child that is unequivocally related to the hypnotizability of our college students is punishment used in child rearing — a result confirmed in the follow-up interviews previously mentioned. This was a surprise to us on two grounds. In the first place, we were initially more prepared to accept "basic trust" as a background for hypnosis, and expected this to derive from a nonpunitive relationship between parent and child; in the second place, because of the emphasis upon permissiveness in contemporary middle-class culture, we did not expect enough of our Stanford students to report severe childhood punishment to make possible a study of its effect. We were wrong on both counts. The relation between reported severity of punishment in childhood and hypnotic susceptibility at the college age is shown in the accompanying tabulation ($\chi^2 = 10.62$, $p<.01$; data from J. R. Hilgard, 1970, p. 208).

| | Low (0–5) Hypnosis | High (6–12) Hypnosis | Total |
|---|---|---|---|
| High punishment (5–7) .. | 22 | 41 | 63 |
| Medium punishment (4) . | 36 | 30 | 66 |
| Low punishment (1–3) .. | 37 | 21 | 58 |
| Total .............. | 95 | 92 | 187 |

Of those reporting high punishment in childhood, two-thirds fall in the highly hypnotizable group; of those low in punishment, only one-third are highly hypnotizable. The medium punished group falls between the others. Expressed as a coefficient of correlation, punishment correlates .30 ($p<.001$) with hypnotizability, compared with a sum of the involvements which correlates but .35 ($p<.001$). Because punishment correlates a nonsignificant .12 with the sum of involvements, it is essentially a separate "factor" predictive of hypnotic susceptibility (J. R. Hilgard, 1970, p. 243), and punishment plus involvements produce a multiple correlation with hypnosis substantially higher than either one alone.

The second surprise about punishment was its prevalence in the childhood background of our Stanford students; about one-third of them reported punishment rated by our interviewers as severe, 5–7 on a 7-point scale. These are not mild reprimands, such as going without dessert or being sent to bed; they include spankings to the age of twelve, occasionally with a "big black belt," and severe deprivation for minor infractions of the rules.

We were puzzled about the effects of punishment, and have tried to understand how these effects influenced hypnotizability. For one thing, we wondered whether the stereotype of a cold, forbidding parent in a punitive home might be incorrect. Our conjecture here was right: of those reporting severe punishment in childhood, twice as many reported high mother warmth as reported low (J. R. Hilgard, 1970, p. 217). The cases interviewed later throw additional light on how childhood discipline may be related to subsequent hypnotic susceptibility.

The two main possibilities are, first, that the discipline produces an automatic conformity and desire to please those in authority, which may then be transferred from the parents to the hypnotist. We have no independent check on this, except to the extent that the ready acceptance of hypnotic suggestions is taken as evidence. The second possibility is that the discipline may give rise to a fantasy life, and this developed fantasy life then serves as a background for hypnotic susceptibility, in accordance with our general finding on the importance of imaginative involvement. This second possibility is indeed supported by the interview data. In the follow-up cases, roughly half (9 of 20) reported that they habitually indulged in active fantasy as an accompaniment or aftereffect of a severe episode of discipline. The fantasy they engaged in was seldom hostile – such as a fantasied counterattack on the punishing parent – instead it was usually pleasant, an escape from an unpleasant reality to a more enjoyable world experienced in imagination. This escape from reality to pleasant fantasy corresponds closely to the hypnotic experience.

It should be pointed out as a caution against overgeneralization that in a group of successful university students reporting on their childhood backgrounds, we do not have a representative sample of the population as a whole. Among the total of punished children, we have had a selective process so that we can interview only the *successful outcomes* of strict discipline and punishment. Recall that the mothers of our punished students were not reported as cold, but predominantly as warm and loving. We

45

have no way of knowing how much antisocial behavior, and how many school dropouts have been created in punitive homes; we do not know whether maternal coldness may be a factor in such cases. The generalizations from this study, although limited, do tell us something we did not know about university students and their childhood backgrounds.

SEX ROLE AND NON–SEX ROLE IDENTIFICATIONS

We began all these investigations by studying the personality background of hypnosis, but we ended by studying what hypnosis could tell us about personality. In the course of our interviewing, we found that many distinctions had to be made that were often not made in the personality studies with which we are familiar. The material in this section does not bear directly on the theme of childlikeness, but it is related to the development of hypnotic susceptibility because of its implications for the ways in which parents influence children.

The distinction to be made is that between *sex role (or gender)* identification and *non–sex role (or non-gender)* identification. Under the influence of psychoanalysis, so much attention was paid in the recent past to how a boy becomes a man and a girl a woman, with appropriate sex roles the criteria of good mental health, that nonpsychoanalytic writers as well became preoccupied with sex typing as the important outcome of parental identification. Although there has been an occasional voice against this preoccupation (Slater, 1961), it continues to this day; one need only look at the current child psychology textbooks to see how little attention is paid to social behavior learned from the parent of the opposite sex, and how little attention is given to the "normal" imitation that there is of this other parent — that is, an imitation *not* associated with reversed sex roles.

It soon became clear in the interviews that there are many aspects of personality and temperament that are not strongly sex typed in our culture; in such aspects there is no taboo against imitating a parent of either sex, if that parent is found attractive in respect to some of the aspects of behavior that are not sex specific. Thus most of the involvements — reading, enjoyment of nature, adventure — can be picked up from either parent. Sense of humor, playing a musical instrument, friendliness, and sociability are not the property of one sex alone.

We might suppose that the degree of dependence on the same-sexed parent would be higher in some spheres of activity than in others. Thus, in working life we might expect the son to imitate his father, and to learn

46

attitudes from the father's business or profession; the mother, more likely to be domestic, would presumably influence her daughter more. In recreation we would expect somewhat less specific imitation, because either parent can enjoy the theater or music, or a hike in the country, or playing tennis or golf. Temperament, as reflected in general cheerfulness or moroseness or moodiness, is probably little sex specific. Table 5 gives the results of an examination of the student's statement of his own similarity to a father or a mother in these three different categories. The male subjects are only a little more likely to say that they resemble the father only rather than the mother only in their work habits, recreational interests, or temperament. The same is true for the girls, except that numerically more say they are like their fathers (rather than their mothers) in recreation and temperament. A substantial number say they resemble both parents in all of the characteristics. It thus appears that when one gets away from specific sex role behavior, personality is not at all highly based on identification with the same-sexed parent alone.

Table 5. Identifications of Young Adults with Their Parents in Work, Recreation, and Temperament[a]

| Identification | Work | Recreation | Temperament |
|---|---|---|---|
| Sons with: | | | |
| Father only ........ | 33% | 44% | 47% |
| Both parents ....... | 27 | 11 | 19 |
| Mother only ....... | 23 | 25 | 30 |
| Neither parent ...... | 13 | 18 | 3 |
| Not ascertained ..... | 4 | 2 | 1 |
| Total ($N = 115$) .. | 100% | 100% | 100% |
| Daughters with: | | | |
| Mother only ........ | 37% | 31% | 29% |
| Both parents ........ | 28 | 25 | 33 |
| Father only ......... | 26 | 33 | 35 |
| Neither parent ...... | 6 | 10 | 3 |
| Not ascertained ..... | 3 | 1 | 0 |
| Total ($N = 72$) ... | 100% | 100% | 100% |

[a] After J. R. Hilgard, *Personality and Hypnosis: A Study of Imaginative Involvement* (Chicago: University of Chicago Press, 1970), pp. 191, 192. © 1970 by the University Chicago. All rights reserved.

We might suppose that there is some bias in this because the socioeconomic class from which university students come makes less of sex specific behavior in cultural settings than lower socioeconomic classes do. That is, college men are likely to express interests in art and music that might be considered somewhat effeminate in the blue-collar culture, and women are likely to go in for politics or engage in business promotion in a way considered a little masculine in other strata. The families of twins cover a somewhat wider spectrum than the university sample; although essentially a middle-class group, it is not so limited as the university sample. Furthermore, instead of children (as young adults) describing their similarities to their parents, we have parents describing their young children's resemblances to themselves, with, of course, some of the uncertainties involved in such judgments (Roff & Ricks, 1970). The results for sons are given in the top half of Table 6. When the results on the eleven ratings are averaged, almost the identical number of sons resemble mothers as resemble fathers in these characteristics, with a substantial number resembling both. In six of the characteristics the sons resemble the father more often than the mother; in five they resemble the mother more often than the father. Obviously, resemblance is not merely a father-son matter.

The same comparisons are shown for the daughters in the bottom half of Table 6. The results are much the same — the daughters slightly more often resembling the mother than the father, with an excess in favor of the mother on eight of the scales, in favor of the father on one, and one tie. The main point is that there is not very strong sex typing, although one can pose some hypotheses from the table. The daughters tend more often to resemble their fathers in strong ego traits, such as orderly compliance, striving for perfection, and taking pride in tasks well done. (These are not traits correlated with hypnotizability; the fathers are in fact less hypnotizable than the mothers in this study.) Except for the self-control rating, the traits in which daughters resemble mothers are those associated with hypnotizability. Could it be that the failure of the daughters to correlate with their mothers in hypnosis results from the cancellation of much of this effect by identification with the compulsive traits of the father, when these are present? It would take a larger sample, carefully studied, to answer questions of this kind, but it is intriguing to play with the possibilities.

Within our college population there are some evidences of a cross-sex parental identification in hypnosis. We did not find this in the family population from which the twins were drawn, where the only correlation that amounted to anything was a father-son one. But in the two studies we are dealing with children at a very different stage of development (averaging 10 years in the child study and nearly 20 years in the college sample) and of somewhat different socioeconomic backgrounds, and we do not know

Table 6. Similarity of Children and Parents $(N = 83)$

| Traits | Father | Mother | Both | Neither | Total |
|---|---|---|---|---|---|
| | *Sons* | | | | |
| More often like father | | | | | |
| Striving for perfection ... | 31 | 18 | 29 | 22 | 100 |
| Adventuresomeness ...... | 28 | 18 | 38 | 16 | 100 |
| Curiosity ............. | 27 | 24 | 37 | 12 | 100 |
| Pride in tasks .......... | 24 | 14 | 46 | 16 | 100 |
| Humor ............... | 22 | 15 | 46 | 17 | 100 |
| Fearfulness ........... | 16 | 13 | 35 | 36 | 100 |
| More often like mother | | | | | |
| Imagination ........... | 20 | 33 | 27 | 20 | 100 |
| Cautiousness .......... | 18 | 32 | 28 | 22 | 100 |
| Sensitivity ........... | 13 | 28 | 43 | 16 | 100 |
| Self-control ........... | 19 | 24 | 33 | 24 | 100 |
| Compliance ........... | 13 | 18 | 51 | 18 | 100 |
| Mean .................. | 21 | 22 | 37 | 20 | 100 |
| | *Daughters* | | | | |
| More often like mother | | | | | |
| Curiosity ............. | 35 | 13 | 39 | 13 | 100 |
| Imagination ........... | 35 | 15 | 35 | 15 | 100 |
| Cautiousness .......... | 35 | 22 | 26 | 17 | 100 |
| Sensitivity ........... | 33 | 16 | 33 | 18 | 100 |
| Self-control ........... | 33 | 21 | 23 | 23 | 100 |
| Humor ............... | 26 | 13 | 42 | 19 | 100 |
| Adventuresomeness ..... | 26 | 22 | 26 | 26 | 100 |
| Equally like mother and like father: | | | | | |
| Fearfulness ........... | 21 | 21 | 32 | 26 | 100 |
| More often like father | | | | | |
| Compliance ........... | 14 | 21 | 42 | 23 | 100 |
| Striving for perfection ... | 17 | 21 | 41 | 21 | 100 |
| Pride in tasks .......... | 13 | 17 | 45 | 25 | 100 |
| Mean .................. | 26 | 18 | 35 | 21 | 100 |

enough to make firm assertions about the meaning of these differences. In the university sample, males resembling their mothers in temperament and females resembling their fathers scored higher in hypnosis than did sons resembling fathers and daughters resembling mothers $(p<.01$; J. R. Hilgard, 1970, p. 197). Mother warmth was significantly correlated with hypnotic susceptibility of male subjects, but correlated not at all with female subjects; father warmth nearly reached significance in correlation with female subjects, but correlated not at all with male subjects.

If these cross-identifications should be confirmed in subsequent studies, some interesting theoretical possibilities arise. One is that a child may find something attractive in a parent who has the childlike qualities associated with hypnosis, regardless of that parent's sex. The child who chooses an opposite-sex model, against the pressure for a same-sex choice, may beyond chance choose one who is hypnotizable. Such selectivity could explain our findings that those who model after an opposite-sex parent are more hypnotizable than those who model after a same-sex parent. The second possibility is based on a dissociation concept. If it is assumed that most everyday social behaviors are modeled upon the same-sex parent, then the prevailing reality-oriented behavior will be of this kind. But there may be a concealed fascination with some of the qualities of the other parent, not typically revealed in behavior, but perhaps present in the fantasy life. If that should be the case, hypnosis, allowing these concealed strands to find expression, will reflect some of the hidden identification with the parent of the opposite sex. The fact that some temperamental similarity to that parent is openly acknowledged does not destroy this argument; the dissociated material need not be "unconscious," but it may simply be restrained under the ordinary pressures of social behavior. The restraint may be similar to that of a father who likes to play with trains but waits for a son to come along in order to enjoy this pastime; this does not mean that his desire has all along been unconscious.

### DISSOCIATION OR REGRESSION?

The use of the word *childlike* to describe some of the characteristics that make an adult hypnotizable calls for an answer to the question, Is hypnosis a regressive state? It may be recalled that Gill and Brenman (1959) subtitled their book on hypnosis "Psychoanalytic Studies in Regression." The word *regression* as used by a psychoanalyst has a great many connotations embedded in that theory, such as the distinction between primary and secondary processes in thought, between the primitive irrational or impulsive and the more mature, rational, or conceptual. There is also the inviting concept of regression in the service of the ego, a kind of adaptive regression within which Gill and Brenman fit much that happens in hypnosis. I find the psychoanalytic concept of regression too vague to be useful, partly because there is no clear distinction within it between the childish and the childlike.

A term that I prefer, although it is not widely in favor, is *dissociation*. I believe that the concept of the unity of consciousness and personality is very misleading, that there are indeed many cleavages in thought, motivation, and feeling that are better described as dissociated than regressive activities. Thus, a constructive life of fantasy, even though it partakes of irrationality, is not regressive in the sense that it is childish and immature;

ERNEST R. HILGARD

it may require a temporary setting aside of a scientific viewpoint, but the subject may be no more regressed than the writer of science fiction who, on another occasion, writes standard works of science. Regression theory and dissociation theory have this in common: an adult may subtly exhibit the unchildish qualities of maturity, and yet be capable of exhibiting and enjoying, upon occasion, childlike qualities. If he can, he is more likely to be hypnotically susceptible and has whatever advantages for experiencing satisfactions that this ability provides.

*References*

Barber, T. X., & D. S. Calverley. "Hypnotic-like" suggestibility in children and adults. *Journal of Abnormal and Social Psychology*, 1963, 66, 589–597.
Betts, C. H. *The distribution and functions of mental imagery.* New York: Teachers College Contribution to Education, 1909.
Bowers, K. S., & S. J. van der Meulen. Effect of hypnotic susceptibility on creativity test performance. *Journal of Personality and Social Psychology*, 1970, 14, 247–256.
Gill, M. M., & M. Brenman. *Hypnosis and related states: Psychoanalytic studies in regression.* New York: International Universities Press, 1959.
Gottesman, I. I. Heritability of personality: A demonstration. *Psychological Monographs*, 1963, 77 (9, Whole No. 572).
———. Genetic variance in adaptive personality traits. In M. Manosevitz, G. Lindzey, & D. D. Thiessen, eds., *Behavioral genetics: Method and Research*, pp. 606–617. New York: Appleton, 1969.
Hilgard, E. R. *Hypnotic susceptibility.* New York: Harcourt, 1965.
———. *The experience of hypnosis: A shorter version of hypnotic susceptibility.* New York: Harcourt, 1968.
Hilgard, J. R. *Personality and hypnosis: A study of imaginative involvement.* Chicago: University of Chicago Press, 1970.
London, P. Developmental experiments in hypnosis. *Journal of Projective Techniques and Personality Assessment*, 1965, 29, 189–199.
———, J. T. Hart, & M. P. Leibovitz. EEG alpha rhythms and susceptibility to hypnosis. *Nature*, 1968, 219, 71–72.
Morgan, A. H., E. R. Hilgard, & E. C. Davert. The heritability of hypnotic susceptibility of twins: A preliminary report. *Behavior Genetics*, 1970, 1 (No. 3), 213–223.
Nowlis, D. P., & J. C. Rhead. Relation of eyes-closed resting EEG alpha activity to hypnotic susceptibility. *Perceptual and Motor Skills*, 1968, 27, 1047–1050.
Roff, M., & D. F. Ricks. *Life history research in psychopathology.* Minneapolis: University of Minnesota Press, 1970.
Schaie, K. W., & C. R. Strother. A cross-sequential study of age changes in cognitive behavior. *Psychological Bulletin*, 1968, 70, 671–680.
Slater, P. Toward a dualistic theory of identification. *Merrill-Palmer Quarterly*, 1961, 7, 113–126.
Smith, R. T. A comparison of socioenvironmental factors in monozygotic and dizygotic twins, testing an assumption. In S. G. Vandenberg, ed., *Methods and goals in human behavior genetics*, pp. 45–62. New York: Academic Press, 1965.
Stukát, K. G. *Suggestibility: A factorial and experimental analysis.* Stockholm: Almquist & Wiksell, 1958.
Vandenberg, S. G. Contributions of twin research to psychology. *Psychological Bulletin*, 1966, 66, 327–352.
Weitzenhoffer, A. M., & E. R. Hilgard. *Stanford Hypnotic Susceptibility Scale, Forms A and B.* Palo Alto, Calif.: Consulting Psychologists Press, 1959.

# Explorations into Patterns of Mental Development and Prediction from the Bayley Scales of Infant Development

THE topic of infant mental development, or, more precisely, parameters of infant development relevant to later mental ability, is interesting for both theoretical and practical, social reasons. A common denominator in many of the contemporary studies of infancy is the attempt to fathom the components of early human development which bear upon later status. This unifying goal is often apparent despite the great variety of research methods used, questions posed, and theoretical models put forward. In this paper we shall discuss past and present research using the Bayley Scales of Infant Development as predictors of subsequent intellectual status and review some of the issues and methodological problems encountered.

## The Berkeley Growth Study

The Bayley infant scales have only recently become available for general use, following revision and broad standardization (Bayley, 1969). Hitherto, they have been used for research in various ways, including the Collaborative Perinatal Research Project (Mendelson, 1967), assessments of infants in other cultures (Francis-Williams & Yule, 1967; Kohen-Raz,

NOTE: This paper is based on research of the Berkeley Growth Study of the Institute of Human Development, University of California, Berkeley. The research has been funded in part by the University of California, by grant MH-08135 from the National Institute of Mental Health, and by grant HD-03617 from the National Institute of Child Health and Human Development, United States Public Health Service.

1967, 1968; Phatak, 1968, 1969), and a longitudinal study of mentally retarded infants (Bayley, 1966b; Bayley, Rhodes, Gooch, & Marcus, in press; Stedman & Eichorn, 1964). However, the major research use of the scales has been in conjunction with the Berkeley Growth Study, a longitudinal study which began in 1928 and has continued to the present (Jones & Bayley, 1941). The Bayley infant scales, devised to provide measures of infant development for the study, included a variety of "mental" items which incorporated many aspects of intelligence, such as perception, memory, imitation, adaptation, problem solving, social responsiveness, and vocalization. They also included items of fine and gross motor development, descriptions of behaviors relating to infant traits and temperament, and observations of maternal behaviors. The mental and motor items were first standardized on the initial group of 61 Berkeley Growth Study infants to produce the California First Year Mental Scale (Bayley, 1933a) and the California Infant Scale of Motor Development, from birth to three years (Bayley, 1935). The Berkeley Growth Study continuation of mental scale items through three years (Bayley, 1933b) forms the basis for this scale's extension in its present form to thirty months; the companion scales of motor development and behavioral assessment cover the same age range.

Because the infant measures were comprehensive, it has been possible to return again and again to these data whenever trends in the longitudinal sample or theoretical questions have suggested that such a review might be profitable. The babies were tested at monthly intervals from ages one to fifteen months, then at three-month intervals to thirty months of age. Because of the short intervals between tests, it has been possible to ascertain the emergence of specific abilities on the scales for each infant with considerable precision. Replacement cases, added to the sample over a period of several years, have been included in Berkeley Growth Study reports published after 1959. Long-term data over thirty-six years are based on the 63 subjects who were tested at most ages.

Data collected from this group of subjects over the years have included many kinds of measures, but a dominant and consistent research interest has been the development of mental abilities (e.g., Bayley, 1955, 1968a). Particular emphasis has been given to a search for relations between differential variables in infancy and differences in mature cognitive abilities (Bayley, 1940, 1965; Bayley & Schaefer, 1964).

Additional longitudinal data are available from the test records of ap-

53

proximately 130 children of the Berkeley Growth Study subjects. Many of these second-generation members of the Study were tested with the Bayley infant scales on a systematic, but less intensive, schedule. Annual assessments since infancy have included a number of tests and measures used with the original, parent group. Many of these children have now reached adolescence and their cumulative records provide a potential source for updating and corroborating previous data.

## The Search for Prediction

The earliest results of the Berkeley Growth Study contradicted some theoretical notions of the day and indicated the complexities inherent in a search for prediction based on infant measures. By the time the children were three years old, it was clear that the notion of IQ constancy, based on the popular, simplistic concept of the IQ as a pure reflection of genetic mental capacity, did not hold. It was also clear that individual rates of infant growth on the mental scales were unstable and that prediction based on IQ was not possible except over very brief periods of time (Bayley, 1933b, 1949). The orderly relation of prediction to age of testing and to interval between tests has been shown for other studies, as well (Honzik, 1938; Honzik, Macfarlane, & Allen, 1948; Sontag, Baker, & Nelson, 1958). Although there have been those who have suggested that these early results were both inevitable and conclusive (Eyesenck, 1953; Hunt, 1961; Irwin, 1942), the search for prediction from infant performance has continued to interest many investigators (Escalona & Moriarty, 1961; Knobloch & Pasamanick, 1960; Simon & Bass, 1956). There are reasons for such persistence.

First, there is evidence that infant test scores differentiate in a general way between normal and retarded individuals, although they are not predictive for the intellectually superior. When the test of IQ is augmented by other observations of behavior, the prediction improves (Ames, 1967; Werner, Honzik, & Smith, 1968). Although broad trends lack the precision necessary for prediction within a relatively homogeneous normal population (such as the Berkeley Growth Study), they do suggest that one is viewing the tip of the predictive iceberg.

An important factor in the continuing search for prediction is the influence of theoretical constructs which portray development in terms of processes or stages evolving progressively from earliest infancy (Erikson, 1950; Piaget, 1960). If each new stage or process builds upon previous ones, then past experience becomes relevant for present behavior; prior development is related to subsequent development. There is no reason to exclude cognitive development from this argument. Mental abilities do not arise spontaneously, but have their roots in earlier stages of development — just as the onset of walking, though dramatic, has its precursors in earlier stages of locomotion. Where individual differences exist, one may search for the continuous, differentiating thread through development, even though its form and substance may be altered by changing developmental processes.

There are studies that report elements within infant tests which discriminate between infant groups. Honzik, Hutchings, and Burnip (1965) found specific differences at eight months of age between infants judged normal and those suspected of being neurologically impaired according to birth record data. In this study, items within all three of the Bayley infant scales (Mental, Motor, and Behavior Record) were discriminating. Escalona (1968) found specific differences in normal infants at eight months of age when she investigated the interactive effects of innate traits and maternal behaviors. For some of her comparisons she found differences in developmental rates, whereas for others, the differences were reflected in the kinds of test items passed, even though total scores were equal. The results of these studies are not, in themselves, predictive. One cannot presume, for example, that the distinctive patterns of Honzik's impaired infants are necessarily related to cognitive development, even though the later sequelae of the damage may include mental retardation. Nor can one assume that the early establishment of visual or sensorimotor differences at eight months will predict adult differences for Escalona's normal infants. However, these studies lend support to the idea that individual differences in infant test performance may be due, at least in part, to factors other than genetically controlled maturational rates. Indeed, it appears that subtle, differential variables may be influencing the infant's capacity or opportunity to interact with his environment, and that these influences are expressed as differences in the early organization of specific patterns of ability. Using the longitudinal research model, we may be able to trace back through the developmental history of an individual, or a group of individuals who are unique in some trait, to determine the early manifestations of the mature ability. This method has been used for the Berkeley Growth Study data by looking for correlations between mature traits and early behavior.

55

One technique used was to compare the six subjects who earned the highest IQ's on tests given from 14 to 16 years of age with the six who earned the lowest IQ's during the same period, by examining discriminating items from their previous performance on the infant mental tests. There were thirty-one test items which had been passed at least two months earlier in infancy, on the average, by the brighter teenage group; only one item was found which discriminated in the opposite direction. These were a heterogeneous assortment of items with no obvious communality (Bayley, 1949). When these items were combined and scored as a separate test, they did not prove predictive for the whole group at ages 16–18 (Bayley, 1955).

The consistency correlations of the Berkeley Growth Study mental test data for the first 18 years were subjected to factor analysis (Hofstaetter, 1954). Three distinct, age-related factors were obtained. The infancy factor, predominant during the first two years, was named Sensory Motor Alertness; between two and four years the factor Persistence was identified; after four years, a predominant factor was isolated and named Manipulation of Symbols. The finding of a persistent factor after the age of four years is in accord with the increasing predictive power noted for tests given after this age. The validity of the factor analysis was subsequently challenged in a criticism by Cronbach (1967).

The search for a unitary intellectual predictor shifted to a search for specific elements in the infant records which might be predictive of later general or specific abilities. A major study (Bayley & Schaefer, 1964) and subsequent follow-up (Bayley, 1968a) present correlations among temperament in infancy, maternal behaviors in infancy, and adult mental scores. Both the numbers and the magnitude of correlations were greater for the males than for the females. The persistent sex differences found in these data led to consistent separation by sex in all subsequent investigations using the infancy measures of the Berkeley Growth Study. Sex differences are also reported for adult measures of intellectual ability. Subscales of the Wechsler tests given at different adult ages show sex differences both in patterns of ability and in changes in these patterns over time (Bayley, 1966a, 1968b). However, there is also evidence of considerable individual stability in adulthood for a number of both personality variables and mental abilities (Bayley, 1966a).

Specific infant test items have been re-examined for functional properties which might be used for predictive purposes. The miniature scale of heterogeneous items in the test, which had been passed at an earlier age by the high IQ adolescent group, was not predictive in subsequent years for the group as a whole, but it seemed possible that there might be other homogeneous groups of items which would have better predictive power. An a priori construction of subscales according to item content was not attempted because most of the items assess behavior in more than one functional domain and because developmental changes in the infant may give different portent to superficially similar items placed at different ages on the scale. Instead, the infant scores on specific items were subjected to the Tryon cluster analysis. This was possible because the babies had been tested at monthly intervals so that an age-of-first-passing could be determined for each item on the scale. By computing product-moment correlations for each item with each of the other items, it was possible to find clusters of items which hung together, in that precocity on one resulted in precocity for all. Six subscales were identified (Bayley, 1966b, 1968a, 1970) which were clearly related to separate functions but also were restricted to specific age placement rather than extending across the range of the test. In chronological order, they are, Visual Following (2–3 months); Social Responsiveness (3–7 months); Perceptual Interest (1–2 and 15–17 months); Manual Dexterities (4–7 months), Vocalizations (8–14 months) and Object Relations (10–17 months). The correlations of these First Year Factors with later IQ have been reported (Bayley, 1968a, 1970; Cameron, Livson, & Bayley, 1967). Of the six, only Vocalizations was predictive. This factor showed a dramatic sex difference in its prediction of IQ beyond 3 years of age, remaining high and consistent for females but dropping and remaining very low for the males from age 4 years through 36. This scale was found to be independent from the socioeconomic status of the subjects' parents. The earliest subscale, Visual Following, showed no consistent relation with mature intelligence but did show positive and increasing correlations for males with Wechsler digit symbol subtests, which had been given five times from ages 16 to 36. A predictive mental factor was found in the preschool scale for items ranging from 20 to 60 months. This factor, labeled the Memory for Forms scale, predicted Stanford-Binet intelligence scores from 5 to 10 years of age, for males only. It is not until the interval of 2½ to 6 years that a reliable predictor emerges for both sexes, and its items tap the child's mastery of basic abstract words.

## Item Analyses

At the present time there are two different analyses of the Infant Mental Scale in progress which we can report in a preliminary manner. Both are attempts to pinpoint specific items in the test which illustrate differences in cognitive development in infancy and to relate these to later intellectual status.

### ITEM ANALYSIS OF PRECOCITY SCORES

One approach has been a re-examination of the infant precocity scores for the Berkeley Growth Study and their relations to later indices of intelligence. This study, by Dieter Bruehl (in preparation), departs from the concept of cluster scores described above (Cameron et al., 1967). In the earlier study, items given during infancy were cluster analyzed, and the resultant cluster scores were then related to performance on tests of intelligence given at adulthood. With one exception, the clusters were nonpredictive for the infancy period. The present analysis relates individual infant scale items to later test performance, to determine the specific predictive power of each item on the infant scale. According to Bruehl, this approach is based on the assumption that intellectual factors found to be correlated at one point in a developmental sequence need not be correlated at another — that is, the factor structure of intelligence in infancy may differ from that in adulthood.

Each of the 115 items on the original mental scale was correlated with a number of prediction criteria at adulthood. These prediction criteria were the eleven subscales of the adult Wechsler tests, and five scales derived from the Wechsler tests, including IQ measures. The Wechsler-Bellevue had been administered at age 16, 18, 21, and 26 years; the Wechsler Adult Intelligence Scale (WAIS) at 36 years. Not all subjects were available at each of the five adult ages. At 36 years, 54 of the subjects were tested. Items on the infant scale were scored by age-at-first-passing in a way such that a positive correlation of an item with a later index of intelligence would indicate that a subject who was precocious in a given item was also "smarter" on the later measure of intelligence.

Analyses were made for the whole group and for each sex separately. Groups were subdivided by odd and even numbers. An item was kept as a predictor only when it correlated consistently, either positively or negatively, with all measures of a particular criterion and for both odd and even subject groups. For example, an item was retained as a positive predictor of digit span for males if it correlated positively with all measures of digit span on the five Wechsler tests for both the odd and even male groups.

Using these criteria, 170 predictors were derived from the total sample, 80 positive and 90 negative. There are some indications that these predictors are more than chance results. For example, there are eleven positive predictors of Full Scale IQ and only one negative predictor; similarly, there are eight positive predictors of block design performance and no negative predictors.

The analyses for the separate sexes are based on small groups when the method of odd and even division is used. However, a sex difference is seen in the results. For the females, the total number of predictors is 69, with 53 positive and 16 negative; for the males, the total number of predictors is similar, 76 total, but only 19 of these are positive and 57 are negative. This sex difference is also evident for the specific predictors of Full Scale IQ. For the females, there are eight positive predictors with correlations ranging from .19 to .71: three negative predictors are generated, two of these occurring in items placed below two months of age. For the males, there are no positive predictors of Full Scale IQ and there are eight negative predictors, with correlations ranging from .20 to .34.

For the total group, positive predictor items for Full Scale IQ are located along the age range of the scale except for a conspicuous absence in the interval from five and a half to seven months. The negative predictors for the males begin at about the five-month level and are seen for all three IQ measures (Verbal, Performance, and Full Scale). The females show strong positive predictors from five to seven months for Full Scale and, especially, for Performance IQ. Items which are positive predictors for Verbal IQ in the females are not found until the eight-month level.

From these results, statistically derived scales can be constructed. The resulting scales may predict adult intelligence or specific abilities at higher levels than have been observed in earlier investigations.

The finding of greater positive prediction for the infant scores of females in Bruehl's correlation analysis of the mental scale is in accord with the results obtained in the earlier cluster analysis (Cameron et al., 1967). However, the correlational results further suggest that equally powerful negative predictors exist for the males. Definite sex differences in infant data have been consistently reported in Berkeley Growth Study research. It is possible that this relatively small group is idiosyncratic and hence comparisons with a different sample of subjects would be desirable. Replication of the precocity score data presents problems. The precocity scores, derived from age-at-first-passing, depend upon a systematic and frequent testing schedule in infancy. There have been no other longitudinal studies using the Bayley scales with such frequency which permit comparisons with adult performance. The twin study of Freedman and Keller (1963) presents an interesting possibility for such an analysis, since these twenty pairs of infants were tested on the Bayley scales at monthly intervals during the first year. However, a comparable analysis could not be made for many years. Even the second-generation children of the Berkeley Growth Study do not qualify for this particular analysis, for they were tested, on the average, only twice during the first year of life.

### ITEM ANALYSIS OF SINGLE TEST PERFORMANCE

A different method of analysis for the infant mental scale, currently in progress, uses data from a single test performance by each subject. This approach seems appropriate for analyzing test data collected in a variety of clinical and research settings. Stated simply, the method used is to locate those test items which are relatively "hard" or "easy" for a particular group of subjects. The 163 items of the present form of the scale are ordered chronologically (median age at passing) from below one month to thirty months and more, specific placements being derived from the large and representative standardization sample (Bayley, 1969). The infant's performance is scored by summing the total number of items passed. Typically, each infant has an assortment of passes and failures toward the upper level of his performance, resulting in some items being failed below his total pointscore ("hard" items) and others being passed above his pointscore ("easy" items). In assessing group performance we should expect to find that individual differences in passes and failures are randomly distributed, in that their occurrence would be more dependent upon the distance of the item from the individual's pointscore than upon specific item content. If we find certain items which are significantly difficult or easy for a particular group, these reflect qualitative differences between the group and the standardization sample.

By using a method of item weighting to reflect the distance of an item from the pointscore, it is possible to assign a specific value to each item passed above or failed below each pointscore. Specific item values can then be combined for subjects to locate "hard" and "easy" items for a group with varied pointscores.

JANE V. HUNT

## ITEM ANALYSIS IN MENTAL RETARDATION

The item analysis method was used to analyze 207 protocols of the mental scale which had been administered to infants and young children during diagnostic assessment of mental retardation. The tests were obtained from 150 children, multiple tests being included in the analysis when no item overlap between tests occurred. The children were chosen from the clinic population by alphabetical order of last names and are representative of the clinic group receiving the Bayley mental scale.

Table 1. Characteristics of a Clinical Population Tested on the Bayley Mental Scale, According to Level of Retardation ($N = 207$)

| AAMD Level | IQ Range | N | Percent-age | CA/ Mo. | MA/ Mo. | Ratio IQ | Point-score |
|---|---|---|---|---|---|---|---|
| Normal .......... | 84–100+ | 17 | 8.2 | 16.9 | 15.6 | 92 | 114 |
| Borderline ........ | 68–83 | 29 | 14.0 | 20.6 | 15.4 | 75 | 113 |
| Mild ............. | 52–67 | 49 | 23.7 | 28.6 | 16.6 | 58 | 118 |
| Moderate ......... | 36–51 | 69 | 33.3 | 38.9 | 16.5 | 42 | 117 |
| Severe ........... | 20–35 | 36 | 17.4 | 44.8 | 12.8 | 29 | 100 |
| Profound ......... | 1–19 | 7 | 3.4 | 48.9 | 8.2 | 17 | 79 |
| Total .......... |  | 207 |  | 33.1 | 14.2 | 52 | 107 |

Table 1 shows the composition of the retarded group. The average chronological age at testing was 33 months, with a range (not shown) of from 5 to 75 months; the average mental age was 14 months; the average ratio IQ was 52. The IQ was computed by using the mental age equivalent of the pointscore and dividing it by the chronological age. Although this is not a recommended test procedure, we have found that, for retarded children whose scores are below the range of the normal distribution, the ratio IQ derived from the mental scale agrees closely with subsequent Stanford-Binet scores.

The 207 tests were divided by IQ level, according to accepted classifications of the American Association on Mental Deficiency (AAMD) (Heber, 1959) of normal, borderline, mild, moderate, severe, and profound retardation. The greatest number of scores, 57 per cent, are in the mild and moderate categories. The group with severe retardation makes up 17 per cent of the sample, 14 per cent are in the borderline category, and relatively small groups fall in the classifications of normal and profound retardation. The average pointscore for the different classifications is fairly comparable for the first four subgroups — normal, borderline, mild, and moderate — but drops for the last two. This comparison can also be seen in the average mental ages for the different classifications.

Table 2 indicates the pointscore distribution of the tests in relation to the different levels of retardation. The lower range of the test is poorly represented by the group, with only 5 per cent scoring below 61 points and only 12 per cent scoring below 81 points. The greatest number of tests have pointscores between 81 and 140 (74 per cent of the sample), and 14 per cent are scored between 141 and 163. This means that the test protocols yield considerable information for subjects in the mental age range of 7–22 months, but limited information below and above this range.

Table 2. Distribution of Scores

| | Pointscore Range | | | | | | | | Mean |
|---|---|---|---|---|---|---|---|---|---|
| AAMD Level | 1–20 | 21–40 | 41–60 | 61–80 | 81–100 | 101–120 | 121–140 | 141–163 | Point-score |
| Normal (N = 17) ... | 0 | 0 | 1 | 1 | 3 | 3 | 7 | 2 | 114 |
| Borderline (N = 29). | 0 | 0 | 1 | 2 | 5 | 9 | 8 | 4 | 113 |
| Mild (N = 49) ..... | 1 | 0 | 1 | 1 | 8 | 11 | 18 | 9 | 118 |
| Moderate (N = 69) .. | 1 | 1 | 0 | 3 | 11 | 18 | 23 | 12 | 117 |
| Severe (N = 36) .... | 0 | 2 | 2 | 5 | 8 | 8 | 10 | 1 | 100 |
| Profound (N = 7) .. | 0 | 0 | 1 | 3 | 2 | 0 | 1 | 0 | 79 |
| Total .......... | 2 | 3 | 6 | 15 | 37 | 49 | 67 | 28 | |
| Percentage ....... | 1 | 1 | 3 | 7 | 18 | 24 | 32 | 14 | |

To find the test item characteristics for the whole group, each item is examined for the mean weighted value of the times it was passed above the pointscore ("easiness") and for the mean weighted value of the times it was failed below the pointscore ("hardness"). The difference between these values reflects the relative easiness or difficulty of an item. Wherever possible, multiple $t$ tests have been computed, based on the total number of times the item was given. One item may serve as an example. Item 88, with an age placement of nine months, tests the infant's ability to lift a cup and purposefully pick up a cube which he has seen an examiner hide under the cup. In the present study, the item was given 45 times. It was scored in the expected direction (i.e., failed above pointscore or passed below it) 27 times. It was passed above the mean ("easy") 5 times, with a mean weighted value for those 5 times of .56, or less than 1 point above the mean, overall. It was failed below the mean ("hard") 13 times and with a mean weighted value of −5.76 (more than 5 points below the pointscore, on the average). The difference between the two is −3.12, a "hard" item. Using the $t$ test, probability is .02. We can say, with some confidence, that this particular item is more difficult for the retarded population than it is for normal infants of comparable mental age.

The statistical method used is not satisfactory across the range of the test for this group of subjects, and results must be considered preliminary. At the upper and lower extremes it is not possible to make comparisons between mean weighted values because one of the values may be entirely missing or based on only a few scores. In these instances, we can indicate the hard and easy items, but probabilities are lacking. The standard deviations for the weighted values are sometimes very large, reducing the significance of a particular item. This divergence suggests a lack of homogeneity in subjects scoring in the same direction. In future comparisons it may be possible to identify the subjects with more precision, according to specific characteristics.

The hard and easy items identified by this preliminary analysis have been grouped on an ad hoc basis to conceptualize the categories of items which appear to be represented (see the list on p. 64). The first item, disproportionately difficult for the retarded group, playful response of the infant to his mirror image, is placed under the classification of social awareness. There are a number of items, ranging from just under one month to six months, which are based on very small groups of subjects but show extreme "hardness" for these small numbers. Several of these items seem to be related to "social awareness." Included are reactions to novel and familiar social situations as well as reactions to the infant's own mirror image.

The second category of difficult items is associated with object awareness. These items seem to be those measuring the comprehension of object relationships or object constancy. The earliest items, based on small numbers of tests and not included in the list, combine visual with auditory features — the infant looks at what he hears. The two significant items in this group are object constancy items — finding the hidden cube and finding one of two hidden objects. The last item also includes language comprehension and illustrates the difficulties of isolating test items by content.

The third category of hard items for the retarded has been labeled motor-adaptive. The significant item in this category tests the child's ability to attempt to accept a third cube while already holding two other cubes. Other, earlier-placed "hard" items in this group appear to be related to ability in holding or grasping two cubes at once.

The motor-imitative items are an extension of the motor-adaptive group, and are placed at 9.4 to 16.7 months. These all require that the

## Items on the Bayley Mental Scale "Hard" and "Easy" for Mentally Retarded Subjects

| Classification and Item | Age Level (Mo.) | |
|---|---|---|
| *"Hard" Items (Failed below Pointscore)* | | |
| Social awareness | | |
| 76. Playful response to mirror ........ | 6.2* | |
| Object awareness | | |
| 88. Picks up cup: secures cube ........ | 9.0** | |
| 131. Finds 2 objects ................. | 19.7** | |
| Motor-adaptive | | |
| 82. Attempts to secure 3 cubes ........ | 7.6** | |
| Motor-imitative | | |
| 90. Puts cube in cup on command ...... | 9.4* | |
| 92. Stirs with spoon in imitation ....... | 9.7* | |
| 119. Builds tower of 3 cubes .......... | 16.7* | (moderate) |
| Language | | |
| 101. Jabbers expressively .............. | 12.0* | |
| 106. Imitates words .................. | 12.5** | |
| 113. Says 2 words ................... | 14.2** | (mild) |
| 124. Names 1 object ................. | 17.8*** | (moderate) |
| 130. Names 1 picture ................ | 19.3*** | |
| 138. Names 2 objects ................ | 21.4*** | |
| 139. Points to 5 pictures ............. | 21.6** | |
| 141. Names 3 pictures ............... | 22.1*** | |
| 146. Names 3 objects ............... | 24.0* | (moderate) |
| 148. Points to 7 pictures ............. | 24.7** | |
| 149. Names 5 pictures ............... | 25.0*** | |
| *"Easy" Items (Passed above Pointscore)* | | |
| Motor-adaptive | | |
| 66. Bangs in play .................. | 5.4* | |
| Motor-imitative | | |
| 103. Turns pages of book ............. | 12.0* | |
| 105. Dangles ring by string ........... | 12.4* | |
| 112. Spontaneous scribble ............ | 14.0* | |
| 114. Puts 9 cubes in cup ............. | 14.3*** | |
| 122. Attains toy with stick ........... | 17.0* | |
| 135. Differentiates scribble from stroke.. | 20.5** | |
| Language | | |
| 116. Uses gestures to make wants known.. | 14.6* | |
| Spatial concepts | | |
| 102. Uncovers blue box .............. | 12.0* | |
| 108. Places 1 peg repeatedly .......... | 13.0** | (mild) |
| 115. Closes round box ............... | 14.6*** | |
| 120. Pink board: places round block .... | 16.8** | |
| 122. Attains toy with stick ........... | 17.0* | |
| 134. Pegs placed in 30 seconds ........ | 20.0* | |
| 137. Pink board: completes ........... | 21.2* | |
| 142. Blue board: places 6 blocks ....... | 22.4** | |

*p<.10          **p<.05          ***p<.01

64

child combine materials in a specific way, following a demonstration. Verbal instructions and encouragement are added for items 90 and 119.

The last and most significant group of hard items is related to language ability. This group covers the mental age range 12–25 months. Item content includes both language comprehension and speech, but with more emphasis on speech. Four of these items (101, 106, 113, 124) were included in the original Bayley infant scale given to the Berkeley Growth Study infants, and all four differentiated the high IQ group from the low IQ group at adolescence. Of these four items, 124 ("names 1 object") is the most powerfully discriminating. The high IQ group passed this item, on the average, eight months earlier than did the low IQ group. This item is also a positively correlated predictor, for females, of the Wechsler test Performance IQ in Bruehl's analysis of the Berkeley Growth Study data described above. Item 101 ("jabbers expressively") is a positively correlated predictor for the three adult IQ measures for the females. It is not surprising to find that verbal items appear to differentiate between retarded children and normal infants of comparable mental ages, but it is encouraging to find significant differences appearing as early as the twelve-months level on the scale. The earliest items assessing vocalization do not appear to be difficult for the small numbers of the retarded group who were given them. There appears to be a transition to items measuring verbal ability following earlier difficulty with items related to social awareness and object awareness. However, Honzik et al. (1965) found that early vocalization items differentiated, for males, between the "definitely suspect" group and less suspect groups, and the interpretation of the retardation data for items below seven months is highly speculative.

The bottom half of the list on page 64 indicates the items which are disproportionately easy for the retarded in comparison with the normal population. The earliest category of items seems to be motor-adaptive, from three to six months, with one item, "bangs in play," reaching significance. Three other items in this category, again showing a strong trend for small samples, are behaviors that include mouthing, fingering, and noise production from objects. Unlike the "hard" items in this same category, these seem to have a common quality of motor control and manipulation, with maturational overtones. (An examination of the precocity score correlations for the four easy items reveals one positive and two negative predictors of IQ. There are three positive predictors and one negative one in the three items which constitute the hard items in the category of motor-adaptive. None of the predictors is for an IQ measure and the items give poor discrimination.) The easy items include repetitive behaviors which appear to be those which develop relatively more normally in the retarded child, even though their development may be considerably delayed in comparison with chronological age.

A second group of easy items, motor-imitative, includes examples of de- layed imitation from general environmental experiences (turning pages, scribbling) as well as responses of direct imitation (dangling the ring, using a stick). The items range in age placement from 12 to 20 months. There are two items which demonstrate an ability to handle crayon and paper. This ability may be closely allied with spatial concepts. The third easy category, language, has one item with no speech requirements.

The largest and most statistically significant group of easy items has to do with spatial concepts. This group extends from 12 to 22 months and includes a variety of concrete, problem-solving tasks, ranging from un- covering a box to completing formboards and pegboards. On these tasks, the retarded group performs with relatively more ease than does the nor- mal child of the same mental age. The difference may be an artifact of language difficulty — that is, failed language items in the test protocols may result in a lower total pointscore, which has the effect of inflating the weighted value of the performance tasks. However, there is a clear di- chotomy here of a qualitative sort, and spatial concept items are not rep- resented in the difficult items at any age level on the scale.

These tentative results are presented to show the trends in the kinds of items falling into the difficult and easy categories. The next step which must be taken is that of enlarging the sample considerably, to allow more tests of significance for the items, and to permit analyses of meaningful subgroups. It is difficult, but particularly important, to increase the subject pool in the lower pointscore range. The early infant items show a pattern- ing for this retarded group which is unique. There is no communality among these groups of items and the precocity scales derived from the normal Berkeley Growth Study population (Cameron et al., 1967). The suggestion of a progression of item difficulty from social awareness to ob- ject awareness to language needs confirmation from a larger group of in- fants with delayed development. The trend of "hard" versus "easy" items for the relatively small group represented in items placed below six months is consistent. For example, there is only one easy item which might be construed as social awareness — item 61, "enjoys frolic play." This is an intrusive type of social communication on the part of the adult, and seems to have little in common with the social awareness items which constitute the "hard" group.

Separate analyses of the IQ subgroups for the retarded population were essentially unrevealing, primarily because of the small numbers included. An examination of the hard items for the whole group reveals some subgroup trends. The group of seventeen normal children contributes very little to the pool of hard items, with an average of only one test represented in the weighted score for any item. Only two of the hard items show a tendency for increasing difficulty with increasing severity of retardation, 82 ("attempts to secure 3 cubes") and 106 ("imitates words"). There are four items which reach significance for a specific IQ group but not for the group as a whole. They are found in the mild and moderate IQ groups and are indicated in the top of the list on page 64. Three are verbal items, and the fourth is motor-imitative. Degree of retardation may not be the most discriminating subcategory of the sample. Even within a retardation subcategory there are discrepancies which suggest the existence of other important differences. For example, item 101 ("jabbers expressively") is significantly difficult ($p<.10$) for the subgroup with IQ's in the severe range of retardation. There are six tests in which it is failed below pointscore and the mean weighted value is greater than $-15$. However, despite this significance, there are four instances of this item's being passed above pointscore in this same subgroup of severe retardation, with a mean weighted score of 5.4.

Enlarging the sample considerably may permit both the identification of those individuals with common item patterns and the analysis of the item scores of subgroups with different etiological or diagnostic characteristics. If qualitative differences in the infant test performance of retarded children can be identified, they may help us to formulate developmental definitions of retardation which cannot be expressed by quantitative measures such as IQ or maturational level.

## Prediction of Change versus Constancy in Longitudinal Research

The use of the Bayley infant scales in studies of the mentally retarded suggests a different, important aspect of prediction. This is, the prediction of *change*, rather than prediction of constancy, in a disadvantaged group of infants subjected to therapeutic efforts to alter an adverse course of development. The methods of item analysis presented above may contribute to the understanding of early patterns of cognitive integration in normal and disadvantaged groups and, thereby, point the way for specific, meaningful attempts at intervention. The success of these attempts may be measured by subsequent test performance. In some instances, significant changes in developmental rate, measured by total score, may be observed, especially in cases of severe deprivation followed by intensive intervention.

An example of the use of the Bayley infant scales to assess a program of intervention is the study of the effect of language training on a group of institutionalized retarded children with Down's syndrome. Various aspects of this longitudinal study have been reported elsewhere (Bayley et al., in press; Stedman & Eichorn, 1964). The interesting feature of the study, from the perspective of prediction of change, is that the rate of mental growth, as measured by frequent administrations of the Bayley mental scale, took a sharp turn upward following the onset of special training between the ages of five and six years, so that the rate of development was comparable for some months to that seen in normal children. No such upturn was observed during the year before the special language training, even though attendance at the institutional school had been inaugurated between four and five years. No corresponding increase in the rate of development was noted for the motor scale between the ages of five and six years. The effect of a specific program on a specific measure of development is evident.

Prediction of constancy in mental, emotional, or social characteristics presupposes either constancy of major environmental influences for the individual over time, or else the relatively greater importance to development of some specific experiences or genetic traits which will have effects persisting over time regardless of subsequent, intervening environmental circumstances. Mental abilities in adulthood are surely the result of complex, interacting variables of traits and experiences. The longitudinal approach permits an assessment of the relative contributions of a number of influences on the individual during his life span. Prediction from infancy to adulthood, as attempted in the numerous studies of Berkeley Growth Study data outlined above, represents a continuing attempt to investigate specifically the degree of correspondence between infant cognitive style and adult functions. Although it is clear that the degree of general developmental precocity in infancy is not correlated with adult IQ (except perhaps in the case of defective development), it also appears that, to some extent, adult abilities may have identifiable roots in infancy which are found in such diverse measures as specific item clusters in the infant mental scale or maternal behaviors. Important sex differences found in the data of the Berkeley Growth Study suggest the true complexity of prediction from infancy, for it would appear that subtle cultural differences between the sexes are at least as likely an explanation of the data as would be a "genetic" explanation for sex differences in the constancy of those mental abilities commonly regarded as polygenic.

The examples of past and ongoing research outlined above indicate that prediction from infant test performance continues to provide a challenge for developmental research. With the more general availability of the Bayley infant scales, their use for research purposes will increase. It seems highly likely that they will be used in the future, as they have been used during the course of their construction and revision, to probe the complex and elusive variables of prediction in mental development.

## References

Ames, L. B. Predictive value of infant behavior examinations, in J. Hellmuth, ed., *Exceptional infant*, Vol. 1, pp. 207–239. New York: Brunner/Mazel, 1967.

Bayley, N. *The California First-Year Mental Scale*. Berkeley: University of California Press, Syllabus Series, No. 243, 1933. (a)

————. Mental growth during the first three years. A developmental study of 61 children by repeated tests. *Genetic Psychology Monographs*, 1933, 14, 1–92. (b)

————. The development of motor abilities during the first three years. *Monographs of the Society for Research in Child Development*, 1935, 1 (No. 1).

————. Factors influencing the growth of intelligence in young children, in G. M. Whipple, ed., *39th Yearbook, National Society for the Study of Education*. Part 2. *Intelligence: Its nature and nurture*, pp. 49–79. Bloomington, Ill.: Public School Publishing, 1940.

————. Consistency and variability in the growth of intelligence from birth to eighteen years. *Journal of Genetic Psychology*, 1949, 75, 165–196.

————. On the growth of intelligence. *American Psychologist*, 1955, 10, 805–818.

————. Comparisons of mental and motor test scores for ages 1–15 months by sex, birth order, race, geographical location, and education of parents. *Child Development*, 1965, 36, 379–411.

————. Learning in adulthood: The role of intelligence, in H. J. Klausmeier & C. W. Harris, eds., pp. 117–138. *Analyses of concept learning*. New York: Academic Press, 1966. (a)

————. *The two-year-old: Is this a critical age for development?* Durham: Durham Education Improvement Program, 1966. (b)

————. Behavioral correlates of mental growth: Birth to thirty-six years. *American Psychologist*, 1968, 23, 1–17. (a)

————. Cognition and aging, in K. W. Schaie, ed., *Theory and methods of research on aging*, pp. 97–119. Morgantown: West Virginia University Library, 1968. (b)

————. *Manual, Bayley Scales of Infant Development*. New York: Psychological Corporation, 1969.

———. Development of mental abilities, in P. H. Mussen, ed., *Carmichael's manual of child psychology* (3rd ed.), pp. 1163–1210. New York: Wiley, 1970.

———, L. Rhodes, B. Gooch, & M. Marcus. Environmental factors in the development of institutionalized children, in J. Hellmuth, ed., *Exceptional infant*, Vol. 2. New York: Brunner/Mazel, in press.

Bayley, N., & E. S. Schaefer. Correlations of maternal and child behaviors with the development of mental abilities: Data from the Berkeley Growth Study. *Monographs of the Society for Research in Child Development*, 1964, 29 (6, Serial No. 97).

Bruehl, D. Correlations of individual items in the Bayley scale of mental development with later measures of intelligence. In preparation.

Cameron, J., N. Livson, & N. Bayley. Infant vocalizations in their relationship to mature intelligence. *Science*, 1967, 157, 331–333.

Cronbach, L. J. Year-to-year correlations of mental tests: A review of the Hofstaetter analysis. *Child Development*, 1967, 38, 283–289.

Erikson, E. H. *Childhood and society*. New York: Norton, 1950.

Escalona, S. K. *The roots of individuality*. Chicago: Aldine, 1968.

———, & A. Moriarty. Prediction of school-age intelligence from infant tests. *Child Development*, 1961, 32, 597–605.

Eyesenck, H. J. *Uses and abuses of psychology*. London: Pelican Press, 1953.

Francis-Williams, J., & W. Yule. The Bayley infant scales of mental and motor development: An exploratory study with an English sample. *Developmental Medicine and Child Neurology*, 1967, 9, 391–401.

Freedman, D. G., & B. Keller. Inheritance of behavior in infants. *Science*, 1963, 140, 196–198.

Heber, R. A manual on terminology and classification in mental retardation. *American Journal of Mental Deficiency*, 1959, 64 (Monogr. Suppl. 2).

Hofstaetter, P. R. The changing composition of "intelligence": A study of *t*-technique. *Journal of Genetic Psychology*, 1954, 85, 159–164.

Honzik, M. P. The constancy of mental test performance during the preschool period. *Journal of Genetic Psychology*, 1938, 52, 285–302.

———, J. J. Hutchings, & S. R. Burnip. Birth record assessments and test performance at eight months. *American Journal of Diseases in Children*, 1965, 109, 416–426.

Honzik, M. P., J. W. Macfarlane, & L. Allen. The stability of mental test performance between two and eighteen years. *Journal of Experimental Education*, 1948, 18, 309–324.

Hunt, J. McV. *Intelligence and experience*. New York: Ronald, 1961.

Irwin, O. C. Can infants have I.Q.'s? *Psychological Review*, 1942, 49, 69.

Jones, H. E., & N. Bayley. The Berkeley Growth Study. *Child Development*, 1941, 12, 167–173.

Knobloch, H., & B. Pasamanick. An evaluation of the consistency and predictive value of the forty-week Gesell developmental schedule, in C. Shagass & B. Pasamanick, eds., Child development and child psychiatry. *Psychiatric Research Reports of the American Psychiatric Association*, 1960, 13, 10–13.

Kohen-Raz, R. Scalogram analysis of some developmental sequences of infant behavior as measured by the Bayley scales of mental development. *Genetic Psychology Monographs*, 1967, 76, 3–21.

———. Mental and motor development of kibbutz, institutionalized, and home reared infants in Israel. *Child Development*, 1968, 39, 489–504.

Mendelson, M. A. Interdisciplinary approach to the study of the exceptional infant: A large scale research project, in J. Hellmuth, ed., *Exceptional infant*, Vol. 1, pp. 15–77. New York: Brunner/Mazel, 1967.

Phatak, P. Mental and motor growth of Indian babies of 1 month to 30 months. Research Reports No. 1, 2, & 3. Unpublished MSS. Department of Child Development, Faculty of Home Science, Maharaja Sayajirao University of Baroda, India, 1968, 1969.

Piaget, J. *The psychology of intelligence*, trans. M. Piercy & D. E. Berlyne. Paterson, N.J.: Littlefield, Adams, 1960.

Simon, A. J., & L. G. Bass. Toward a validation of infant testing. *American Journal of Orthopsychiatry*, 1956, 26, 340–350.

Sontag, L. W., C. T. Baker, & V. L. Nelson. Mental growth and personality development: A longitudinal study. *Monographs of the Society for Research in Child Development*, 1958, 23 (2, Serial No. 68).

Stedman, D. J., & D. Eichorn. A comparison of the growth and development of institutionalized and home-reared mongoloids during infancy and early childhood. *American Journal of Mental Deficiency*, 1964, 69, 391–401.

Werner, E. E., M. P. Honzik, & R. S. Smith. Prediction at ten years from twenty months pediatric and psychologic examinations. *Child Development*, 1968, 39, 1063–1075.

◈ GERALD R. PATTERSON AND JOSEPH A. COBB ◈

# A Dyadic Analysis of "Aggressive" Behaviors

THIS paper outlines the hypothetical process by which individuals acquire and maintain mutually supporting roles as "victim" and "aggressor." In these interchanges, the victim's behavior provides the cues which produce the attack and, paradoxically, also the reinforcer which increases the probability that in the future he will be assaulted again. The training contingencies for both victim and attacker are contained within the elements of dyadic interaction. For each member, the controlling stimuli, the responses, and the reinforcing contingencies are ubiquitous components found in the behavior of the other person.

This report outlines the two processes by which some aggressive behaviors are learned and maintained. The two processes represent only a general outline of the determinants for a limited set of children's and parents' aggressive behaviors. The aggressive behaviors analyzed were limited to those readily observable in the classroom and the home. The two processes are positive and negative reinforcement. The paper describes a series of laboratory and in vivo studies which have explored the utility of con-

NOTE: This research was supported by grants MH-10822, RO1-MH15985, and career development award 4-K1-Mh-40,518. Computing assistance was obtained from the Health Sciences Computing Facilities at the University of California at Los Angeles, sponsored by National Institutes of Health grant FR-3.

We are particularly grateful to our colleagues L. Goldberg, W. Sheppard, B. Martin, D. Shaw, and F. Kanfer for their painstaking critiques of earlier versions of this manuscript. We also owe a great deal to the members of the laboratory group who patiently tolerated our repeated intrusions into the Tuesday seminars. It was during these interchanges that many of the problems were clarified and methods of analyses developed. We owe special thanks to Roberta Ray, Vern Devine, Hy Hops, Karl Skindrud, Helen Walters, Steve Johnson, John Atkinson, and the "pernicious" R. Jones.

ceptualizing aggressive behavior as being under the control of these two mechanisms. Probably this limited scope formulation would not account for the wide spectrum of aggressive behaviors encompassed by such writers as Wolfgang and Ferracuti (1967) or Lorenz (1966).

The writers assume that for many types of children's, and to a lesser extent, parents', aggression the primary contingencies consist of positive reinforcers dispensed by the victim, the peer group, and/or society. This paradigm is probably most relevant for the aggressive behaviors characterizing the classroom bully, gangs, scapegoating, boxing matches, or football games. In these instances society — either explicitly as in the case of warfare, boxing, and football, or implicitly as in the case of scapegoating or the classroom bully — "neglects" to impose negative sanctions. The studies reviewed here establish the fact that positive reinforcers *can* be used in the laboratory to control aggressive behaviors. In addition, field studies demonstrated that positive reinforcers were indeed dispensed by victims in nursery school interactions. The data showed that these contingencies increased the probability of future attacks. At this juncture only a few studies are available which directly test the assumption that the peer (nonvictims) group also provides positive reinforcers for aggressive behaviors. An observation study by Buehler, Patterson, and Furniss (1966) showed that the institutionalized delinquent peer group provided positive social reinforcers contingent upon verbal report of past delinquent behaviors. In three studies, an average of 80 per cent of these behaviors received immediate support from at least one peer.

It is assumed that there is an initial stage of training which is a prerequisite for producing positive reinforcers for aggression. Whether the aggression involves a boxing match, or functioning as the playground bully, reinforcers will not be forthcoming unless the individual possesses a high order of skill. Although the subculture *can* provide training programs for skills such as may be found in the boxing class or the gang culture, it is assumed that most novices undergo training in a small, closed group and under the aegis of negative reinforcement. This process is not planned, but it *is* tightly programed; we have labeled it "coercion process." The coercion paradigm describes aggressive behaviors maintained by the withdrawal of aversive stimuli rather than by peer-dispensed positive reinforcers. It tends to characterize dyads interacting within relatively small closed systems rather than large or open systems in which membership is changing rapidly. Coercion has more ominous overtones to it, in that both victim and attacker may find themselves compelled to escalate to ever more intense exchanges of pain.

For both processes, the interlocking sets of stimuli controlling the victim and aggressor are investigated within the general matrix of sequential interactions among family members. The dependent variables consist of the minute-by-minute and day-to-day fluctuations in observed rates of aggressive behavior. The prosaic minutiae encompassed by the immediate behaviors of the other person constitute the controlling variables. In vivo observations of aggressive behaviors point to one overriding fact: not only do observed rates for such an aggressive response as hitting vary *from one setting to another, but within any given setting, the rates vary over time.* These fluctuations in rate constitute the dependent variable which will be used to test our understanding of aggression. Only when we can account for the major components of variance in the intra-subject distribution of these rates may we assume that a theory of aggression exists.*

In this paper variables significant for an understanding of aggression will be identified by the changes which their presence produces in the response probabilities for hitting. Within the context of thousands of classroom or familial interactions, the base rate $p(\text{Hit})$ serves as a means of assessing the significance of the independent variable. To be considered significant, the variable X should produce a conditional probability, $p$-(Hit/given that X has occurred), which differs in some demonstrable fashion from $p(\text{Hit})$. As a research strategy we have opted to examine the impact of events which immediately precede the occurrence of Hit and those which immediately follow. Presumably, certain events increase the probability that Hit will occur, whereas others are characterized by reduced probabilities of occurrence. The former are labeled "facilitating stimuli" ($S^F$); the latter are "inhibitory stimuli" ($S^I$). The surplus meaning attached to the analogous traditional concepts of $S^D$ and $S^\Delta$ make their usage cumbersome and, in fact, inaccurate, when applied to some of the functional analyses central to this report.† The assumption was that the

---

* Presumably, the various stimuli and setting components which account for these variations could be viewed as variables in a multiple regression equation where the criterion consists of rates of observed hitting. The $N$ in this case would be defined by the number of observation sessions or blocks. Although beta weights for each independent variable might vary somewhat from individual to individual, it is our hypothesis that there are broad consistencies in programing contingencies in Western society, such that certain classes of behavioral events would hold across individuals.

† The term *Hit* is used whenever a subject physically attacks or attempts to attack another person. The attack must be of sufficient intensity to *potentially inflict*

social stimuli occurring in the *immediate* situation govern a significant amount of the variance associated with changing probabilities for the occurrence of an aggressive response such as Hit. Analyses planned for the future will be concerned with the impact of complex classes of social stimuli preceding the behavior in extended time periods, but such analyses require larger samples of behavior than are available at the present time. For this reason, the present analysis will focus primarily upon the impact of events occurring within immediately adjacent time intervals.

The day-by-day rate of Hitting is assumed to covary with the availability of the relevant facilitating and inhibitory stimuli.* The rate covaries with the relative "density" of the stimuli which control Hitting and those which control competing, concurrent operants. The immediate consequences provided in the social environment determine whether the individual will continue to Hit or shift to a competing, more social and acceptable response. Stimulus density interacts with these reinforcing contingencies to determine rate of Hitting.

Social interaction events may be arranged along a time line in which the occurrence of some events, such as $S^F$s or $S^I$s, signal alterations in the probability of a given behavioral event following within the next time interval. It is further assumed that, given the occurrence of a Hit, some events which follow it will increase the probability of its *immediate* recurrence, whereas others will decrease it. The terms *accelerating* and *decelerating* consequences suggested by O. Lindsley seem uniquely suited as

*pain* — for example, kicking, biting, slapping, hitting, spanking, and taking an object roughly from another person. The circumstances surrounding the act need not concern the observer, only the potential of inflicting pain. For example, children may be playing and part of the play involves wrestling. If during the wrestling, one child hits the other child or pins him down to the point where pain could result, then the act of hitting or pinning down should be coded Hit.

* The terms *facilitating* and *inhibitory* stimuli bear more than a passing resemblance to the traditional concepts *discriminative stimulus* on the one hand and $S^\Delta$ on the other. However, when these traditional concepts are applied to sequential interactions, it becomes apparent that they are simply too complex. For example, the term *discriminative stimulus* defines an occasion in which behavior will be reinforced by positive or aversive consequences. By describing both types of arrangements, it also describes contingencies which could result in increases or decreases from baseline levels. Similar complexities are found for the term $S^\Delta$. Within the present context what was needed was a term that simply specified that, given the occurrence of event $X_1$, at time one, there was an increased probability that $Y$ would occur at time two. The terms $S^F$ and $S^I$ fulfill the requirement. They are simple descriptive terms which describe specific stimulus control properties but do not specify the reinforcing contingencies which maintain this status.

labels which describe this functional relation between a response, a following event, and the impact upon the probability of recurrence.

These terms are *not* synonymous with the traditional concepts of positive reinforcement and punishment. In fact, the concept of positive reinforcer is neither a necessary nor a sufficient condition characterizing consequences which are accelerators. For example, some social behaviors which constitute positive reinforcers also provide stimuli for a new chain of behaviors, such that the prediction would be that the preceding response would be unlikely to recur within the immediately following time interval. Holding the door open for a young lady might well produce a "thank you," which would function as a positive reinforcer for the response's recurring on some future occasion. However, in terms of its impact upon ongoing behavior, the outcome would lead the consequence to be coded a decelerator.

Both accelerators and decelerators may function as positive or negative reinforcers which have long-term implications for strengthening the responses involved. Although these reinforcement effects will not be analyzed in the present report, it is important to keep in mind that such arrangements could be explored within the matrix of sequential dependencies. For example, if shouting at the children reduced the noise level, the mother will cease to shout; but on future occasions she is even more likely to use this behavior to control shouting. In this arrangement we have a decelerating consequence which is also a negative reinforcer. If she had shouted at her husband for coming home late and received a slap which led to further shouting and an eventual beating, we would have an accelerating consequence which was also associated with eventual punishment for her shouting. Consequences, then, can have a dual impact: one upon the immediate future and the other upon the "distant" future.

Our eventual understanding of any given class of responses presupposes a means by which these long-term shifts in response probabilities can be expressed. This type of analysis requires repeated samplings of behavior for the same individuals over extended periods of time. Given such samplings, it would be possible to specify both short-term and gradual long-term changes in response probabilities for any given class of antecedent stimuli. Presumably these shifts would result from observable consequences provided by the social environment. The long-term alterations would be reflected both by changes in the overall rates of a given response and/or by the changes in conditional probability values for the stimuli which control that behavior. For example, given a "mother attend" followed by the response "child talk" and the consequence "mother praise," there should be an increase in the conditional probability for "child talk," given future presentations of the $S^D$ "mother attend."

The general perspective obtained by viewing behavior within the sequential interaction matrix is rather odd, to say the least. The point of emphasis is not upon enduring traits, but rather upon the analysis of behavior *change* as reflected in minute shifts in response probabilities. From this molecular viewpoint one is immersed in an organized but shifting matrix of probabilities which describe moment-by-moment alterations in the behavior of members of a dyad. As a counterpoint there are also the background themes of long-term, tempered, but gradual shifts in the control or lack of it exerted by certain stimuli over behavior. The dissonance generated by this perspective lies in the fact that at a molar level, the behavioral realities seem more static.

Everyday experiences emphasize the sameness of the behavior of a colleague, a spouse, or our children. Interactions with them, across settings, suggest a coherence and patterning of behavior at variance with the chaotic picture of constantly changing response probabilities' shifting across both time and settings. The dissonance perhaps may be resolved by noting that descriptions of colleague or spouse are based upon sporadic samplings. In addition, the data are integrated in such an unsystematic manner that the modest shifts in rate investigated in this paper would simply go unnoticed. The casual observer operating within the limiting scope of the traditional trait theory records only cataclysms and overlooks the changing increments in rates. At a molar level there actually are few changes, unless the individual is thrust into some new setting where he must learn new skills or alter existing ones. Most adults shop, and then permanently adopt settings which are maximally reinforcing and thus ensure stability. However, the stability is relatively illusory and can be maintained only by a myopic fascination with a macrocosm which is not clearly perceived. The situation is somewhat analogous to the sensible assertion based upon phenomenological evidence, that objects are "static." The introduction of data from longer time spans or from more careful observation of these objects with an electron microscope suggests yet another reality that coexists with these perceptions. The perception of frozen immobility obtained by casual examination of the heavens is quickly dispelled by more careful observation with a telescope.

77

Presumably the analysis of sequential dependencies characterizing children as they interact with one another, and with the adults in their environment, would tell us something about the nature of aggressive behavior. Such an analysis assumes that one has some presuppositions about which behaviors are important determinants, and which are not. The presuppositions determine the kind of coding system which one will use, the data collected, and the general strategies used in the analyses. The section which follows traces the gradual development of the hypotheses (positive and negative reinforcement) which have governed our attempts to understand aggressive behavior in children. The initial, naive hypotheses led to the collection of data in both the laboratory and the field. These data, particularly the experience of actually *observing* aggressive behaviors, led to new hypotheses, and the gradual evolution of a much broader base for viewing the problem. This report is *not*, by any stretch of the imagination, a theory of aggression, for the process of the investigators' shaping is, as yet, far from complete.

Although the actual shaping experience has by no means been neatly chunked or labeled with clearly defined beginnings and endings, the material in the next section is organized around two general topics. The first concerns the control of aggressive behavior by means of positive reinforcement, and the second, negative reinforcement.

## Control of Aggression by Positive Reinforcement

The early 1960's were characterized by a general excitement over the discovery that a marvelous range of social and nonsocial behaviors could be controlled by social reinforcers. Head nods, smiles, attention, and words of approval seemed to be powerful tools that could be used to sculpt complex social behaviors from the raw material of ongoing interactions. It was in this context that the decision was made to "try it on aggression." In an unpublished study by Gina Lerner, 12 nursery school children were randomly assigned to experimental and control groups. Each of the children spent twelve minutes playing with dolls; the subjects in the experimental group received reinforcement for aggressive behavior and the control group, reinforcement for nonaggressive doll play. The experimental group showed a significant increase in aggressive doll play and the control group did not. Aside from reiterating our faith in the law of effect, the results also led to more carefully controlled studies to test the general assumption that some aggressive behaviors were under the control of positive social reinforcers.

It was assumed that the peer group, or the father, might model aggressive behavior, and in addition make praise and approval contingent upon the occurrence of such behaviors. It was thought that this kind of training might characterize young boys in a machismo culture. In the next unpublished study by Ludwig and Sonoda, 38 boys and girls between the ages of 6 and 11 interacted with Bobo the rubber clown. Following a three-minute baseline, half of the children were given social reinforcers for each blow by an adult seated in the room. The other children were given social reinforcers for nonaggressive behaviors. The mean hits per minute for the control group were 19 and 26 for the first and last minutes of the baseline and 19 for the remainder of the trial. The respective means for the experimental group were 21, 23, and 32. The latter figure suggests an increase in rate of hitting as a function of the social reinforcement.

At about the same time, other investigators also demonstrated that positive reinforcers could accelerate hitting in a laboratory analogue task. Walters and Brown (1963) and Lovaas (1961) showed that positive reinforcers could be used to increase the hitting response and that the effects generalized to other settings. These findings, together with those from our own laboratory, were encouraging, and led to a series of methodological studies investigating the characteristics of rate and amplitude measures of reinforcement effects. The original Bobo was forced to give up his freefloating status and was instead rooted to the floor. He became completely automated to deliver continuous data on rate and amplitude of behavior. However, in retrospect it must be said that all of these improvements produced little output of new information about aggressive behavior. R. Jones, in an extended baseline study, showed rate measures significantly increased in the absence of external reinforcers. These findings led us to mistrust rate measures of the kind usually found in Bobo studies. In an unpublished study by D. Sichel, 22 third-grade boys responded to the instructions to attack this elegant target. Following a three-minute baseline, they received 120 social reinforcers dispensed on a variable ratio schedule for hitting, kicking, or pushing Bobo. The reinforcers produced a significant increase in the amplitude of the blows delivered, but only modest increases in rate. Of some interest was the finding that the magnitude of the baseline amplitude of the blows correlated .66 with peer sociometric ratings of aggressiveness in school and also with variables on a personality test measuring aggression. An additional study by Hinsey, Patterson, and Sonoda (1961) suggested some further relations between behavior in the laboratory analogue situation and teachers' ratings of aggressive behavior in the classroom.

The Walters and Brown study (1963) had shown that aggressive behaviors reinforced in the laboratory might generalize to the world outside. Data from our own pilot studies suggested that boys who had learned to be aggressive in the school setting would display more aggressive behavior during the baseline period in the laboratory. Although the laboratory analogue model seemed to have promise, it was decided to go into the real world and to determine the relevance of the model constructed thus far. How much aggressive behavior was actually maintained by positive social reinforcers dispensed by spectating peers or fathers? A pilot study was carried out in which the in situ aggressive behaviors of nursery school children were observed. A few weeks of observation showed that aggressive behavior *did* occur and consequences which seemed, a priori, to be positive reinforcers also occurred. However, these consequences *were seldom delivered by onlooking peers or adults*! In retrospect, it should not have been necessary to carry out this pilot study; common sense should have sufficed. However, the data did suggest that whether the hypotheses tested by the laboratory analogue model were true or false, they were not relevant to a significant portion of aggressive child behaviors. So much for lab *analogue* models.

The field observations suggested that the positive reinforcers were provided *by the victim* of the attack! In this sense, certain children seemed to be the discriminative stimuli whose presence set the occasion for reinforcement of the attacks by other children. When these children were attacked, they gave up the toy with which they had been playing or withdrew from the area. In many cases, if the victim did not immediately comply, the aggressor accelerated the amplitude or intensity of his attacks until the victim produced the reinforcer. The behavior of the victim was immediate, and it seemed intuitively to be "reinforcing." There seemed to be a few general classes of victim behavior which characterized most of the interactions; these included behaviors such as "withdraw," "passive," and "cry." The problem was to determine how frequently these events occurred as consequences and to "prove" that they indeed were reinforcers.

In 1963 an observation study was initiated in two local nursery schools. During the 16 weeks of observation in the fall and 10 weeks in the following spring, a total of 2,583 aggressive behaviors were observed (Patterson, Littman, & Bricker, 1967). On the occasion of each event, the observer dictated relevant information about the response and the consequence which followed. The data showed that consequences such as victim "cry," "give up object," or "withdraw" followed 80 per cent of such aggressive behaviors; the latter included responses such as "bodily attack," "attack with an object," and "invasion of territory." Similar findings have been noted in the earlier pilot study and by other investigators from observations made in nursery schools (Dawe, 1934; Green, 1933).

The fact that such consequences regularly follow aggressive behaviors does not, of course, prove that they are reinforcers. If these consequences function as positive reinforcers, they should strengthen the aggressive behavior. It was hypothesized that a positive reinforcer would be followed by an increase in the probability that the same class of aggressive behaviors would be delivered to the same victim on the occasion of the next attack by the aggressor. An aversive consequence, such as a counterattack, should be followed by the selection of a new victim or a shift in the class of aggressive behaviors dispensed. The analysis of the sequential behaviors for the nine most aggressive children showed that these relations held.

The idea that reinforcers dispensed by peer-victims did in fact control some types of assertive or aggressive behaviors was used to develop intervention procedures for hyperaggressive boys (Patterson & Brodsky, 1966). In these approaches an effort was made to make aggressive behavior "nonreinforcing" by briefly removing the attacking child from the reinforcement situation. However, there remained a great many unanswered questions. It would seem important to understand the process by which some children learn to respond to a victim's pain reactions, such as crying, as a positive reinforcer. Secondly, it would seem important to define the stimuli that set the occasion for aggressive behavior. In the hope of understanding both of these matters and to check on the cross-situationality of our nursery school findings, we next focused upon family interaction. Three years of effort were required to construct a coding system sufficient to the task (Patterson, Cobb, & Ray, 1970; Patterson & Reid, 1970).

It seems that different segments of our society arrange for different types of contingency programs for aggression in this new setting, the home. The reinforcing contingencies which controlled aggressive behavior seemed quite different from those observed in the nursery school. Rather than positive reinforcers, the withdrawal of aversive stimuli was most often crucial. The formulation relevant to the control of aggressive behavior by aversive stimuli is termed *coercion process*, and is outlined in the section which follows. Some of the hypotheses outlined there will be tested by sequential observation data obtained in the homes of hyperaggressive boys.

## The Control of Aggressive Behavior by Aversive Stimuli

### CONTROL BY PAIN

This general formulation of control by aversive stimuli has evolved gradually as a result of the clinical intervention studies, extensive observations in homes, and laboratory studies. The initial statement suggested that the aggressive child controlled his victim (Patterson et al., 1967) and his parents (Patterson & Reid, 1970) by aversive stimuli. More recent analyses suggest that *in some settings both* the victim and the aggressor may be controlled by aversive stimuli. At the present time our statements about this coercion process extend considerably beyond the data which are available.

It is hypothesized that positive social reinforcers are prime determinants for most children's pro-social behaviors, whereas negative reinforcement is a ubiquitous presence in the acquisition and maintainance of many deviant child behaviors. It is also hypothesized that coercive processes provide tighter control over the behavior of another person, and this makes his behavior more predictable than is the case when positive reinforcers are being exchanged.

The increase in predictability seems to have several sources. First, it is a response event which partially defines the response expected from the other person. If the consequence occurs, then the aversive stimulus is withdrawn. In this sense it is analogous to the concept of *mand* noted by Skinner (1957). The mand is an event which specifies a narrow range of responses as appropriate. For example, the mand "Please close the door" delineates a narrow set of responses which constitute a reinforcer for that request. "Closing the door" will be reinforced, and all other responses are likely to be ignored or "punished" by a repetition of the mand. It is assumed that this careful delineation of an acceptable response gives situations in which high rates of mands occur a mildly aversive quality. However, this is perhaps offset by the fact that etiquette requires immediate reinforcement for compliance to mands. "Thank you" is the carefully prescribed outcome for compliant responses.

82

Aside from the exigent quality implied in the specification of the response expected of the other member, coercive behaviors have an additional characteristic which gives control. It is hypothesized that noncompliance will be followed by a repetition of the coercive behavior with, perhaps, an increase in intensity or amplitude. Noncompliance is severely punished; the punishment continues until the desired behavior is obtained. After many training sessions, the child may train his sibling or mother to comply at the first presentation of the coercive behavior, or even at the threat of its coming into play.

In the coercion process, behavior is controlled by the presentation and withdrawal of aversive stimuli. The process begins when one member presents what the other member *perceives* as an aversive stimulus. His reaction in turn, is to present an aversive response to the other person. The interchange continues until one member withdraws his aversive stimulus, at which point the other reciprocates and withdraws his. Thus, there are *two* identical sets of escape processes, one for each member of the dyad; each member provides aversive stimuli for the other. By the same token, each is reinforced by the withdrawal of the aversive stimulus presented by the other. If either member does not terminate, then the interaction is likely to continue with a steady escalation in the intensity of the pain being delivered.

Negative reinforcement is the keystone to the process. Coercion is an additional, although perhaps special, case of the more general escape/ avoidance paradigm. In the avoidance learning paradigm, the organism learns to escape from the aversive stimuli, whereas in the coercive process he *remains* in the situation and behaves in such a manner that he *changes the stimulus*. The aversive stimulus in the coercive process is social in nature, which in this context implies that the stimulus can be changed. The individual does not withdraw from the situation, but instead alters the conditioned or unconditioned aversive stimulus.

Experimental data already available attest to the reinforcing effects of this arrangement. Recently some investigators have also provided data which suggest a physiological basis for negative reinforcement. Hokanson, Willus, and Koropsak (1968) and Edwards and Treadwell (1967) have produced data which suggest that cardiovascular activation occurs following the occurrence of seemingly aversive stimuli. Presumably removal of the stimuli would not only be reinforcing but would also be accompanied by a drop in blood pressure to baseline level. However, the latter has not yet been demonstrated.

The key concepts are "aversive" and "changeable." If one attempted to list those aspects of human behavior which may, under some circumstances, be aversive to someone else, the list would be impressive indeed. It would probably run the gamut from physical pain resulting from blows or intense sounds to statements implying a negative evaluation. It might include more subtle manifestations included under short- or long-term extinction schedules in which the other person simply ceases to reinforce for a time. Probably, too, such a list would vary from person to person, in that some stimuli could acquire status as conditioned aversive stimuli by their contiguous association with other events which are already functionally aversive. For these reasons, it does not seem feasible to attempt the construction of a taxonomy of aversive stimuli. The problem of defining aversive stimuli is discussed in the section which follows.

AVERSIVE STIMULI

The aversive stimulus is dispensed by another person who may or may not label his behavior "aversive." The operational definition used here requires that the other person react to the stimulus *as if it were aversive.* Aversive stimuli, then, will not be defined by their physical characteristics or topographies; rather, they will be identified by two different effects which they have upon the behavior of other persons. First, when an aversive stimulus occurs as a consequence for the behavior of another person, it produces a reliable suppression in rate of ongoing behavior. Second, its occurrence is likely to be followed by a coercive response from the other person. It might be noted that some, not all, stimuli which operate as punishment for the behavior of other people also become facilitating stimuli for coercive behaviors.

The general formulation that aversive stimuli function as facilitating stimuli for aggressive behavior is analogous to that presented in the concept of "pain-elicited aggression" described by Azrin, Hutchison, and Hake (1963) and Ulrich and Flavell (1970). They describe a series of laboratory studies which demonstrate that painful stimuli, such as an electric shock, produce reliable increases in aggressive attacks upon cagemates. The range of aversive stimuli which will produce this effect is impressive and includes, among other things, intense noise, heat, prolonged deprivation, and brief periods of nonreinforcement. The position taken in these studies is that the relation between "pain" and "aggression" is innate. For example, Azrin et al. (1963) showed that animals reared in relative isolation made aggressive responses when exposed to aversive stimuli. Ulrich and Flavell (1970) take the position that lower animals are under innate stimulus control. Tinbergen (1951), Scott and Fredericson (1951), Lorenz (1966), and Graham, Charivat, Honig, and Weltz (1951) also emphasize the unlearned function of certain stimuli in controlling the aggressive behavior of lower organisms.

There is one respect in which findings from animal studies perhaps ought to be qualified when generalizing to human subjects. The evidence for complex sexual interactions suggests that, as one moves up the phylogenetic scale, instinctual determinants play a less important role (Beach & Jaynes, 1954). Ulrich (1966) also notes differences in strains of rats, as well as differences among species in pain-elicited aggression (guinea pigs did not display aggressive attacks when presented with an aversive stimulus). The studies he reviewed also showed that previous social experience and training in aggression influenced these reactions. By the same token, the connection between aversive stimuli and aggressive attacks might be of lesser magnitude and more easily "unlearned" for human subjects.

There are some aversive stimuli which seem, a priori, to be good candidates for status as $S^F$s for aggression. One might expect, for example, that an attack by another child would be such a stimulus; verbal attacks or threats would be another. Observation data collected by Rausch (1965) showed that among adolescent boys the general class of "unfriendly acts" had a probability of .75 of being followed by an unfriendly act. A physiological basis for classifying negative evaluations as aversive has been demonstrated. Hokanson (1961) showed that both painful stimuli and negative evaluations are followed by autonomic reactions in the victim.

Edwards and Treadwell (1967; 1969) showed cardiovascular arousal in situations where it was necessary for the subject to continue responding for prolonged periods of time with his behavior maintained by negative reinforcement. This situation is analogous to that which characterizes the settings lived in by many housewives and graduate students. This belongs to a general class of contingencies which would seem to warrant a priori status as facilitating stimuli for aggression. It would also include nonreinforcement or extinction, and stimuli that signal reinforcement will be delayed indefinitely (i.e., the child runs to the sandbox to find that someone is already there). These constitute arrangements similar to the operational definitions of the construct "frustration" given in the laboratory work by Amsel (1958) and others. We might note here that relatively *brief* intervals of a few seconds of nonreinforcement *may* function as effective aversive stimuli.

Emotional outbursts accompanying laboratory extinction procedures are noted regularly by investigators working with animals. Even during discrimination training procedures, pigeons have been observed to engage in emotional behaviors during the brief interval when the $S^\Delta$ was presented (Terrace, 1966). Rheingold, Gewirtz, and Ross (1959) and Sheppard (1969) obtained emotional outbursts from infants during early stages of extinction schedules. In view of the absence of a victim, one may or may not choose to label such outbursts "aggressive." However, Ulrich and Flavell (1970) showed that for lower organisms nonreinforcement *is* a powerful stimulus for aggressive attacks upon other animals.

Fawl's ecological study (1963) provides data which suggest that there are many frustrating stimuli presented to a child which *could* function as $S^F$s for Hit. He noted an average of 7.58 disturbances per hour in the lives of six preschool children and 5.42 per hour for six school-age children. Presumably, these were all potential $S^F$s for the acquisition of coercive behaviors. Another common source might be found in such deprivation states as fatigue and hunger. For example, Goodenough (1931) showed that conflicts of preschool children vary as a function of the time since their last feeding.

Probably the most direct test of the hypothesized relation between brief extinction periods and increases in coercive behavior is that reported by Atkinson (1970). In his study two- and three-year-old children were placed in a laboratory situation with their mothers. Baseline interaction patterns were tallied for such coercive behaviors as whining, yelling, crying, kicking, and commanding. Following the baseline period, the mother sat behind a low barrier and concentrated fully upon a task; hence, she was present but unavailable. The child's coercive behaviors were recorded during baseline and experimental phases, an ABAB design. The data offered impressive support for the hypothesis that *brief* periods during which the mother was present, but nonreinforcing, increased the rate of coercive behaviors dramatically for young children. Atkinson noted that even 10 to 15 seconds of nonreinforcement was an effective arrangement for many of the children. Four of the behaviors met the criteria for identification as behaviors under appropriate stimulus control. Cry, Destructive, Whine, and Yell all showed greater rates during experimental manipulations than during the preceding baseline periods. In addition, the analyses of variance of repeated measures were significant for these responses.

It is hypothesized that status as an aversive stimulus is a necessary but not sufficient basis for establishment as a facilitating stimulus for coercive behavior. The aversive "stimuli" are social behaviors which can in turn be altered; it is this changeability which structures the second, necessary characteristic. Presumably, each child learns which aversive behaviors dispensed by which agents can be terminated by a coercive behavior such as Hit. Some children, for example, might learn that a temper tantrum will terminate the mother's, but not the father's, scolding; others learn that whining will terminate scolding.

It is further assumed that low-order consistencies exist across children and across families, in terms of which agents are "coercible." It is these agents whose presence will function as facilitating stimuli for behaviors such as Hit. To the extent that the cultural mandates and myths are in any way commensurate with actual role behaviors, it might be expected that the father's presence will function as an $S^I$ and the younger brother might be an $S^F$ for Hit. Data analyzed later in this report will search for such consistencies in family roles.

It is assumed that stimuli associated with the withdrawal of a stimulus might acquire status as a positive reinforcer for the coercive behavior. The laboratory findings reviewed by LoLords (1969) suggest that this means of obtaining a conditioned reinforcer is a reliable one. In addition, Lovaas, Schaeffer, and Simmons (1969) demonstrated that social stimuli associated with shock termination showed increased effectiveness as social reinforcers in controlling the behavior of autistic children. Within the present context, it is assumed that there are some behaviors which regularly signal the end of an aversive interaction. Little brother's teasing leads to a Hit by his older sister; his crying signifies that the teasing is terminated. A large number of such pairings could create the situation in which crying becomes a conditioned positive reinforcer and the brother a discriminative stimulus setting the occasion for attacks. Training within coercive interchanges controlled by negative reinforcement could then be viewed as a necessary preliminary training in which victim responses become positive reinforcers and the victim's presence, $S^D$s for attacks. Scott's classic studies of the training of fighting rats noted a similar phenomenon (Scott & Fredricson, 1951; Scott, 1958). Earlier in the training of these animals the withdrawal of the UCS was made contingent upon an attack upon another animal. The termination of the UCS was often accompanied by squeals and other pain reactions of the victim being attacked. Scott noted that later in their training these reactions seemed to excite the "fighters."

This general formulation would suggest that in more advanced stages of training the $S^F$ for a coercive behavior may not be "aversive." For the well-trained aggressive child, the appearance of a responsive victim could set the occasion for an attack as noted earlier in the nursery school study (Patterson et al., 1967). The aggressive behavior of such a child is under both positive and negative reinforcement control. The responsive victim could find himself being coerced in a wide variety of settings in which no clearly defined aversive stimulus was present. For example, the mother may be coerced by the temper tantrum behaviors of her son who wants a candy bar. The school bully may push, pummel, or trip a victim who just happens to be passing by. At this stage of training the coercer possesses a high order of skills which bring him immediate and reliable reinforcement. He is a highly skilled person who makes others miserable.

### COERCION SETTINGS

To understand differences in rate of Hit behaviors which one might find among various social settings, it is necessary to consider two key dimensions along which systems might vary. First, systems may differ in the density of aversive stimuli which they provide the child; second, they vary in the proportion of aversive stimuli which become conditioned as $S^F$s for Hit. For example, it might be expected that a ghetto, with its high rates of aversive stimuli, might also have higher rates of hitting. However, this would also assume that the controlling agents, the adults, are uncommitted to their supervisory roles in that they allow the coercer to be reinforced.

Limited space produces frequent intrusions upon the individual, and might therefore be described as a setting characterized by a high density of aversive stimuli. Jersild and Markey (1935) emphasized this point with observation data showing more aggressive behaviors indoors than on the playground. Biernoff, Leary, and Littman (1964) have shown that assertive interactions among monkeys vary as a function of the amount of living space available.

Perhaps there are stimuli, easily identifiable, which signify that in a particular setting, sanctions will not be applied for coercive behaviors. For example, the boxing ring and the football field actually set the occasion in which positive reinforcers will be supplied for these behaviors. The study by Berkowitz (1970) showed that the mere presence of weapons was a significant variable which increased the frequency of attack behaviors. In the same vein, aggressive films or actual modeling behaviors could serve the important function of signifying that the peers or adults in that setting will not only abrogate the usual negative sanctions, but in addition might even supply positive reinforcers for skill at coercion (Bandura & Walters, 1963; Lovaas, 1961). Actually observing the model being reinforced or, better yet, seeing the model reinforcing someone for such behaviors should also function as a setting stimulus which increases the probability of attack behaviors. For example, in the studies reviewed by Berkowitz (1968) the data showed that if the subjects were reinforced for aggressive words, then in that same setting there was an increased likelihood of aggressive attacks upon an agent who had frustrated the subject. Presumably, each of us learns to decode the subtle, and not so subtle, cues which signify the presence or absence of sanctions against our use of coercive behaviors. In part, it is these cues which define a setting.

Thus far, there are few data available for testing the hypotheses that systems characterized by high rates of coercive behaviors will also be characterized by high densities of aversive stimuli and supervisors who are unskilled or uninvolved. Data from observations made in the homes of seven families showed that deviant boys tend to receive the highest rates of aversive stimuli from other family members (Patterson & Reid, 1970). The fact that the differences were not significant, plus the fact that the cause-and-effect relations cannot be ascertained with such data, make these findings only suggestive at best.

Clinical intervention in the homes of hyperaggressive boys has led to some speculations about these families (Patterson, Cobb, & Ray, 1971). The first, and most frequent, was labeled the "diffusion parent." Characteristically, the parents are uncommitted and unskilled. They are only peripherally involved in tracking and arranging contingencies for their children's behavior. In the second pattern of interaction, "selective diffusion," the parents *are* involved and they *do* track child behaviors; indeed, they may do a creditable job in rearing several children. But for this one child they neither track nor apply contingencies. A case in point is the working mother who is told that by working she deprives the child of mothering; this leads to her belief that she should permit his coercive behaviors to occur. For other parents, serious illness or a diagnosis of retardation leads the parent to *allow* the coercive behaviors to be reinforced because the child is "sickly." The third program, "sadomasochistic arabesque," requires the mutual efforts of both parents. Their separate reactions to the child are delicately balanced in such a way that neither parent carries out a successful program. One parent plays the harsh punitive role; the other parent attempts to balance the severity of the first by being overly permissive. The net result is a loss of control of the child's behavior.

These families do not supply effective sanctions for coercive behaviors; many of them supply, in addition, very high densities of aversive behaviors. These speculations have not yet been directly tested, but they have provided a basis for generating social engineering procedures which have been effective in reducing observed rates of aggressive behaviors.

### CLASSES OF COERCIVE BEHAVIORS

Coercive behaviors have no particular typology. The only general characteristic which they possess lies in the consistency with which they are reacted to by others as aversive stimuli. Hitting would be but one special case of this more general process. For example, the child who acquires high rates of hitting behavior is likely also to display *other* behaviors which similarly produce immediate and reliable reactions from the social environment. These other behaviors might include temper tantrums, yelling, arguing, destroying, whining, crying, or teasing.

If each child is idiosyncratic with regard to the responses which function as coercers, then the hope of constructing a theory of aggression would quickly become mired in a morass of disconnected fragments of data which describe $S^F$s, $S^I$s, and the accelerating consequences separately for each response for each child. In this sense it would not be possible to construct a "theory" which adequately accounts for the behavior of even a single child, let alone one which generalizes to others. Thus it becomes necessary to consider how such classes of responses might be constructed.

It is assumed that to the extent that two response events are under the same stimulus control, they constitute a "class of responses." For example, if "younger sister teasing" proves to be a significant $S^F$ for older brother's Hit and for his Yell, we might assume that for him, these constitute a class of coercive behaviors. At this point no attempt is being made to specify the degree of overlap in stimulus control necessary to warrant assignment to class membership. For example, if there are a dozen $S^F$s which are significant in the control of both Hit and Yell for this boy and the stimulus sets overlap for only one event, are they then members of the same class? Should it also be required that the conditional probabilities for the overlapping $S^F$s be exactly the same?

One means of approaching this problem would be to use a series of decision rules to form classes and then to carry out a functional analysis to validate the structure of the classes derived. For example, once a class is formed, a multiple baseline design could be used to determine the generalization among class members resulting from intervention procedures which focus upon only one member of the class. In this manner, it would be possible to test the "efficiency" of various decision rules in constructing classes. A report by Patterson and Bechtel (1970) describes comparable analyses. Classroom observation data for a hyperactive child were subjected to a $P$-type correlational analysis to determine which behaviors covaried over time. This crude means of constructing response classes identified three responses which were presumably under similar, but unspecified, stimulus control. For this child, "aggressiveness," "talk to neighbor," and "noisy" all intercorrelated at significant levels. The data also showed higher rates during "group activity" than for the setting "individual desk work." This suggests some additional commonality in stimulus control for the three responses. Another response event, "movement about the room," showed just the reverse, in that higher rates occurred during "individual desk work" than during "group work." The effects of a classroom intervention program were analyzed to test the validity of this classification. The data showed that all three members of the class displayed marked reductions in rate following intervention, whereas the unrelated response, "movement about the room," showed no change. Class membership "predicted" the outcome of intervention. Using more precise data, such as the conditional probability values for the overlapping $S^F$s controlling the responses, should provide an even more powerful basis for making predictions about the "generalization" of effects among responses.

The construction of a "theory" would require that some of the response classes obtained for individuals be replicated among other subjects. A lack of replication would suggest a completely idiographic theory; which may indeed prove to be the case.

## HIGH-AMPLITUDE AGGRESSION

Most children's aggression interactions are of short duration and presumably of relatively low amplitude. For example, the observation study by Dawe (1934) showed that the average preschool quarrel lasted only 23.6 seconds. It is assumed that most high-amplitude aggressive behaviors are the outcome of extended interactions in which the intensity of the pain being delivered escalates until one member is seriously injured. Presumably such escalation can also occur in the behavior of adults. Studies reviewed by Wolfgang and Ferracuti (1967) showed the most likely participants in a homicide to be members of a family. It is hypothesized that either positive or negative reinforcement could produce such an escalating process.

In the observation study by Patterson et al. (1967), a surprising number of these "chains" were noted for preschool children. A "chain" of aggressive behaviors was defined as a sequence in which the aggressor dispensed five or more attacks. In the two schools studied, such chains occurred an average of more than one an hour!

It is hypothesized that some victims provide a positive reinforcer for Hit ("crying") only when the Hit is of high amplitude. In effect, the reinforcing contingency is such that the victim shapes the aggressor to dispense high-amplitude aggression. Victims who "cry" early might very well avoid intense pain. On the other hand, observations made in this same study suggested that immediate reinforcement is not without its limitations. On some occasions victims' crying seemed to function as an $S^D$ which produced attack behaviors from several aggressors at the same time.

There is another kind of situation which could produce a sequence of interactions with escalating intensities of pain being delivered. It is hypothesized that this second instance is most likely to occur when the initiator of the chain is himself under the control of powerful aversive stimuli and the two protagonists are evenly matched in their abilities to deliver pain. If the initiator is not under the control of aversive stimuli, the recipient's reaction to his behavior may lead him to immediately withdraw the stimulus and perhaps even apologize, "I didn't mean it that way." For this dyad, the interchange ends at this point. However, if the first agent is controlled by either a prolonged deprivation state or some other aversive stimulus and his initiations are met with a coercive behavior instead of compliance, this could lead to escalation. He will respond to the noncompliance with an increase in the amplitude of his demands and thus lead to another round of coercive interchanges. This chain will continue accelerating until one of the individuals terminates the interaction and thus reinforces the other member. If either one of the members is obviously more skilled, it should decrease the probability of continuation. If one of the members has a "protective convoy," such as a mother or big brother, as a back-up dispenser of pain, this would also decrease the likelihood of escalation. Helpless victims or inexperienced victims should also mean short interchanges and less likelihood of high-amplitude aggression. An obvious exception to this would be a situation in which attacks made upon a helpless victim receive positive reinforcement from peers who are present and assist in the attack.

## A COERCION TRAIT?

The trait label is a crude summary term which implies predictability across settings for a given child *and* specifies some point along a continuum in terms of individual differences. To the extent that a child displays comparatively high Hit rates across a number of settings, he might be said to have a trait of hitting. If he displayed high rates of behaviors such as Hit, Tease, Noncomply, and Destructive across many settings, he might be said to have a trait of aggressiveness. The previous discussion of the construction of response classes suggests that such summarizations and comparisons are extremely gross, but even so, they may be of some predictive power. This section discusses the means by which across-settings correlations might be obtained and reviews some of the existing literature showing across-settings, across-time correlations and long-term implications for early evidence of coercive "traits."

The general assumption is that response classes, or summaries across response classes, will be stable across settings and/or time to the extent that the settings are similarly programed to support these behaviors. If the program for the setting changes over time, then the "stability" correlations will be low; similarly, across-settings correlations will be low if the reinforcing contingencies provided the behaviors vary from one setting to the other. The design required to test this hypothesis would require in situ observations of the reinforcing contingencies across time or settings together with the across-subjects correlations for frequencies of the response class(es). There are no such data available at the present time.

There are a number of reports of sizable correlations across time for behavior settings which are presumably constant. Jersild and Markey

93

(1935) showed that children highly aggressive in nursery school also tended to be aggressive in the first grade. Patterson et al. (1967) gathered observational data from preschool children on mean rates of aggression over a seven-month period and found a correlation of .56 for one school and .69 for another. Kagan and Moss (1962) found surprisingly high associations between boys' "temper tantrums" and "aggression to peers" during the preschool years and comparable variables scored from ages 10 to 14. However, these across-time correlations may have been spuriously inflated, since the same Es made the ratings at the different age points.

It can be predicted from a state framework that across-settings comparisons at the same point in time would produce lower correlations than across-time comparisons of the same settings. Sears, Rau, and Alpert (1965) found little correlation among aggression observed in the nursery school, the laboratory, and the home. In the observation data provided by Schalock (1958), there were few significant correlations on variables describing twenty pairs of mother-child interactions across settings such as the laboratory and home. Four observations were made in each of the settings; these findings replicated an earlier study by Schalock (1956).

Coercive behaviors are best conceived as a general style for handling aversive stimuli. They probably occur first during infancy, where they would seem to have definite survival value. An infant's crying functions as an effective aversive stimulus producing the mothering behavior necessary to alleviate the source of the pain. By this means, the infant can train the uneducated mother and thus survive. As the child matures, the social environment no longer reinforces earlier specific coercive behaviors such as "cry," "kick," or "scream" — in fact, most parents begin to track them and intensify punishment for their continued use. However, the parents may reinforce some other type of coercive behaviors. For this reason, the typology of the coercive responses may or may not be the same at different stages of life or in different settings. But coercion becomes a general mode of dealing with aversive stimuli. The alternative would be to develop the wide range of social skills necessary to anticipate many unpleasant situations and to deal noncoercively with those which do occur.

There is a set of findings consonant with the hypothesis that the coercive process constitutes a style of dealing with aversive stimuli which persists long past childhood. The sociometric studies reviewed by Moore (1967) consistently showed that coercive children (aggressive) tended to be rejected by their peers. This steadfast reaction from the social environ-

94

ment should be a major determinant of the manner in which a child describes himself and other people. In follow-up studies of former child guidance clients by Roff (1961), a wide range of adult pathologies were characterized as having had early difficulties in interacting with peers. Morris (1956) followed up 71 children between the ages of four and fifteen who had been characterized as conduct disordered, a category including "extremely aggressive" youngsters: as young adults, 18 per cent were psychotic and 10 per cent had a criminal record; in fact, only about 21 per cent were characterized as "adjusted." This dismal picture was corroborated in Robins's (1966) thirty-year follow-up study of 406 antisocial children who had been treated in an outpatient clinic and a group of matched controls. Of the aggressive children, 39 per cent had been diagnosed as psychotic, compared with 6 per cent of the controls; only 16 per cent were considered well adjusted, in contrast with 52 per cent of the controls. As adults, 44 per cent of the males were arrested for major crimes versus 3 per cent of the male controls; they also had marginal employment records and were more likely to rear antisocial children. Similar evidence was provided by Pritchard and Graham (1966) in a follow-up study of 71 adults in a psychiatric hospital who had been seen as children. Those children characterized as conduct disordered or delinquent were more likely to be diagnosed as antisocial or inadequate personality as adults.

Both Robins (1966) and Macfarlane, Allen, and Honzik (1954) identified a general "deviancy factor" in their longitudinal data. Macfarlane reported a correlation of .73 between the total number of problems reported for the boys by their parents at age six with the total number of problems reported during ages nine through fourteen. Robins's findings supported a notion that aggressive child behaviors are one facet of a general style of interaction which eventually is applied across a variety of social settings.

### HYPOTHESES TO BE TESTED

The hypotheses to be examined in the present report pertain only to the control by aversive stimuli of the aggressive response Hit. The analyses will be based upon sequential observation data collected within the homes of families of aggressive boys. Analyses of sequential dependencies will focus upon the following:

a. It is assumed that stimuli occur within family interaction which function as punishment for pro-social behaviors. The various consequences for the behavior Talk will be examined to identify events which significantly decelerate that behavior from its base rate. In that some, but not all, of these will be "aversive," this constitutes a necessary but not sufficient basis for classifying events as aversive.

b. It is assumed that all of those events which function as significant facilitating stimuli for Hit will have previously been identified as significant decelerating consequences for Talk.

(1) The events which are significant $S^F$s for Hit will differ from those which are significant $S^F$s for Talk. The $S^F$s for Hit will include events related to nonreinforcement, negative evaluation, and attack.

(2) There will be differences among family members with regard to the effect of their presence as $S^F$s for Hit and Talk. Presumably the parents' presence will function as $S^I$s for Hit, and siblings' will function as $S^F$s.

c. There are events which, when arranged as antecedents, significantly decrease the probability of a Hit.

(1) These events will tend not to be aversive and therefore will not have been identified either as decelerating consequences for Talk or as $S^F$s for Hit.

(2) There will be differences among family members with regard to their status as $S^I$s for Hit and Talk.

d. An aversive event which follows Hit will tend to increase the probability of the response occurring again within the immediately following time interval.

(1) These will tend to be events which were previously identified as decelerating consequences for Talk and $S^F$s for Hit.

## Procedures

### SAMPLE

The sample consisted of 24 families referred to the Social Learning Project by community agencies because one or more of the children had displayed high rates of aggressive behavior. The deviant children were boys age six to thirteen years; two (Zeim and Waldo) had received tentative diagnosis of possible brain damage, and five (Zeim, Tal, Waldo, Mac, and Sam) were on medication at the beginning of the study. None of the parents or children had been diagnosed as psychotic. Most of the families had dealt with several social agencies, and as a group they represented some of the more difficult families one might encounter in a community child guidance clinic. All of the families consisted of at least three persons living within a 20-minute drive of the laboratory. The parents were informed about the required home observation procedure before the intake interview, and interestingly enough, few objected.

Table 1 summarizes the demographic data collected for the families. By this classification, a majority of the families were from the lower socioeconomic levels defined by Hollingshead and Redlich (1958). In one-third of the families, the father was not present in the home. The median age of the deviant boys was eight and one-half. Referrals came most frequently from the school, the juvenile court, the mental hygiene clinic, and the child welfare department.

Secondary data will also be used, obtained from observations made in the homes of ten "normal" families matched for number of family members, fathers' presence or absence, and socioeconomic level with the first ten families of deviant children. Most of these had volunteered for the study in response to a newspaper advertisement and were paid on a sliding fee schedule whereby the amount increased as the family participated in more sessions. Others were obtained through the local child welfare department.

### OBSERVATION

*Baseline Assessment.* Ten hours of baseline observation were collected in the home; the data were collected five days a week for approximately an hour each day for two weeks. The observers usually collected the data between 4:00 and 7:00 P.M.; the members of the family were required to remain either in the kitchen or the adjoining room, with the television set turned off. No outgoing telephone calls were made, and no visitors were present.

Each observer was equipped with a clipboard with a built-in timing device; at thirty-second intervals the observer received both a visual (light) and an auditory stimulus (via earphone). On those occasions when reliability data were being collected by two or more observers, the timing devices were synchronized.

A randomly ordered list of family members determined the sequence in which they were observed. The target's behavior was coded, as were the consequences provided by others for his behavior. This yielded a continuous account for each family member for a five-minute period. After each

Table 1. Demographic Data for Families

| Name | Number of Family Members | Age of Deviant Child | Referral Problems | Source of Referral | Socio-economic Status[a] | Father |
|---|---|---|---|---|---|---|
| Kim | 4 | 10 | Negativistic, school failure, steals, disrupts class, poor peer relations | psycho-educational clinic | 1 | present |
| Rom | 8 | 8 | Disrupts in school, fights, fails in school, poor peer relations | school | 6 | present |
| Mo | 6 | 13.5 | Assaults mother & siblings, steals, breaking & entering | juvenile court | 6 | absent |
| Al | 5 | 12 | Violent temper, sets fires, fails in school, truant, negativistic, destructive, aggressive | psychology clinic | 3 | absent |
| Hep | 5 | 7 | Lies, cheats, steals, screams, rocks, negativistic, cries | child welfare | 3 | present |
| Fird | 6 | 11 | Assaults mother, disrupts school | school | ...[b] | absent |
| Tal | 5 | 7 | Temper, fights siblings | mental health clinic | 4 | present |
| Cal | 4 | 13 | Rages, disrupts in school, negativistic | juvenile court | 4 | absent |
| Waldo | 4 | 9 | Runs away, steals, lies | juvenile court | 4 | present |
| Holly | 4 | 10 | Temper, fights siblings | children's hospital, school | 5 | present |
| Sam | 7 | 8 | Temper, fights, steals, lies, disrupts school | mental health clinic | 5 | present |
| Zeim | 5 | 10 | Temper, fights siblings, disrupts school | psychiatrist | 6 | present |
| Mac | 5 | 8 | Temper, immature, disrupts school | mental health clinic, school | 6 | present |
| Stein | 6 | 10 | Fights at home & school, disrupts in school | school | 3 | absent |
| Jack | 4 | 8 | Disrupts in school, temper | school | 4 | present |
| Ole | 3 | 7 | Noncompliance, poor peer relations | psychologist | 7 | absent |
| Yok | 4 | 6 | Fights at home, temper | school | 3 | absent |
| Curt | 5 | 7.5 | Lies, enuretic, cries, fails in school, nervous, noncompliant, aggressive | school | 3 | present |

Table 1 – Continued

| Name | Number of Family Members | Age of Deviant Child | Referral Problems | Source of Referral | Socio-economic Status[a] | Father |
|---|---|---|---|---|---|---|
| Fen ........ | 3 | 7 | Hyperactive, temper tantrums, noncompliant | mental health clinic | 7 | absent |
| McKee .... | 6 | 13 | Steals, fights, fails in school, no friends | mental health clinic, school | 4 | present |
| Cully ..... | 6 | 10 | Disrupts, poor peer relations, fights | school | 1 | present |
| Brem ..... | 8 | 7 | Lies, fights, hyperactive, steals, temper tantrums, noncompliant | school | 5 | present |
| Loman ... | 5 | 6 | Steals, fights, hyperactive, fights with siblings, allergies, enuresis, noncompliant | school | 5 | present |
| Olly ....... | 7 | 12 | Steals, lies, noncompliant | school | 3 | present |

[a] Based on Hollingshead and Redlich's (1958) system: 1 = higher executive or major professional; 2 = business managers, proprietors of medium-sized businesses, and lesser professionals; 3 = administrative personnel, owners of small businesses, and minor professionals; 4 = clerical and sales workers, technicians, and owners of little businesses; 5 = skilled manual employees; 6 = machine operators and semiskilled employees; 7 = unskilled employees.

[b] Mother is a college student.

99

member had been the target, the whole series was repeated once during that session.

The coding system was developed gradually beginning in 1966 (Reid, 1967) as a function of extensive observations in forty or fifty homes of both deviant and nondeviant children. It is designed to test some specific hypotheses based upon social learning principles and is therefore *not* an omnibus system. Currently, it consists of thirty categories which describe various behavioral events: Approval, Attention, Command, Command Negative, Comply, Cry, Dependency, Destructiveness, Disapproval, High Rate (hyperactive), Hit, Humiliate, Ignore, Indulge, Laugh, Negativism, No Response, Noncomply, Normative, Physical Positive, Play, Proximity, Receive, Self-stimulation, Talk, Tease, Touch, Whine, Work, and Yell. A manual providing operational definitions for these categories together with the rules for their use has been deposited with the National Auxiliary Publications Service.*

*Observer Training and Reliability.* The observers were intelligent, middle-aged women for the most part, and had already met the usual obligations of motherhood. During training they first studied the manual and then practiced with video tapes of family interaction. Following about twenty hours of training, they went into the homes with the experienced observers until their agreement with that observer reached 75 per cent.

Observation protocols from two observers were compared unit by unit for agreement during each thirty-second interval. Errors in identifying the behavioral event, the persons involved, or the sequence of events were subtracted from total agreement for each thirty-second interval. The overall percentage agreement was calculated by summing the events observed for both observers and dividing this into the total number of events (behavioral events, persons, and sequences) for which they were in agreement. All of the observers employed by this project were compared with one another in the field regularly. Mean percentage of agreement figures among five observers were as follows: 83, 81, 85, 81, and 85.

Thomas, Loomis, and Arrington (1933) and Reid (1971) have demonstrated that a few hours of field experience following adequate training can produce abrupt decreases in observer reliability. For example, Reid's data showed a median of .76 for observer agreement after

* To obtain it, order document 01234 from ASIS National Auxiliary Publications Service, c/o CCM Information Sciences, Inc., 909 Third Avenue, New York, New York 10022; remit $2.00 for microfiche or $5.30 for photocopies.

extensive training. However, when the observers assumed that they were no longer being monitored, agreement with the code standard *immediately* dropped to a median of .51! Observer agreement, then, is not fixed; it can and does change over time as a function of many variables. For this reason, we held biweekly training sessions in order to "re-calibrate" the observers. There, they regularly coded video tapes of family interaction from homes of deviant children and then, as a group, compared their observations with a master sheet prepared by Cobb. Discrepancies were discussed, and the video tape rerun until *all* observers agreed.

Rosenthal (1966) has reviewed studies which emphasize the distortions that can occur as the result of observer bias. The empirical findings reported by Scott, Burton, and Radke-Yarrow (1967) and by Rapp (cited by Rosenthal, 1966) leave little doubt that assumptions held by observers lead to distortions of the data. To counteract this effect, a "calibrating observer" was added to the staff. Unaware of which families were being treated and which were controls, she saw other staff members only when she picked up her time schedule for the week, attended television training sessions, and went into the homes with the regular observers. Each observer codes in a home with the calibrating observer once a month. Observer agreement with the calibrating observer ranged from 66 to 98 per cent. Although this suggests minimal bias, an analysis is being carried out to determine whether there are any consistent biases in the errors.

*Data Sampling.* Observer time is a precious commodity and therefore is invested as sparingly as possible. For this reason we needed to determine the minimal amount of sampling required to obtain stable estimates of the frequency of occurrence of behavioral events. It was hypothesized that, in large part, variations in rate of behavioral events reflect changes in the availability of relevant stimuli (Patterson & Bechtel, 1971). If the stimuli within settings do not vary appreciably, the rates of the observed behavioral events should be stable over time. Furthermore, the amount of sampling necessary to establish a stable estimate should increase as a function of the complexity of the setting. Complexity may be defined by the range of stimuli which exist in a setting.

Ascertaining stability of estimation assumes that one has a "taxonomy" of settings and/or stimuli readily at hand. No such schema exists, and in lieu of its development, we have determined stability empirically, given various amounts of event sampling. Osborn (1952) observed 33 mother-child pairs in their homes for five one-hour periods. There was little stability in the mothers' behavior until the fourth session, at which point the correlation between frequency estimates of code categories obtained in sessions four and five was significant. Stability data for the 12 families included in the present report were analyzed separately for mothers, deviant children, and oldest sibling (Patterson et al., 1971). For each of the thirty categories, the correlation was calculated between the estimates based upon the first session and the estimates based upon the remaining nine sessions. Then the correlations were calculated for the first three with the remaining seven, and the first five with the last five sessions. When data for the first and the last five sessions were correlated, the median was .71 for the response categories and .60 for the consequence categories. It should be noted, however, that those categories whose frequency was less than one event per hour could not be analyzed (Dependency, Destructiveness, High Rate, Humiliate, Physical Positive, and Whine). Two of the code categories were identified as unstable (Self-stimulation and Work).

Although the correlational analysis suggested that ten sessions give minimal stability in ordinal ranking for subjects, it did not provide a basis for determining the significance of systematic changes in level over time. For example, it is possible that families "habituate" to the presence of the observer and demonstrate significant shifts in mean level even though the ordinal ranking for subjects remains highly stable. An analysis of variance for repeated measures was calculated for each of the thirty categories, separately for 12 mothers, fathers, deviant children, and oldest siblings (the analysis has been deposited with NAPS; to order, see note on p. 100).

Of the 116 $F$ values, only two were significant at the .05 level. Comply showed a significant increase for mothers, and Laugh showed significant shifts in mean level, but no consistent trend over time. These two findings are less than what would be expected by chance and strongly suggest that there were no significant shifts in level over the ten sessions. However, the fact that there were only 12 subjects in each group would suggest that the analysis may not have been powerful enough to identify small shifts in mean level. For this reason, a satisfactory resolution of this problem must await the outcome of analyses based upon larger samples.

The next event-sampling problem to be raised here relates to the comparability of estimates for subjects when they are the primary targets being observed in contrast with estimates based upon data obtained for the subjects when some other person is the target. In their classic study, Thomas et al. (1933) found a median correlation of .76 between data obtained from subjects' own protocols and estimates based upon protocols of the other children. Using both samples of a child's behavior would, of course, increase the stability of any estimate *if* one could assume they sample the same population. A comparable analysis was made of our data to determine whether the same population of events was being sampled when the subject was the target versus sampling his behavior when other children were the target.

The proportion of the child's social interaction characterized by each of the thirty code categories was computed separately for data obtained from subject-as-target and for the same subject when another person was the target. Across-subjects correlations were calculated to determine the agreement in subject ranks obtained from the two sets of data. In addition, an analysis of variance for each code category tested the significance of the difference in means for the two sets of data (the findings from this analysis have been deposited with NAPS; to order, see note on p. 100). They are based upon the data obtained from the 21 of the 24 deviant boys in the sample for this paper.

By and large, ordinal rankings of subjects were maintained across data sampling their own and others' protocols. The mean correlation (after $z$ transformation) was .74, which compares favorably with the analysis of preschool interaction by Thomas et al. (1933). Only the variables Comply, Normative, Self-stimulation, and Talk did not show significant correlations.

An analysis of variance was also computed for each of the code categories to determine the significance of differences in mean level obtained from sampling own versus others' protocols. The variables for which the $F$ tests were significant included: Attention, No Response, Comply, Normative, Self-stimulation, and Talk. To some extent, these differences obtained are a function of constraints imposed by the coding system. For example, by definition it is unlikely that No Response would be credited to a *particular* target subject; rather, the behavior is more likely to be coded as the "total group did not respond." This would result in lower estimation of No Response from others' than from the subjects' own protocols. Similar constraints apply to coding Normative.

In light of the small number of significant $F$ tests and the mean correlation of .74, these data may be interpreted to mean that the two data sets are in fact the same. On the other hand, the fact that *any* of the $F$ tests were significant and some correlations were not significant can be interpreted to mean that the two samples were drawn from different populations of settings. For the present, we choose to gamble. The average increase of 114 per cent constitutes a sizable increase in sampling for most code categories. Combining the data also means that more settings are being sampled, and has the additional advantage of increasing the generalizability of the data. The combined data were used in the analysis of stability outlined earlier in this section and were used to calculate the dependent variables in the analyses to be discussed below.

*Observer Effect.* Within the present context, the presence of the observer in the home is viewed as a significant social stimulus which should have some effects upon family interaction. The question, however, concerns the magnitude and the duration of such effects. The parents in our studies report that observers do not see the "really extreme" deviant behaviors. Observers feel that they are not getting a valid sampling of some families' interaction, presumably because the families seem to program their activities carefully during the observation period. It is our impression that for most families the effect of the observers' presence is short-lived and that, aside from the possible omission of the intense violent interchanges, the portrayal of family interactions is relatively free of major distortions. The hypothesis that most families habituate to the observers' presence is also shared by the Kansas group on the basis of their extensive experience in observing parent-child interaction (Barker & Wright, 1954).

The data reviewed earlier showed that there were no significant habituation effects. For example, if one hypothesized that family members gradually habituate to the presence of observers, one might then expect increases in rates of deviant behaviors over time. If one assumes that such an effect would occur in ten sessions, the findings disconfirm the hypothesis. On the assumption that the effect might be more ephemeral, the data were reanalyzed to test for habituation effects in the first three sessions. It was assumed that a habituation effect would be manifested by increases in rates of deviant behavior from the first to the second session and a corresponding slight decrease in rates of pro-social behaviors. The following code categories have been classified a priori in other studies as deviant: Command Negative, Cry, Dependency, Destructiveness, Disapproval, High Rate, Humiliate, Ignore, Negativism, No Response, Physical Negative, Tease, Whine, Yell. All other categories were classed as pro-social. The average proportion of total social interaction characterized as pro-social was .059 for session one, .056 for session two, and .058 for session three. The corresponding proportions for the deviant behaviors were .0044, .0056, and .0047, which suggests that there was indeed about a 27 per cent increase in deviant behavior for all family members during the second observation session. Much of this effect was a function of marked increases in behaviors coded Hit and Negativism. Taken together, these data suggest that a *single* observation session in the home may produce an underestimate of rates of deviant behavior.

Two studies have been completed in which data collected surreptitiously by mothers in their own homes are compared with data collected by observers who are not family members (Harris, 1969; Hoover & Rinehart, 1968; Patterson & Harris, 1968). Each study employed a control group of mothers who collected the data for the entire series of ten sessions and experimental groups in which mothers observed for the first five sessions and outside observers for the last five (in which the mothers were absent). In neither study were there significant main effects between trials or groups or interactions for a measure of social interaction. Patterson and Harris analyzed a summary group of deviant behaviors, and again, no significant effects were obtained.

It was assumed that a subtler measure of the effect of the observers' presence might be reflected in the alterations in "predictability" of subjects' behavior from one point in time to another. Social interaction rates were several times more predictable when mothers were the observers (Harris, 1969). Harris also speculates that the observer effect might differentially affect individuals and families as a function of their initial levels of social interaction, and provides some data which show this to be the case. Such shifts, however, are comparable with what would be expected on the basis of regression to the mean and are therefore particularly difficult to pin down.

Clearly, the problem of observer effect demands further attention. For the time being, we continue to assume that the effects of observers' presence are not a major problem.

## Analyses

The method of coding used to analyze social interaction sets imposes constraints upon the perspectives which one adopts in conceptualizing the nature of the process. In the present system, the observer records the behavior of $A$, then codes $B$'s reaction to $A$, then codes $A$'s reaction to $B$, and so on. In this manner, interaction is organized into relatively discrete units, and these units are arranged along a single time line. Once the interaction is initiated, then each event which follows is set within a context of other events. As coded here, the context is always the behavior of another person, in that it is something which the other person does that both precedes and follows the behavior of the target subject. The present analysis concentrates only upon two or three "links" in such interactions. Events which accelerate a response following its first occurrence may have no significant status if introduced later into the same chain. These subtle interactions between the structure of ongoing behavior and immediately impinging stimulus events will have to be outlined by the data, for no existing theory can elucidate these relations.

Within the present context, a given class of events may decrease the probability of a "response" which it follows, but may at the same time serve to increase the probability of certain events which follow it. In fact, as hypothesized earlier in the report, aversive stimuli have just such a dual impact. The point in sequence in which an event occurs interacts with its aversive or nonaversive status to determine its impact upon events which form the context.

The first step in testing the coercion hypotheses necessitates an independent means for the identification of stimuli which are "aversive." The operational test outlined earlier involved identifying events which served to suppress ongoing rates of pro-social behaviors. This will form a necessary, but not sufficient, basis for constructing a list of aversive stimuli whose occurrence increases the probability of a Hit. Although it is hypothesized that not all "aversive stimuli" will be $S^F$s, all $S^F$s have previously been identified as aversive.

### AVERSIVE STIMULI

It was hypothesized that certain events serving as consequences for Talk would result in a decreased probability that Talk would occur again within the immediately following time interval. To test this hypothesis, all interactions were considered in which the same member of the dyad provided both the antecedent stimulus and the consequence for the behaviors of the other member. Those interactions were excluded which contained more than one person or more than one behavior as antecedent stimulus.

With these exclusions, over a hundred thousand interactions were available for analysis; of these, 56,632 were Talk.*

Given that some member of the family had Talked, and this was followed by the behavior of another family member, the base rate probability that the person would continue to Talk was .519. This was calculated with the numerator being the frequency with which individuals continued to Talk, given that they had been Talking in the immediately preceding time interval. The denominator was the total frequency of Talks, plus all non-Talks, given that the subject had been Talking during the immediately preceding time interval. A decelerating consequence would be one whose occurrence led to a significant reduction in the probability that Talk would recur. For each comparison, the base rate conditional probability, $p$(Talk/Talk, followed by Consequence $X_i$) was recalculated. In correcting these base rate values, the contribution of each unit for which Consequence $X_i$ occurred was subtracted from both the numerator and the denominator. These corrected base rate values for the recurrence of Talk were compared with the conditional probability of Talk, given that the consequence for the previous Talk had been consequence $X_i$. A $t$ test was used to compare the two proportions calculated for each consequence.

Presumably, there are several classes of events which might decelerate Talk. One kind signals that reinforcement has occurred and that further responding will probably *not* be reinforced. The other kind signifies that punishment has occurred and future responses are likely to be either non-reinforced or punished. Either kind of event signals a shift to concurrent operants. It is for this reason that significant deceleration was labeled as a necessary, but not sufficient, condition for status as an "aversive stimulus." Table 2 lists the consequences identified as significant decelerators. They have been grouped into a priori classes of consequences which signify punishment and positive reinforcement.

There is a surprisingly large number of decelerating consequences for Talk, some of which produce massive decreases in the conditional probabilities for the continuance of Talking (Command, Hit, Dependency, Touch). For example, if the speaker is Hit, the likelihood that his next response will be Talk alters from its base rate value of approximately .5 to

---

* The category Talk was not recorded if any other behavior category was more appropriately descriptive of the behavior which occurred. For example, if Yell, Cry, Whine, Command, Command Negative, Disapproval, Negativism, Noncomply, or Laugh *could* serve as labels, then the event was coded as such. Talk, then, was a residual category, used when nothing else applied.

Table 2. Significant Decelerators for Talk

| Consequence | Frequency | $p$(Talk/Previous Talk followed by $X_1$) | $t$ |
|---|---|---|---|
| *Punishment* | | | |
| Command ......... | 633 | .0142 | 97.91*** |
| Command Negative .. | 69 | .0145 | 34.36*** |
| Hit ............... | 45 | .0889 | 10.01*** |
| Dependency ........ | 19 | .1579 | 4.25*** |
| High Rate .......... | 25 | .2800 | 2.60** |
| Noncomply ......... | 9 | .2222 | 2.10* |
| Tease ............. | 98 | .3061 | 4.46*** |
| Yell .............. | 78 | .3205 | 3.65*** |
| Disapproval ........ | 1001 | .3407 | 11.63*** |
| Ignore ............ | 518 | .3320 | 8.81*** |
| No Response ....... | 3148 | .3431 | 20.67*** |
| Laugh ............ | 507 | .3728 | 6.58*** |
| Whine ............ | 151 | .4106 | 2.57* |
| Negativism ......... | 470 | .3851 | 5.74*** |
| *Positive Reinforcement* | | | |
| Touch ............ | 123 | .0325 | 29.88*** |
| Approval ........... | 169 | .3609 | 4.14*** |
| Comply .......... | 26 | .1538 | 5.08*** |
| Physical Positive .... | 100 | .2200 | 7.09*** |
| Receive ........... | 58 | .2759 | 4.05*** |
| Play ............. | 990 | .4202 | 6.00*** |

\* $p<.05$ \*\* $p<.01$ \*\*\* $p<.001$

.09. Similarly, if the speaker receives a caress (Physical Positive), the chances drop to .22 that he will continue to Talk in the next time interval. According to the coercion hypothesis, the $S^F$s for Hit will be drawn from this list of decelerating consequences.

It should be noted that this particular analysis is not without its problems. The assumption being tested here was that there is a *general* set of consequences which function across families, across sex, and across ages of family members such that they decelerate Talking. It would seem more reasonable to proceed with a separate analysis of each family separately and then across families. However, there were not sufficient data for such an analysis.

Even more serious is the problem of the independence of the events analyzed. It is likely, for example, that different families, and different individuals, contributed varying frequencies of Hit. To the extent that some individuals or families contributed a disproportionate number, the events may not be independent. Again, the method of handling such a problem would be to analyze each family separately — and there were not enough data available for any single family to permit such an analysis. Now that the problem has been recognized, the data collecting procedures have been corrected; future analyses will be based on single families. In the meantime, an inspection of the computer output on Talk, by individual families, showed that across-family relations described in Table 2 were also applicable to most of the individual families. A second check to determine the extent of confounding was to run an across-family analysis for the ten matched normal families. To the extent that the summary in Table 2 represented the contribution of only a few families, one would not expect generalization to a new sample.

The analysis identified all but three of the decelerators classed as punishment in Table 2. The conditional probabilities from this analysis were as follows: Command, .006; Command Negative, .000; Hit, .000; Dependent, no data; High Rate, .000; Noncomply, no data; Tease, .000; Play, .275; Ignore, .469; No Response, .459; Laugh, .111; Negativism, .000; and Whine, .000. This pilot analysis was based upon only 10,541 interactions; hence, no attempt was made to determine the significance of the differences between these conditional probability values and the base rate for continuance of Talk (.447). A more intensive analysis will be forthcoming in a later report for a larger sample of normal families. However, these preliminary findings suggest that the analysis of decelerators for the deviant families may not be far off the mark, in that the list of decelerators seems to be descriptive of normal families as well.

It was hypothesized earlier that some agents are more likely than others to withdraw an aversive stimulus if it is followed by Hit. Agents might also differ with regard to the frequency of $S^F$s they provide. The presence of those agents who provide negative reinforcement would increase the likelihood of a Hit's occurring, whereas those likely to counterattack would be associated with low probability values for Hit. The section which follows constitutes an indirect test of this hypothesis. The effect of agents' presence upon the probability of Hit are examined for mothers, fathers, older sister and brother, younger sister and brother, and older and younger deviant boys.

### AGENTS' PRESENCE AS AN ANTECEDENT STIMULUS

Presumably, differences among family members in size, experience, skills, time available for interaction, and tasks to be performed lead to the delineation of various family "roles." Differences among roles are partly defined by the stimuli which set the occasion for the behavior of other family members. In addition, the role is also defined by the consequences provided for the behaviors of others. It is assumed that there would be some low-level consistencies in the programs of antecedent stimuli and consequences which, for example, characterize the oldest, strongest male in a family (father), the oldest female in the family (mother), and the youngest female or youngest male.

For each class of agents the conditional probabilities were calculated for Hit and Talk, given the presence of that agent $[p(\text{Hit}/\text{agent}_i)]$. This specified the likelihood that *some other* family member would display a Hit, given the presence of that particular agent. This value was compared with a corrected base rate value describing the probability of a Hit in the presence of all agents other than agent $i$. The corrected value was based upon agent $i$'s contribution as an antecedent stimulus being subtracted from both the denominator (total interaction) and the numerator (frequency of Hit). If the presence of a particular agent served as a facilitator stimulus for others' Hit, then the conditional probability value for that agent should be greater than the corrected base rate probability, and if his presence acted an an inhibitory stimulus, then $p(\text{Hit}/\text{agent}_i)$ should be lower than $p(\text{Hit})$. If neither effect occurred, the agent was considered a neutral stimulus.

The significance of these effects was tested by a two-by-two chi-square analysis to determine the degree of association between presence or absence of the agent and the occurrence or nonoccurrence of others' Hit. All interactions were considered in which the same member of a dyad provided both the antecedent stimulus and the consequence for the other member's behavior. Those interactions were excluded which contained more than one member as stimulus agent or more than one behavior for the stimulus agent. With these exclusions, 117,033 interactions were available for analysis; of these responses 273 were Hits and 37,176 were Talks.

The data from the second column of Table 3 provide base rate estimates of Hitting and show that, in general, Hit could be expected to occur about two or three times in every thousand events. The most likely person to function as facilitating stimulus for Hit was a child. If the child was the younger sister, the older brother, or the older deviant boy, there was at least a twofold increase over base rate values in the likelihood of Hit's oc-

Table 3. Conditional Probabilities for Others' Hit and Talk Given the Antecedent Stimuli of Agents' Presence

| Agents Present | $p$(Response/ Agent$_1$) | $p$(Response/ Non-agent$_1$) | Direction of Change[a] | $\chi^2$ |
|---|---|---|---|---|
| | | *Hit* | | |
| Mothers .............. | .00091 | .00279 | − | 32.77*** |
| Fathers .............. | .00046 | .00267 | − | 31.45*** |
| Deviant boys | | | | |
|   Younger ........... | .00293 | .00225 | | 2.70 |
|   Older ............. | .00435 | .00210 | + | 23.54*** |
| Brothers | | | | |
|   Younger ........... | .00309 | .00288 | | 2.38 |
|   Older ............. | .00462 | .00210 | + | 27.82*** |
| Sisters | | | | |
|   Younger ........... | .00454 | .00211 | + | 25.17*** |
|   Older ............. | .00117 | .00249 | − | 8.25** |
| | | *Talk* | | |
| Mothers .............. | .37778 | .29836 | + | 626.37*** |
| Fathers .............. | .36059 | .31007 | + | 175.66*** |
| Deviant boys | | | | |
|   Younger ........... | .31586 | .31794 | | 0.27 |
|   Older ............. | .26799 | .32343 | − | 154.73*** |
| Brothers | | | | |
|   Younger ........... | .22970 | .32406 | − | 304.05*** |
|   Older ............. | .28835 | .32068 | − | 42.70*** |
| Sisters | | | | |
|   Younger ........... | .34049 | .31529 | + | 29.35*** |
|   Older ............. | .23751 | .32791 | − | 433.07*** |

[a] + = increase over base rate probability; − = decrease.
** $p<.01$      *** $p<.001$

curring. It is interesting to note in this regard that the identified "deviant" child, who presumably displayed high rates of deviant behavior, also served as a facilitator in *producing it in others.*

These data strongly suggest that there are well-structured roles which tend to be replicated with appreciable consistency across families. Among deviant families, one of the most interesting roles is occupied by the younger sister. One wonders if her sex, and her age, do not constitute a protective sanctuary for her role as poltergeist in provoking the Hitting behavior of others. Interestingly enough, she is also a powerful facilitating stimulus for Talk. One would suspect that, as provocateur, she is setting up her brothers, who are then punished by the parents for Hitting. Probably the parents are also most likely to talk to her when she is present. Younger boys do not share in this high-status role; presumably the younger brother is less likely to be protected if Hit, and less likely to be talked to by parents when he is present. The parents and older sister function as effective inhibitors in that their presence is associated with reduced conditional probabilities. In the case of the father, the reduction is a sixfold decrease from base rate values. Presumably, the father occupies this status because of his reputation for dispensing intense punishment.

The situation described by these data is analogous to one in which there are three segregated populations within the same household: boys, girls, and parents. Each has specific roles in setting the stage for both pro-social and deviant behaviors. Considering only the deviant response Hit, the three agent groups (older brother, older deviant boy, and younger girls) constitute the trainers whose function it is to train others to Hit. Presumably they train not only one another, but in some families, even the parents.

Table 4. Conditional Probabilities Associated with Antecedent
Behaviors for Others' Hitting[a]

| Antecedent Stimuli | $p(\text{Hit}/X_i)$ | $p(\text{Hit}/X_i)$ | $p(\text{Hit}/X_i)$ | $p(\text{Hit}/X_i)$ |
|---|---|---|---|---|
| | Mother | Father | Younger Deviant | Older Deviant |
| Approval | .00000 | −.00000*** | −.00000** | .00000 |
| Attend | .00167 | .00144 | .00042 | .00251 |
| Command | .00126 | .00000 | .00000 | .00000 |
| Command Negative | .00000 | +.02632*** | −.00000*** | .00000 |
| Compliance | −.00000** | −.00000*** | .00000 | .00000 |
| Cry | .00000 | .00000 | +.10000*** | −.00000*** |
| Disapproval | .00295 | .00000 | +.03192*** | .01177 |
| Dependency | −.00000*** | .00000 | .00000 | −.00000** |
| Destructiveness | .00000 | .00000 | .00000 | .00000 |
| High Rate | .00000 | −.00000*** | +.07692*** | .04506 |
| Humiliate | −.00000*** | −.00000*** | .00000 | .00000 |
| Ignore | .00067 | −.00000 | −.00000** | .00000 |
| Indulge | −.00000** | −.00000*** | .00000 | .00000 |
| Laugh | .00000 | −.00000 | .00000 | .01852 |
| Noncompliance | −.00000*** | −.00000*** | +.03636*** | .01471 |
| Negativism | .00000 | −.00000*** | .00909 | +.05556*** |
| Normative | .00000 | .00000 | −.00026*** | −.00000*** |
| No Response | .00248 | .00205 | .00867 | .00673 |
| Play | .00000 | .00080 | .00161 | .00101 |
| Physical Negative | +.21426*** | −.00000*** | +.21622*** | +.23810*** |
| Physical Positive | .00000 | −.00000 | −.00000*** | .00000 |
| Proximity | −.00000*** | −.00000*** | .00000 | .00000 |
| Receive | .02778 | −.00000*** | .00000 | +.09091*** |
| Self-stimulation | −.00000*** | −.00000*** | .00000 | .00000 |
| Talk | .00024 | .00019 | .00091 | −.00138** |
| Tease | −.00000*** | −.00000*** | +.09836*** | +.09756*** |
| Touch | .00000 | −.00000*** | .00000 | .00000 |
| Whine | .00000 | .00000 | .04348 | .00000 |
| Work | .00000 | .00000 | .00000 | .00000 |
| Yell | −.00000*** | .00000 | +.09375*** | .03571 |

Table 4 — Continued

| Antecedent Stimuli | $p(\text{Hit}/X_1)$ | $p(\text{Hit}/X_1)$ | $p(\text{Hit}/X_1)$ | $p(\text{Hit}/X_1)$ |
|---|---|---|---|---|
| | *Younger Brother* | *Older Brother* | *Younger Sister* | *Older Sister* |
| Approval | −.00000*** | −.00000*** | −.00000** | −.00000*** |
| Attention | .00155 | .00268 | .00322 | .00043 |
| Command | +.22222*** | .00000 | .00000 | .00000 |
| Command Negative | −.00000*** | .00435 | −.00000*** | −.00000*** |
| Compliance | .00585 | +.00917*** | .01389 | .00000 |
| Cry | .02564 | −.00000*** | +.06667*** | .00000 |
| Disapproval | .01961 | .00000 | .00000 | .00820 |
| Dependency | .00000 | −.00000*** | .00000 | −.00000*** |
| Destructiveness | .00000 | −.00000 | −.00000*** | −.00000*** |
| High Rate | .00000 | −.00000*** | .02797 | −.00000*** |
| Hit | +.20000*** | +.32308*** | +.25581*** | +.23259*** |
| Humiliate | −.00000*** | .00000 | +.08333** | −.00000*** |
| Ignore | −.00000*** | +.07194*** | −.00000*** | .01020 |
| Indulge | −.00000*** | .00000 | .00000 | .00000 |
| Laugh | +.04348*** | .00578 | +.04762*** | .00532 |
| Noncompliance | .01191 | .03509 | .01460 | +.02083** |
| Negativism | .01087 | +.04908*** | +.07792*** | .01370 |
| Normative | .00190 | −.00085*** | .00158 | .00024 |
| No Response | .00766 | .00700 | .00759 | .00320 |
| Play | .00046 | .00214 | .00434 | .00092 |
| Physical Positive | .00000 | −.00000*** | .00000 | −.00000** |
| Proximity | .00000 | .00000 | .02222 | .00000 |
| Receive | +.02667** | +.17021*** | .00000 | −.00000** |
| Self-stimulation | .00000 | .00000 | .00797 | .01149 |
| Talk | .00390 | .00336 | .00269 | .00039 |
| Tease | −.00000** | .00371 | .01942 | −.00000*** |
| Touch | .00000 | .00000 | .00000 | −.00000** |
| Whine | .00000 | −.00000*** | .00000 | −.00000*** |
| Work | .00000 | −.00000 | .00159 | .00000 |
| Yell | −.00000** | +.15790*** | .00000 | −.00000*** |

ᵃ If the behavioral event produced a chi-square significant at $p < .01$ or better, the conditional probability value is preceded by a plus; if the event is associated with a decreased probability, the conditional probability is preceded by a minus.
\*\*$p < .01$    \*\*\*$p < .001$

Thus, in both the nursery school (Patterson et al., 1967) and in the home, the agents who contribute most to the direct shaping of deviant behaviors are peers rather than the parents.

Agents' presence is a significant antecedent stimulus for Hit and for Talk. However, such status presumably arises because their presence signifies positive or negative reinforcement for Hit and Talk. The section which follows identifies specific agent behaviors which function as $S^F$s and $S^I$s for Hit. The persons who provide tightest training on when not to Hit are those family members who function in the role of adult (occupied by mother, father, and older sister). For these ages there is a disproportionate number of these $S^I$s; at least 80 per cent of the significant antecedent stimuli were inhibiting.

### FACILITATING STIMULI FOR HIT

In Table 4, entries in the first column, $p(\text{Hit}/X_i)$ estimate the conditional probability of Hit, given that the mother displays code behavior $X_i$. This was calculated by dividing the frequency with which Hit followed the mothers' $X_i$ as antecedent stimulus, divided by the total number of family behaviors for which mothers' $X_i$ served as an antecedent. This was compared with the corrected base rate value for Hit; the mothers' contribution was removed from both the numerator and the denominator. The asterisks refer to the level of significance of the two-by-two chi-squares which tested the relation between the presence or absence of the stimulus and the presence or absence of Hitting.

One overriding feature of these findings is the large number of stimuli which have a significant impact on the probability of occurrence for Hit. Interestingly enough, the preponderance of stimuli function as inhibitors. It seems that much of what family members teach one another is when *not* to Hit.

The data suggest an interaction between agent class and behavioral event in determining the status as a controlling stimuli. For example, Cry *increases* the probability of an attack when displayed by the younger sister (.067) or younger deviant boy (.100), but *decreases* the probability when the agent is the older brother (.000) or the older deviant boy (.000). A similar reversal in status is noted for Command Negative, High Rate, Hit, Humiliate, Ignore, Laugh, Negativism, Noncomply, Receive, and Yell. This suggests that one should be cautious in talking about generalized $S^F$s for coercive behaviors.

To make across-agent comparisons possible, the significant facilitating stimuli for Hit are summarized in Table 5. Even a casual inspection of the $S^F$s suggests that most of them, a priori, *seem* aversive for example, Hit, Cry, Command Negative, Disapproval, High Rate, Tease, Whine, Yell, and Ignore. All of these had been previously identified as decelerating consequences for Talk; these effects were significant for all but Cry and Humiliate.

Most of the $S^F$s which controlled the occurrence of Hit were associated with the boys and the younger sisters. The relevant behavioral events

114

seemed to be characterized more as "attacks" (Hit, Yell) and negative evaluations (Command Negative, Disapproval, Humiliate, Tease) and reiatively less often as brief extinction schedules (Ignore, Negativism, No Response). The findings support the hypothesis that aversive events facilitate the response Hit.*

The *most* effective facilitating stimulus for Hit was Hit. The conditional probability values ranged from .22 to .32, which represented substantial increases over the base rate values of .002±. These data replicate the findings by Rausch (1965), to the effect that unfriendly acts by adolescent boys were very likely ($p = .75$) to be followed by unfriendly acts.

### INHIBITORY STIMULI FOR HIT

The events which were significant inhibitory stimuli for Hit summarized in Table 5 seemed to fall into three classes. The first class, positive reinforcement, characterized situations in which the other person had just reinforced the subject — that is, Approval, Physical Positive, or Touch. Positive reinforcement sets the occasion for pro-social behavior and inhibits the likelihood of coercive behavior.

The second class consists of events which suggest that the other person was involved in some reinforcing activity (Normative, Talk, Self-stimulation). The label for this class, concurrent operant, suggests that intrusions by another member will not be reinforced. In fact, it is likely that interruptions constitute an aversive stimulus which increases the probability that the interrupter will be punished. The third class consisted of stimuli which seemed, a priori, to be aversive. It included many of the behaviors which, if dispensed by *other* agents, would constitute S$^F$s for Hit. These findings relate to the hypothesis that being aversive is a necessary, but *not sufficient*, condition for status as an S$^F$ for coercive behaviors. An event will constitute an S$^F$ for Hit only to the extent that *it is dispensed by an agent who can be conditioned to terminate that behavior.*

The rich outpouring of significant and meaningful findings constitutes

---

* The findings that the behaviors Laugh and Receive were facilitators seemed contrary to the hypothesis regarding the nature of stimuli controlling Hits. However, the category Receive is used when a person has physical contact with another and there is no overt response to the contact. Thus, the category is a subset of the No Response category, and implies nonreinforcement in that the person does not exhibit any negative or positive behaviors to the physical contact. The code category Laugh, which was significant for younger brothers and sisters, does not seem to be an artifact of the code system, but a truly unexpected finding which does not readily fit the coercive hypothesis. It suggests that in some circumstances Laugh *may* be an aversive stimulus.

Table 5. Significant Facilitating and Inhibitory Stimuli for Hit

| | Parents | | Older | | | Younger | | |
|---|---|---|---|---|---|---|---|---|
| | Mother | Father | Sister | Brother | Deviant Boy | Sister | Brother | Deviant Boy |
| *Facilitating Stimuli* | | | | | | | | |
| **AVERSIVE** | Hit | Command Negative | Hit Noncomply | Hit Yell | Hit Tease | Hit Cry Humiliate | Hit Command | Hit Yell Tease Cry Noncomply Disapproval High Rate |
| **NONREINFORCEMENT** | Receive | | | Receive Negativism Ignore | Receive Negativism | Negativism | Receive | |
| **NONCLASSIFIABLE** | | | | Compliance | | Laugh | Laugh | |
| *Inhibitory Stimuli* | | | | | | | | |
| **POSITIVE REINFORCEMENT** | Comply | Approve Comply | Approve Physical Positive Touch | Approve Physical Positive | Approve Physical Positive | Approve | Approve | Approve Physical Positive |
| | Proximity Indulge | Touch Proximity Indulge | | | | | Indulge | |

116

Table 5 — Continued

| Parents | | Older | | | Younger | | |
|---|---|---|---|---|---|---|---|
| Mother | Father | Sister | Brother | Deviant Boy | Sister | Brother | Deviant Boy |
| | | | **CONCURRENT OPERANT** | | | | |
| Self-stimulation | Self-stimulation | | Normative | Normative<br>Talk | | | Normative |
| | | | **AVERSIVE** | | | | |
| Dependency<br>Humiliate<br>Tease<br>Noncomply<br>Yell | Humiliate<br>Tease<br>High Rate<br>Noncomply<br>Hit<br><br>Receive<br>Negativism | Dependency<br>Command Negative<br>Humiliate<br>Tease<br>High Rate<br>Whine<br>Yell<br>Destructiveness<br>Receive | Dependency<br>High Rate<br>Whine<br>Cry | Dependency<br>Cry | Command Negative<br><br>Ignore<br>Destructiveness | Command Negative<br>Humiliate<br>Tease<br>Ignore | Command Negative<br>Ignore<br>Yell |

impressive support for the research strategy of using conditional probabilities as a dependent variable in searching for determinants of aggressive behavior. In the section which follows, the analysis will focus on the impact of various consequences upon the probability of the response's occurring again in the immediately adjacent time interval. The speculations about the coercion process outlined earlier suggested that some consequences would increase the probability of a second Hit's following in the immediate series, whereas other consequences would dramatically reduce the likelihood.

### ACCELERATING AND DECELERATING CONSEQUENCES FOR HIT

Behavior is controlled by the antecedent stimuli which produce it *and* by the stimulus events, the consequences, which follow it. On occasion, an event following a response can set the stage such that the other person will present the same response again (accelerating consequence) or it can increase the likelihood he will alter his behavior and present some other response (decelerating consequence). (See pp. 75–76 for a discussion of these terms.) It is assumed that some of these accelerating stimuli are also "reinforcers" in the traditional sense and that some decelerating consequences are also "punishment." However, it is our growing conviction that most of the events in sequential interaction constitute examples of stimulus, rather than reinforcement, control. For this reason it seems reasonable to begin the analysis using the simplest possible descriptive language.

One may think of the advent of each stimulus event, antecedent or consequence, as contributing to the efficiency of predictions about ongoing changes in the subject's behavior. There is no reason to believe that the terms *antecedent* or *consequence* have any particular meaning when one is examining sequences of interactions. In that context, an $S^F$ for one response is at the same time a consequence for the response that preceded it. *All that is there are stimulus events which alter the occurrence of ongoing behavior.* The terms *antecedent* or *consequence* serve only to identify which response, the preceding one or the following one, is of immediate interest.

The appropriate criterion for evaluating the success of this enterprise lies in the adequacy of the predictions which can be made. "Reinforcing" events are seen as making a particularly interesting contribution to predictions in that they provide two pieces of information. If the consequence

118

is just an accelerating stimulus, it indicates that behavior will be repeated in the immediately adjacent time interval. However, if it acts as a reinforcer, the arrangement also says that the discriminative stimulus for the reinforced response is slightly altered in status, such that on future occasions of its presentation, the probability is significantly increased that the response will occur. Thus, a reinforcing event may provide information about both the immediate present *and* the distant future; both sets of information function to increase the magnitude of our predictions.

Given that Hit is followed by a repetition of the aversive stimulus, it would be hypothesized that Hit will occur again, and continue to occur, until either the aversive stimulus is withdrawn or until it becomes so punishing that Hit is terminated. For general predictive purposes it will be assumed that aversive stimuli following Hit will increase the probability of a Hit in the immediately following time interval, and that nonaversive stimuli will function as decelerating stimuli. In effect, Hit followed by any stimulus which was an $S^F$ should function as an accelerator.

A total of 615 Hits were available, contributed by all the members of the family. If the consequence for the Hit was double coded for either persons or responses, it was not included in the present analysis. For the 481 Hits remaining, the base rate $[p(\text{Hit}_{\text{recur}}/\text{Hit}_{\text{previous}})]$ was .237. This represents a considerable increase over the general base rate value for Hit, of two or three per thousand units of social interaction. The analyses were run separately for each family, as well as summed across families. Thirteen of the families showed Hit rates equal to or greater than one event per hour of observation. For each family the conditional probability value for the impact of the consequence upon recurrence of Hit was compared with the base rate probability of Hit for that family. The data were used to calculate the proportion of families for which the direction of the impact upon Hit was the same as those found to be significant in the across-family summary data. The analysis of the effect of various consequences upon Hit followed the same steps outlined previously for Talk. The results are summarized in Table 6.

Although several consequences functioned as accelerators for Hit, only two were significant, Hit and Negativism. For Hit, the effect was demonstrated in most of the families in that Hit functioned as an accelerating consequence. However, the across-families finding for Negativism was due largely to the disproportionate contributions of but *two* families. For the remaining families, Negativism was an uncommon consequence which

119

generally decelerated Hit. Therefore, Negativism should not be considered a significant consequence. Tease and Ignore, though they occurred with lower frequencies, also produced appreciable increases over the baseline value for the recurrence of Hit. All of these accelerators for Hit had previously been identified as significant $S^F$s for that behavior, as well as punishment for pro-social behavior. Some aversive events play multiple roles in sequential interaction in that they are significant $S^F$s for some behaviors

Table 6. Accelerating and Decelerating Consequences for Hit

| Consequence | Frequency | $p(\text{Hit}/X_1)^a$ | $t$ | Percentage of Families Showing Effect |
|---|---|---|---|---|
| Approval | ... | ... | ... | |
| Attention | 57 | −.0702 | 4.72*** | 90 |
| Command | 14 | .2143 | n.s. | |
| Command Negative | 5 | .0000 | ... | |
| Comply | 12 | −.0000 | 12.35*** | 100 |
| Cry | 23 | .2174 | n.s. | |
| Disapproval | 38 | .1842 | n.s. | |
| Dependency | ... | ... | ... | |
| Destructiveness | ... | ... | ... | |
| High Rate | 4 | .0000 | ... | |
| Hit | 90 | +.4444 | 4.57*** | 84 |
| Humiliate | 1 | .0000 | ... | |
| Ignore | 13 | .3846 | n.s. | |
| Indulge | ... | ... | ... | |
| Laugh | 21 | .2381 | n.s. | |
| Noncompliance | 6 | .3333 | ... | |
| Negativism | 21 | +.4762 | 2.26* | 25 |
| Normative | 6 | .1667 | ... | |
| No Response | 23 | −.0870 | 2.54* | 84 |
| Play | 21 | .3281 | n.s. | |
| Physical Positive | 1 | .0000 | ... | |
| Proximity | ... | ... | ... | |
| Receive | 46 | .1957 | n.s. | |
| Self-stimulation | 2 | .0000 | ... | |
| Talk | 28 | .2143 | n.s. | |
| Tease | 12 | .4167 | n.s. | |
| Touch | 1 | .0000 | ... | |
| Whine | 13 | .1538 | n.s. | |
| Work | 2 | .0000 | ... | |
| Yell | 21 | .1429 | n.s. | |
| Total | 481 | | | |

$^a$ If the behavioral event produced a chi-square significant at $p<.05$ or better, the conditional probability value is preceded by a plus; if the event is associated with a decreased probability, the conditional probability is preceded by a minus.
    * $p<.05$          *** $p<.001$

(Hit), decelerators for others (Talk), and accelerators for yet others (Hit). It is clear that aversive stimuli play a powerful role in social interaction.

Behaviors which signify that the aversive stimulus has been withdrawn functioned as decelerating consequences for Hit. Attention, Comply, and No Response all served as significant decelerators. When the victim complies, the attack is terminated. The effect was not only significant for the grouped data, but also characterized almost all of the individual families.

In the study of nursery school interaction (Patterson et al., 1967), the analysis showed that victim behaviors such as Cry functioned as accelerators which increased the probability that the attack would continue.* Many of the attacks seemed initiated as a function of the presence of "a willing victim as $S^D$" rather than as a function of aversive stimuli dispensed by a victim. However, no data on stimulus control were collected in that study, so the hypothesis remains untested. The present analysis suggests that Cry, Yell, and Whine are *decelerators*. However, the two analyses are probably not comparable; the aggressive behaviors in the home seem under the control of aversive stimuli, and those in the classroom under the control of "positive" stimuli. The consequence Cry probably serves very different functions, depending on the kind of stimulus control characterizing the interaction. The present analysis might have separated those Hits which seemed under the control of aversive stimuli from those under the control of nonaversive antecedents. If this had been done, the prediction would be that, for the latter, Cry, Whine, and Yell should function as accelerating consequences. An examination of the records for individual families showed that in 25 per cent Cry did accelerate Hit over base rate values of recurrence. For the present, however, the hypothesis that Cry is a conditioned reinforcer for some children's Hit must remain untested.

---

* The earlier analysis was based to a rather large extent on the prediction of bursts or chains in which one child attacked the other at a high rate for a few moments. However, although most of the predictions were to chained units, some of them were made over consecutive days, and thus the predictions are based upon both accelerating and reinforcing effects. The latter pertain to alterations in the status of the facilitating stimulus as a function of reinforcing arrangements such that future presentations are more likely to produce the response. Because the earlier study summed across both kinds of predictions, the two studies are not directly comparable. A more precise comparison will have to await an analysis of the immediate and future effects of consequences for Hit based upon intensive samplings for individual studies of aggressive boys. Such studies are currently being planned.

The data from the ten matched normal families produced a total of 89 Hits, of which 68 could be used in an analysis comparable with that carried out for the families of the deviant boys. The base rate for recurrence of Hit was .162. Only those consequences which received five or more entries were examined. Hit and Cry seemed to function as accelerators for these families with conditional probability values of .60 and .38, respectively. Attention, No Response, and Comply were decelerators just as they had been for the sample of families of deviant boys. In addition, Command, Laugh, Play, and Disapproval performed a similar function. These secondary findings suggest that the results of the analysis of consequences for Hit may be generalizable across samples of families. This of course would be gratifying in that differences among samples in rates of Hitting would still be accounted for by the same underlying processes of positive and negative reinforcement.

*Specificity of Stimulus Control.* It is our general impression that Hit is under very tight stimulus control. Within each family there are identified victims; the victims present specific $S^F$s to the "deviant person," who predictably provides a Hit. It was also our impression that the effects of an aggressive interchange tend to persist over time, such that if either the victim or the attacker come within "range," the interaction is likely to be repeated. As a preliminary check upon these observations, the data were analyzed for episodes in which the same agent participated as both antecedent and consequator for Hit. In those instances in which a chain of Hits occurred, only the antecedent stimulus for the chain and the consequence which terminated that interchange were included. Those episodes (antecedent, Hit, consequence) which, in turn, were followed during the five-minute block by three interchanges in which the Hitter interacted with an agent other than the one involved in the target episode formed the basis for the analysis. In this approach, an attempt was made to identify Hit episodes which were terminated and then followed by interactions with new agents. A search was then carried out for occasions on which the *same* agent and/or same behavior that had served as antecedent(s) for the previous Hit were again presented to the attacker. The data specify the probability that, given the same antecedent stimuli or components of it, a Hit will again be directed to the previous victim.

There were only ten instances in which the same agent emitting the same behaviors reappeared later within the confines of the five-minute block of observations. Given these circumstances, the conditional probability for a recurrence of Hit was .200. This, of course, is far above the base rate value for Hit of .002±, and suggests the previous interchange still exerts powerful stimulus control. There were sixty-six events in which the same agent appears, but he emits a behavior other than the one associated with the earlier Hit. Given this change in the stimulus matrix, the base rate probability of a recurrence of Hit is now only .061. Similarly, if the same behavior occurred, but dispensed by another agent, the conditional probability of Hit was .064. It would seem that the previous agent plus previous agent behavior is a unique stimulus in that its effects may be much larger than would be predicted by just agent class or response class alone.

## Discussion

The series of laboratory studies reviewed earlier in the paper showed that positive reinforcers could be used to accelerate aggressive behaviors. An observation study showed that delinquent peers dispensed positive reinforcers contingent upon verbal reports of delinquent and aggressive behaviors. A field study showed that in preschool aggressive interactions, victims provided positive reinforcers for assertive-aggressive behaviors that increased the probabilities of these behaviors' being directed toward the same victim on future occasions. Taken together, these preliminary findings suggest that in a few highly selected situations, the social environment is programed to provide positive social reinforcers for certain types of aggressive behaviors.

The analysis of family interaction showed that the behaviors of family members function as significant antecedent stimuli which increase or decrease the likelihood of someone in the family hitting someone else. Events that function as punishment for a pro-social behavior such as Talk were also identified as facilitating stimuli for Hit. The occurrence of the latter increased the probability that a Hit would occur. A Hit followed by one of these aversive events increased the probability that a Hit would recur. There are also events found in the behavior of other family members that are associated with decreased probability of a Hit. In addition, some of these events, when functioning as consequences for Hit, decelerate the recurrence of that behavior. The study of family interaction suggests that Hit, as it occurs within a closed system such as the family, is under the control of negative reinforcement.

In the case of both positive and negative reinforcement, it is clear that aggressive behavior is a *social behavior*, which is to say that it is largely under the control of social stimuli. It is our growing suspicion that both of these training programs are manned almost entirely by peers. Our data have not been organized properly to provide a direct test, but we are beginning to suspect in a small community such as ours, the aggressive behavior of children *and* mothers is acquired and maintained primarily as a function of interaction with children! We suspect that the novice in such training programs is first trained to terminate other children's aversive behaviors by coercive attacks of his own. As shown in the nursery school study, a counterattack has a good chance of terminating attacking behavior, even when it is carried out by a novice. Following several successes, he may initiate his own attacks upon other children. In yet more advanced stages, the pain reactions of victims may come to function as positive reinforcers for attacks, and the presence of willing victims serves to set the occasions for such initiations.

In the case of mothers, it is hypothesized that there are many grown women with no past history of Hitting, who are shaped by interactions with infants and children to initiate physical assaults. Presumably the shaping process is analogous to that provided by children, for children. The mother learns that Hits terminate aversive child behavior. She may then be trained to display behavior of increasingly high amplitude as a function of contingencies supplied by children. We also suspect that many of the child homicides reported are in fact the outcome of such training programs. A young woman, unskilled in mothering, is trained by her own children to carry out assaults that result in bodily injury to her trainers.

For the present the available research does little more than suggest that these speculations are plausible. Large numbers of field and laboratory studies are needed to determine the specifics. Is the termination of an aversive behavior by Hit followed by increases in the probability of Hit, given future occurrences of the antecedent stimulus? Are there conditioned positive reinforcers for Hit which occur outside of preschool interactions? If they exist, what is the process by which they are acquired? What is the density of relevant $S^F$s for Hit in the nursery school, middle-class homes, playgrounds, inner cities, and Sunday school picnics? What is the stability of Hit behaviors across settings? Are there classes of coercive behaviors? Until these, and related questions, are answered, we shall not have an adequate theory of aggressive behavior.

It would, of course, be a vast oversimplification to assume that all aggressive behaviors will neatly fall within the confines of explanations based upon interactions in classrooms and homes. For example, on the larger scene it seems likely that some stimuli reacted to as if aversive have acquired their status by processes more analogous to attitude shaping than by direct experience. Certain groups have been taught to respond to neutral stimuli as if they were aversive; for example, an affront to one's "honor" in the machismo culture, the "establishment" for the hippies, the "nigger" for some whites, the "pigs" for some radicals, and the "hippies" for some conservatives. Thus, members of target groups may become aversive stimuli even though direct experience is missing. However, violence or aggression will not ensue unless these groups are "helpless" by dint of their own lack of training in counteraggression or because "responsible social agents" have indicated by their unwillingness to apply sanctions that these groups may be attacked with impunity.

We also believe that the larger share of aggression in American society occurs either for entertainment or for political purposes. In these instances, the facilitating stimuli are not necessarily aversive, and the reinforcers are as much social approval as the removal of painful stimuli. The rituals associated with the fistfight in the traditional machismo culture are carefully prescribed; once the challenge is issued, a failure to meet it with aggression would be severely punished but success, on the other hand, earns wide-ranging reinforcers. The football game, the boxing match, and much of the socially condoned slaughter in warfare probably rely upon social reinforcement from the peer group for effective aggression and ridicule, or worse, for inept performances. Although society provides penalties and prizes differentially depending upon effective performance, the social mechanism that really keeps these behaviors going is probably the small group.

A proper study of man's behavior requires that we observe man in his natural habitat and focus upon the minutiae which describe the changes in his behavior as he confronts and is confronted by the other people in his world. It is the variables which produce *changes* in his immediate, continuing behavior which are of interest. The major innovation implied in such an approach lies in the assumption that relevant social variables have an immediate impact upon behavior. To the extent that the impact is dramatic, one need only sample a few dozen descriptions of such functional relations; more subtle arrangements between sequential events may require several thousand. But the range of variables and hypotheses which *could* be tested is large indeed, and would provide the foundation for building an understanding of social behavior. The present report is a rather crude first step in determining the characteristics of this kind of data and the hypotheses which can be tested with them.

## References

Amsel, A. The role of frustrative, non-reward in noncontinuous reward situations. *Psychological Bulletin*, 1958, 55, 102–120.

Arrington, R. Time sampling in studies of social behavior: A critical review of techniques and results with research suggestions. *Psychological Bulletin*, 1943, 40, 81–124.

Atkinson, J. Brief deprivation of mother-attention as an antecedent event for coercive mands in the preschool child. M.A. thesis, University of Oregon, 1970.

Azrin, N. H., R. R. Hutchison, & D. F. Hake. Extinction-induced aggression. *Journal of the Experimental Analysis of Behavior*, 1963, 9, 191–204.

Bandura, A., & R. H. Walters. *Social learning and personality development.* New York: Holt, 1963.

Barker, R. G. *The stream of behavior.* New York: Appleton, 1963.

———, P. Gump, W. Campbell, L. Barker, E. Willems, W. Friesen, W. Le Compet, & E. Mikesell. Big school — small school. OEO project No. 594, Progress Report, 1962.

Barker, R. G., & H. Wright. *Midwest and its children.* New York: Row, 1954.

Beach, F. A., & J. Jaynes. Effects of early experience upon the behavior of animals. *Psychological Bulletin*, 1954, 51, 239–264.

Bechtel, R. B. The study of man: Human movement and architecture. *Transaction*, 1967, 4 (May), 53–56.

Berkowitz, L. *Aggression: A social psychological analysis.* New York: McGraw-Hill, 1962.

———. The cue value of available targets for aggression. Paper presented at the meeting of the American Psychological Association, Chicago, September 1965.

———. Control of aggression, in B. Caldwell & H. Ricciuti, eds., *Review of child development research*, Vol. 3. New York: Russell Sage, 1971, in press.

Biernoff, A., R. W. Leary, & R. A. Littman. Dominance behavior of paired primates in two settings. *Journal of Abnormal and Social Psychology*, 1964, 68, 109–113.

Buehler, R. E., G. R. Patterson, & J. M. Furniss. The reinforcement of behavior in institutional settings. *Behaviour Research and Therapy*, 1966, 4, 157–167.

Chittenden, G. E. An experimental study in measuring and modifying assertive behaviors in young children. *Monographs of the Society for Research in Child Development*, 1942, 7 (1, Serial No. 31).

Church, R. M. The varied effects of punishment on behavior. *Psychological Review*, 1963, 70, 369–402.

Cobb, J. A. The relationship of observable classroom behaviors to achievement of fourth grade students. Ph.D. thesis, University of Oregon, 1969.

Crosson, J. E., C. D. Youngberg, M. L. Donley, & M. Waechter. An experimental analysis of natural stimulus function in a special education class. Unpublished MS., University of Oregon, 1968.

Crowder, T. H. Experimental modification of response to frustration in preschool children. Ph.D. thesis, State University of Iowa, 1949.

Davitz, J. R. The effects of previous training on post-frustration behavior. *Journal of Abnormal and Social Psychology*, 1952, 47, 309–315.

Dawe, H. C. An analysis of two hundred quarrels of preschool children. *Child Development*, 1934, 5, 139–157.

Dittman, A. T., & D. W. Goodrich. A comparison of social behavior in normal and hyperaggressive preadolescent boys. *Child Development*, 1961, 32, 315–327.

Dollard, J., L. W. Doob, N. E. Miller, O. H. Mowrer, & R. R. Sears. *Frustration and aggression.* New Haven, Conn.: Yale University Press, 1939.

Ebner, M. An investigation of the role of the social environment in the generalization and persistence of the effect of a behavior modification program. Ph.D. thesis, University of Oregon, 1967.

Edwards, A. E., & T. Treadwell. Cardiovascular response to experimentally induced repressed anger. *Proceedings of the 75th Annual Convention of the American Psychological Association*, 1967, 183–184.

————. Comparative effects of anger and epinephrine upon stomach motility and the cardiovascular system. *Proceedings of the 77th Annual Convention of the American Psychological Association*, pp. 249–250. Washington, D.C.: The Association, 1969.

Fawl, C. Disturbances experienced by children in their natural habitats, in R. G. Barker, ed., *The stream of behavior*, pp. 99–126. New York: Appleton, 1963.

Gewirtz, J. L. Factor analysis of some attention-seeking behaviors of young children. *Child Development*, 1956, 27, 17–36.

Goodenough, F. L. *Anger in young children.* Minneapolis: University of Minnesota Press, 1931.

Graham, F. K., W. A. Charivat, A. S. Honig, & P. C. Weltz. Aggression as a function of the attack and the attacker. *Journal of Abnormal and Social Psychology*, 1951, 46, 512–520.

Green, E. H. Group play and quarreling among preschool children. *Child Development*, 1933, 4, 302–307.

Hanf, C. Modifying problem behaviors in mother-child interactions. Part I. Standardized laboratory situations. Unpublished MS., University of Oregon Medical School, 1969.

Harris, A. Observer effect on family interaction. Ph.D. thesis, University of Oregon, 1969.

Hartup, W. W., & Y. Himeno. Social isolation versus interaction with adults in relation to aggression in pre-school children. *Journal of Abnormal and Social Psychology*, 1960, 59, 17–22.

Henry, M. M., & D. F. Sharpe. Some influential factors in the determination of aggressive behavior in pre-school children. *Child Development*, 1947, 18, 11–28.

Hinsey, C., G. R. Patterson, & B. Sonoda. Validation of a procedure for conditioning aggression in children. Paper presented at the meeting of the Western Psychological Association, Seattle, 1961.

Hokanson, J. E. The effects of frustration and anxiety on overt aggression. *Journal of Abnormal and Social Psychology*, 1961, 62, 346–351.

———— & R. Eddman. Effect of three social responses on vascular processes. *Journal of Personality and Social Psychology*, 1966, 3, 442–447.

Hokanson, J. E., K. R. Willus, & E. Koropsak. The modification of autonomic responses during aggressive interchanges. *Journal of Personality*, 1968, 36, 386–404.

Hollingshead, A. B., & F. C. Redlich. *Social class and mental illness.* New York: Wiley, 1958.

Hoover, L. K., & H. H. Rinehart. The effect of an outside observer on family interaction. Unpublished MS., Oregon Research Institute, Eugene, 1968.

Jersild, A. T., & F. V. Markey. Conflicts between pre-school children. *Child Development Monograph*, 1935, No. 21.

Kagan, J., & H. Moss. *Birth to maturity: A study in psychological development.* New York: Wiley, 1962.

LoLords, V. M. Positive conditioned reinforcement from aversive situations. *Psychological Bulletin*, 1969, 72, 193–203.

Lorenz, K. *On aggression.* New York: Harcourt, 1966.

Lovaas, I. O. Effect of exposure to symbolic aggression on aggressive behavior. *Child Development*, 1961, 32, 37–44.

―――. Interaction between verbal and non-verbal behavior. *Child Development*, 1961, 32, 329–336.

―――, B. Schaeffer, & J. A. Simmons. Experimental studies in childhood schizophrenia: Building social behavior in autistic children by use of electric shock. *Journal of Experimental Research in Personality*, 1969, 1, 99–109.

Macfarlane, J. W., L. Allen, & M. P. Honzik. *A developmental study of the behavior problems of normal children between 21 months and 14 years.* Los Angeles: University of California Press, 1954.

Moore, S. Correlates of peer acceptance in nursery school children. *Young Children*, 1967, 22, 281–297.

Morris, H. H. Aggressive behavior disorders in children: A follow-up study. *American Journal of Psychiatry*, 1956, 112, 991–997.

Osborn, K. D. Dependency in young children in relation to two maternal behavior variables: A methodological study. M.A. thesis, State University of Iowa, 1952.

Patterson, G. R., & G. G. Bechtel. Formulating the situational environment in relation to states and traits, in R. B. Cattell, ed., *Handbook of modern personality study.* Chicago: Aldine, 1971.

Patterson, G. R., & G. Brodsky. A behaviour modification programme for a child with multiple problem behaviours. *Journal of Child Psychology and Psychiatry*, 1966, 7, 277–295.

Patterson, G. R., J. A. Cobb, & R. S. Ray. A social engineering technology for retraining aggressive boys, in H. Adams & L. Unikel, eds., *Georgia symposium in experimental clinical psychology*, Vol. 2. New York: Pergamon, 1971, in press.

Patterson, G. R., & A. Harris. Some methodological considerations for observation procedures. Paper presented at the meeting of the American Psychological Association, San Francisco, September 1968.

Patterson, G. R., R. A. Littman, & W. Bricker. Assertive behavior in children: A step toward a theory of aggression. *Monographs of the Society for Research in Child Development*, 1967, 32 (5, Serial No. 113).

Patterson, G. R., & J. B. Reid. Reciprocity and coercion: Two facets of social systems, in C. Neuringer & J. Michael, eds., *Behavior modification in clinical psychology*, pp. 133–177. New York: Appleton, 1970.

Peterson, D. R. Behavior problems of middle childhood. *Journal of Consulting Psychology*, 1961, 25, 205–209.

Pritchard, M., & P. Graham. An investigation of a group of patients who have attended both the child and adult departments of the same psychiatric hospital. *British Journal of Psychiatry*, 1966, 112, 603–613.

Quay, H., & C. Lorene. Behavior problems in early adolescence. *Child Development*, 1965, 36, 215–220.

Rafferty, J. E., B. Tyler, & F. B. Tyler. Personality assessment from free play observation. *Child Development*, 1960, 31, 691–702.

Rausch, H. L. Interaction sequences. *Journal of Personality and Social Psychology*, 1965, 2, 487–499.

Reid, J. B. Reciprocity and family interaction. Ph.D. thesis, University of Oregon, 1967.

―――. Reliability assessment of observation data: A possible methodological problem. *Child Development*, in press.

Reynolds, G. S., A. C. Catania, & B. F. Skinner. Conditioned and unconditioned aggression in children. *Journal of Experimental Analysis of Behavior*, 1963, 1, 73–75.

Rheingold, H. L., J. Gewirtz, & H. Ross. Social conditioning of vocalization. *Journal of Comparative and Physiological Psychology*, 1959, 52, 68–73.

Roach, J. L., O. Gurrslin, & R. G. Hunt. Some social, psychological characteristics of a child guidance clinic caseload. *Journal of Consulting Psychology*, 1958, 22, 183–186.

Robins, L. N. *Deviant children grown up: A sociological and psychiatric study of sociopathic personality*. Baltimore: Williams & Wilkins, 1966.

Roff, M. Relation between certain preservice factors and psychoneuroses during military duty. *U.S. Armed Forces Medical Journal*, 1960, 2, 152–160.

———. Childhood social interactions and young adult bad conduct. *Journal of Abnormal and Social Psychology*, 1961, 65, 333–337.

———. Some childhood and adolescent characteristics of adult homosexuals. U.S. Army Medical Research and Development Contract No. DA.49-007-MD-2015. Report No. 66-5, 1966.

Rosenthal, R. *Experimenter effects in behavioral research*. New York: Appleton, 1966.

Schalock, H. D. Observation of mother-child interaction in the laboratory and in the home. Ph.D. thesis, University of Nebraska, 1956.

———. Observer influence on mother-child interaction in the home: A preliminary report. Paper presented at the meeting of the Western Psychological Association, Carmel, Calif., 1958.

Scott, J. P. *Aggression*. Chicago: University of Chicago Press, 1958.

——— & E. Fredericson. The causes of fighting in mice and rats. *Physiological Zoology*, 1951, 24, 273–309.

Scott, P. M., R. Burton, & M. Radke-Yarrow. Social reinforcement under natural conditions. *Child Development*, 1967, 38, 53–63.

Sears, R. R., L. Rau, & R. R. Alpert. *Identification and child rearing*. Stanford, Calif.: Stanford University Press, 1965.

Semler, I., L. Eron, L. J. Meyerson, & J. T. Williams. Relationship of aggression in third-grade children to certain pupil characteristics. *Psychology in the Schools*, 1967, 4, 85–88.

Sheppard, W. Operant control of infant vocal and motor behavior. *Journal of Experimental Child Psychology*, 1969, 7, 36–51.

Skinner, B. F. *Verbal behavior*. New York: Appleton, 1957.

Stone, L. J., & J. E. Hokanson. Arousal reduction via self-punitive behavior. *Journal of Personality and Social Psychology*, 1969, 12, 72–79.

Terrace, H. S. Stimulus control, in W. K. Honig, ed., *Operant behavior: Areas of research and application*, pp. 271–344. New York: Appleton, 1966.

Thomas, D. S., A. M. Loomis, & R. Arrington. *Observational studies of social behavior*, Vol. 1. *Social behavior patterns*. New Haven, Conn.: Institute of Human Relations, Yale University, 1933.

Tinbergen, N. *The study of instinct*. Oxford: Oxford University Press, 1951.

Ulrich, R. Pain as a cause of aggression. *American Zoologist*, 1966, 6, 643–662.

———. Research and theory concerning the causes and control of aggression. Paper presented at the meeting of the American Psychological Association, New York, 1966.

——— & J. Flavell. Human aggression, in C. Neuringer & J. Michael, eds., *Behavior modification in clinical psychology*, pp. 105–132. New York: Appleton, 1970.

Ulrich, R., R. B. Hutchinson, & H. H. Azrin. Pain elicited aggression. *Psychological Record*, 1965, 15, 111–126.

Ulrich, R., M. Johnston, J. Richardson, & P. Wolff. The operant conditioning of fighting behavior in rats. *Psychological Record*, 1963, 13, 465–470.

Updegraff, R. L., & M. E. Keister. A study of children's reactions to failure and an experimental attempt to modify them. *Child Development*, 1937, 8, 241–248.

Von Wiltz, M. P., H. H. Hops, I. C. Tacitus, & P. P. Patterson. Serpentes nivorum et mures glaciales. *Agete Scientem*, 1931, 5, 900–1102.

Walters, R. H., & M. Brown. Studies of reinforcement of aggression: III. Transfer of responses to an interpersonal situation. *Child Development*, 1963, 34, 563–571.

Wolfgang, M. E., & F. Ferracuti. *The sub-culture of violence*. London: Social Science Paperback, 1967.

◈ EARL S. SCHAEFER ◈

# Development of Hierarchical, Configurational Models for Parent Behavior and Child Behavior

PROGRESS in the conceptualization of human behavior requires a recurring process of analysis and differentiation followed by synthesis and integration. At different periods and in different studies, investigators emphasize analysis or synthesis, differentiation or integration, and more complex or more simple conceptual systems. The analysis of a domain into a set of discrete concepts is necessary to permit the organization of those differentiated concepts into a simple integrated model. Although preference for more abstract concepts may be contrasted with preference for more concrete concepts, it is possible to integrate both specific and general concepts through a hierarchical, configurational approach to the development of conceptual models.

Efforts to integrate the domains of parent behavior and child behavior have been motivated by the accumulating studies of parent behavior and child behavior, the numerous parent and child behavior variables that have been developed, and the innumerable intercorrelations of parent behavior and child behavior that have been investigated and partially re-

NOTE: I wish to acknowledge with gratitude the contributions of Richard Q. Bell and Nancy Bayley during our collaboration; the contributions of Helen Manheimer, Leo Droppleman, May Aaronson, and Julie Forrest to the development of methods and analysis of data; the cooperation of Alex Kalverboer (The Netherlands), Giselle Renson (Belgium), Resa Arasteh (Iran), Jarmila Kostaskova (Czechoslovakia), Norma Gordon and Marta Schönhals (Germany), A. A. Khatri (India), and Hidea Kojima (Japan), in foreign studies, and John Hurley, Victor Small, and Reyna Larson-Crowther, in American studies.

ported. Attempts to arrive at replicated generalizations from research on parent behavior and child behavior are frustrated by the many different methods and conceptual schemes used by investigators of parent behavior and child behavior. Schaefer (1961) reviewed some of the early attempts to develop conceptual models for parent behavior and child behavior and found evidence of convergence upon two-dimensional or circular conceptual models that had been derived from both theoretical and empirical analyses. Since Schaefer's (1961) review, a number of studies and reviews of personality research have provided further evidence for circular models. However, the accumulated research now reveals the convergence of several different studies upon a three-dimensional spherical model for parent behavior. Other studies, many of them unpublished, that have provided more comprehensive and differentiated analyses of a child's classroom behavior support the development of a replicable three-dimensional spherical model for child behavior.

## CONCEPTUAL CONFIGURATIONS AND CONCEPTUAL DIMENSIONS

Emphasis on the search for underlying dimensions and functional unities through factor analysis and simple structure rotation by Thurstone (1947) heavily influenced American factor analysts to ignore the existence of conceptual configurations. Thurstone (1947), however, was keenly aware of the test configuration from which factors can be derived and indexed the term *configuration* repeatedly in his exposition of factor analysis. Methods for plotting two- and three-dimensional configurations were developed, but with a consistent goal of achieving simple structure and "functional unities." Despite these objectives, Thurstone (1947) recognized that "The choice of a set of fundamental concepts in terms of which any domain of nature is to be comprehended is probably meaningless to nature . . . The choice is for us to make in terms that will attain intellectual control and consistency, as empirically determined, . . . as far as possible with ideas that are already familiar to us. Fundamental scientific concepts that are successful in this sense are as social as other inventions. To hunt for a unique solution to the comprehension of a set of related phenomena is an illusory hunt for absolutes" (p. 332). In his discussion of factors of the mind Burt (1941) likened isolating behavior dimensions to the task of the navigator: "the factors in terms of which the psychologist ultimately expresses his results can at most claim only the same kind of existence as the line or points to which the navigator refers his measurements . . . they are simply items in an *abstract frame of reference*. As such they are naturally presumed to be constant; but they are merely for descriptive purposes; and no one would be tempted to assign them an actual physical existence" (p. 82). Burt (1941) emphasizes that factor analysis cannot discover underlying entities and suggests that the psychologist adopt the same view as the modern physicist, who "finds only an intricate and abstract structure, a pattern of observable relations between observable phenomena — the phenomena themselves being either mere patterns of relations, or else pattern-like sequences of events within a conscious continuum, and so neither substantial nor causal" (p. 220). Burt goes on to argue that "in the field of psychology as a pure but empirical science, we are no longer justified in assuming a universe of individual 'objects' or stimuli acting on an individual 'subject' or mind. The objects or stimuli prove to be merely *Gestalten*: so are the minds; so is the experience that minds have of the objects. We are reduced to the study of a changing structure of relations linking two sets of systems; and these systems themselves are simply structures of relation" (p. 238). Repeatedly Burt urges that psychologists "think in terms of complex patterns rather than isolated units," of systems of relations, of patterns and Gestalten.

Despite Thurstone's (1947) early awareness of configurations and Burt's (1941) sophisticated discussion of systems of relations, explicit awareness of the structures from which factors or dimensions are derived was subsequently reduced and often abandoned completely (Harman, 1960). Lists of isolated factors were produced without explicit reference to the intricate, conceptual configurations from which they were derived. Factors were interpreted as isolated entities; only the points in conceptual space that were identified as factors were recognized, whereas the spaces between those points typically were ignored.

Accompanying this neglect of the configurations from which factors were derived was a tendency to forget Burt's early denial of the actual physical existence of factors and Thurstone's statement that the search for a unique solution is an illusory hunt for absolutes. In a discussion of Guttman's (1966) paper on order analysis of correlation matrices, Cattell (1966) defined factor analysis as "searching for separate factors shown by simple structure to function in Nature as independent determiners." Proponents of this school of thought persist in their search for unique multi-factor organizations despite repeated criticism that they have failed to achieve replicable factors. Some of the critics of the multi-factor, simple structure rotation approach have emphasized the possibility of achieving agreement upon a few major replicable dimensions of behavior (Eysenck, 1953; Peterson, 1961); others have stressed the use of a few major dimensions to achieve replicable conceptual configurations (Schaefer, 1959, 1961). Although the tendency to reify any solution to the problem of scientific description is strong, it is important to recognize all solutions as tentative, subject to modification through further investigation, and as based upon the preferences and decisions of the investigator rather than upon the inherent structure of Nature. However, certain choices of concepts and methods of analysis can yield replicable conceptual structures.

The search for invariant conceptual configurations is probably a more replicable and a more fruitful approach to the search for conceptual structures than is the search for factors, since it is based upon the empirical configuration of tests or measures rather than upon imposing a set of reference dimensions into that empirical configuration. The location of reference dimensions by factor analysis and rotation is determined by the concepts that are selected from the conceptual space. Different samples of concepts would yield different rotated factor locations. The configuration of the selected concepts is invariant and does not depend upon the location of factors. After plotting a two- or three-dimensional configuration, it is possible to remove the reference dimensions and focus entirely upon the configuration of variables.

The location of the factors or reference vectors that allow a plot of a configuration or a map of a conceptual domain may be unimportant. After the conceptual map has been plotted, the reference vectors may be removed, and the spatial arrangement of the concepts will represent the relations among concepts. A spatial plot transforms an algebraic statement of the relations among variables to a geometric representation of those relations, and gives an integrated visual display of the nomological network (Cronbach & Meehl, 1955) in which concepts are embedded. Thus, a search for conceptual configurations may give a more integrated, replicable solution than a search for a set of fundamental parameters of behavior.

Guttman's (1954) radex theory has contributed greatly to a renewed interest in the study of configurations. Particularly influential have been the law of neighboring, which directs attention to systematic variations in the amount of variance shared by variables, and the description of a circumplex order: "It is an order which has no beginning and no end, namely, a circular order. A set of variables obeying such a law will be called a circumplex to designate a 'circular' order of complexity" (p. 260). Guttman (1967) has continued to develop radex theory into methods for non-metrical mapping of variables and has applied those methods to many different kinds of psychometric data. Shepard (1963) also has been developing methods for mapping variables and has applied those methods to experimental data. Tryon and Bailey (1966) included methods for mapping data in their extensive set of computer programs. More extensive use of the statistical methods and computer programs developed by these investigators should greatly extend our knowledge of conceptual configurations. Thurstone's (1947) method of plotting a spherical configuration by extending each test vector to unit length provides a convenient, inexpensive method for visualizing a three-dimensional factor structure that will be used in this paper. Thurstone's method clearly shows the interrelationships of the dimensional and configurational approach to conceptual structures.

## A HIERARCHICAL APPROACH TO THE DEVELOPMENT
### OF CONCEPTUAL STRUCTURES

The development of a parsimonious conceptual model requires the analysis of a domain, which Thurstone (1947) defines as "a field of related measurements," into a set of discrete components. Success in developing an integrated, comprehensive, and comprehensible configuration is highly dependent upon the initial definition of the domain. Combinations of data from different methods — tests, observations — and combinations of different kinds of data — social behavior, attitudes, mental abilities, interests — within a single domain would typically not reveal a clear structure. Also descriptions of a single person by different informants — father, mother, and peer descriptions of a child — or descriptions of different persons by a single informant — descriptions of both father and mother by a single child — should not be intercorrelated and factor analyzed in a single matrix. If several distinguishable kinds of data are collected in a study, separate multivariate domains should be analyzed separately. For example, Schaefer and Bayley (1963) developed separate circumplex orders for maternal behavior and child behavior and then studied the intercorrelations of the two independently ordered sets of data.

Definition of a domain also determines the comprehensiveness of the data included in an analysis and the conceptual structures that can be determined. This fact has led to the judgment — accurate but frequently intended to disparage the method — "you get no more from a factor analysis than you put into it." Apparent differences in conceptual models for child behavior may be due to different definitions of the domain. An analysis of interpersonal behavior of a child or of the social and emotional behavior of a child leads to a more limited configuration than does a domain that includes social, emotional, and task-oriented behavior of a child. More attention to the definition of meaningful domains should lead to improvement in replication across studies and to greater clarity in conceptual structures. A more comprehensive, differentiated analysis of a domain should lead to a more complex, differentiated model for the domain.

Success in achieving a meaningful conceptual model for a domain is also highly dependent upon the analysis of the domain into a set of well-defined discrete variables. Most studies of interpersonal behavior have analyzed trait level scales consisting of sets of specific items, although other studies have analyzed specific behavior items or ratings of general traits. Loevinger (1957) has written at length of the usefulness of developing a priori scales and Schaefer and his collaborators (Schaefer, 1965-a&b; Schaefer & Bell, 1958; Schaefer, Bell, & Bayley, 1959) used this method in a series of studies of parent attitudes and behavior and child behavior. The success of this approach to developing a set of measures for a conceptual domain and the clarity of the conceptual models that have been derived from this approach suggest that further use may rapidly lead to further progress in conceptualizing personality variables.

The development of a priori scales may be contrasted with the development of empirical scales, a method that has been frequently used in developing personality inventories. Empirical scales are frequently developed by factor analyzing a heterogeneous set of items with no explicit hypotheses about the factors that might be derived. This method is expensive, time-consuming, and typically does not yield homogeneous, well-defined scales. In the development of a priori scales, the investigator attempts to assemble a set of homogeneous items to define a more general concept. If a number of items are assembled for each concept, it is usually possible to refine and shorten the scales from analyses of empirical data on item and scale characteristics.

Different approaches can be used in developing scales for a set of constructs for a specified domain. Clinical reports, earlier empirical studies, or the experience of the investigator or of others with knowledge of the domain can be used to generate intuitive concepts that can be operationally defined by writing a set of specific behavior items. A set of behavior items can be sorted into apparently homogeneous groups for which a more general concept can be developed, or a specific behavior description or item can be used as a base for generating a concept and a set of related items for the concept.

The choice of the level of specificity or generality of the concepts to be measured is critical for success in achieving reliable measures and a differentiated analysis of a conceptual domain. Concepts should be as specific as is feasible within the limitations of a study; it is easier to combine differentiated concepts than to analyze global concepts into more discrete components. For example, the concept of parental control is a global, abstract, undifferentiated concept, as is the concept of parental permissiveness. In contrast, the concepts of Intrusiveness, Protectiveness, Possessiveness, Control through Guilt, Control through Instilling Persistent Anxiety, and Control through Withdrawal of Relationship provide a more differentiated analysis. Labels for concepts should be chosen to communicate the item content as accurately as possible.

Items that are written to define the concepts should describe specific observable behaviors and should be designed to elicit adequate variability in description of the target population. Item content must conform to two contrasting demands — psychological and empirical homogeneity and varied behavioral content. After a pool of items have been written for a construct, trained judges can be used to eliminate items which do not meet the criteria. Although it is desirable to use empirical data to determine whether each item shows adequate variability and adequate correlation with total scale score, relatively good internal consistency reliabilities can be obtained for short, unrefined, a priori scales (Schaefer, 1965a).

The definition of a domain, the analysis of the domain into a set of discrete constructs, and the operational definition of those constructs through a set of specific items contribute to the process of analysis and differentiation of human behavior. Measures developed through such methods are immediately useful in scientific research. The measures can also be used to attempt to develop integrated conceptual structures through the isolation of factors and the development of conceptual configurations.

The table of intercorrelations of a set of variables determines a complex configuration for the conceptual domain. Factor analysis is the conventional method for reducing that complex configuration to a smaller number of dimensions. The degree of replication of factorial dimensions across studies, even by the same investigator, has been limited. For example,

Hundleby and Cattell (1968) state of their attempt to isolate replicated factors of child personality that "of the 17 factors, eight were identified with some confidence. Four other factors could not conservatively be matched, though suggestive identifications are possible. Five factors were not identified and have been left for exploration in the light of new studies now about to appear in this field" (p. 52). Both Becker (1960) and Peterson (1965) have criticized the degree of replication for Cattell's claimed matches in earlier studies and conclude that replication of multi-factor analyses of the personality domain has not been achieved.

The controversy between those who propose recognition of only a few major factors in personality research and proponents of multi-factor solutions appears to be related to the need for integration versus the need for differentiation. Proponents of a few major factors emphasize the high degree of replication across studies for a limited number of factors, whereas proponents of multi-factor analyses emphasize the need for differentiated analyses of the personality space. If personality research is to yield a replicable body of knowledge, the proponents of a few major factors would win the controversy, for there is evidence of replication across studies and national groups for such analyses. The need for differentiation can be met by analyzing specific scales and/or specific items in a hierarchical analysis of a behavioral domain that includes items, scales, and factors.

Why has the goal of achieving a highly differentiated, highly replicable multi-factor analysis of behavior been so elusive? Differences in the definition of the domain of investigation and differences in the sampling of concepts from the domain would lead to significantly different factor structures. Also, different labels for the same behavioral content and identical labels for different behavioral content make matching of factors an uncertain task. For example, different personality inventory scales that are labeled extroversion, introversion, and neuroticism may have only moderate intercorrelations.

Differences in the number of factors extracted and rotated from similar correlation matrices also may lead to apparent differences in factor structure. A set of concepts which define a single factor when only two or three dimensions are extracted may be divided into two or three different factors when additional factors are extracted and rotated. Experience suggests that the lesser number of factors can be more clearly replicated than the greater number, as shown by Peterson's (1960) reanalysis of Cattell's behavior rating data.

Despite Guilford's (1952) warning about the need for adequate samples in order to justify factor analysis of a set of data, multi-factor analyses of as few as thirty cases are still being published. Owing to the high standard error of correlation for small samples, the amount of error in rotated factors from small samples would be large. A related problem is the interpretation of small factor loadings in multi-factor analyses for moderate sample sizes.

The analysis of a specified domain into a set of items, scales, and factors provides a hierarchical analysis of that conceptual space. If the factor analysis is limited to two or three major orthogonal factors, those factors can be used to map the interrelationships of the elements of the domain. A two-dimensional configuration can be plotted by merely plotting the two factors. An idealized three-dimensional configuration can be plotted by extending each vector to unit length for the three-dimensional space and plotting the points on the surface of a sphere or a map of the sphere (Thurstone, 1947, p. 131). Although Thurstone's purpose in plotting a spherical configuration was to achieve a simple structure rotation, the factors or reference dimensions can be ignored, and the configuration can be interpreted as a visual display of the interrelationships of the concepts included. The configuration would thus present a system of interrelationships, nomological network, or conceptual structure in which each concept is embedded. If factor loadings, or correlations with orthogonal factor scores, are determined for each item and scale, a plot could reveal the location of each item, scale, and factor in a single, integrated, conceptual configuration.

The map of a conceptual space can reveal at a glance variables that have identical locations in that space, neighboring variables and the degree of neighboring, unrelated variables, and polar opposites. More densely populated sectors of the configuration can be interpreted as clusters or constellations. Less populated or empty sectors of the space indicate that those sectors have not been conceptualized adequately. The few items that are found in a relatively empty sector and items that are adjacent to empty sectors or polar opposites of empty sectors might be used as a guide for further conceptualization and item development.

Plotting conceptual configurations may assist also in reconciling apparently different factor structures for the same domain. As a hypothetical example, three independent investigators would probably develop three different sets of concepts for the same three-dimensional conceptual space. Because of a limited conceptualization of that space, one investigator might identify only two dimensions, and each of the other two investigators might isolate three dimensions that, because of their different samples of concepts, might fall in different sectors of a spherical model. The three investigators, when comparing their analyses, would be confronted with the usual confusing situation of different numbers of factors and only partial similarity or overlapping of factors. Independent plots of the three configurations might allow recognition that all three configurations, after suitable rotation, would be located in sectors of the same conceptual sphere. Of course, an empirical test of that conclusion would be needed to confirm the hypothesis. This analysis of conceptual structure offers hope that the many apparently different factors that have been found in personality research may be integrated into parsimonious conceptual models. However, it would not support a hypothesis that factor analysis and simple structure rotations can isolate factors that "function in Nature as independent determiners."

### DEVELOPMENT OF HIERARCHICAL, CIRCULAR, AND SPHERICAL MODELS FOR PARENT BEHAVIOR

A review of a series of studies in which attempts were made to conceptualize parental attitudes and behavior (Schaefer, 1965b; Schaefer & Bell, 1958; Schaefer, Bell, & Bayley, 1959) illustrates the process of analyzing a domain into a set of relatively differentiated concepts. This review focuses upon: (a) the organization of those concepts into major dimensions and into circular and spherical conceptual models for parent behavior; (b) empirical and theoretical contributions to the development of two-dimensional circular models for parent behavior; (c) research that supports the development of a three-dimensional spherical model based upon more differentiated data on parent behavior; (d) clear replication of three-dimensional organizations of children's reports of parent behavior, across investigators, and across language groups; and (e) the need for more comprehensive investigation of such models for parent behavior using improved methods.

The initial project in this continuing program of conceptualization of parent behavior and attitudes was the development of the Parental Attitude Research Instrument (PARI) by Schaefer and Bell (1958). The mo-

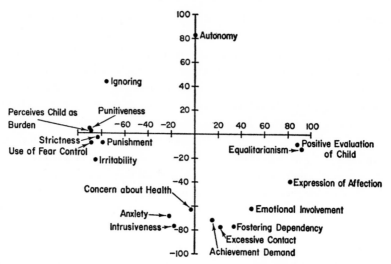

*Figure 1.* A circumplex of maternal behavior ratings. (Reprinted by permission of the American Psychological Association from E. S. Schaefer, A circumplex model for maternal behavior, *Journal of Abnormal and Social Psychology*, 1959, 59, 226–235.)

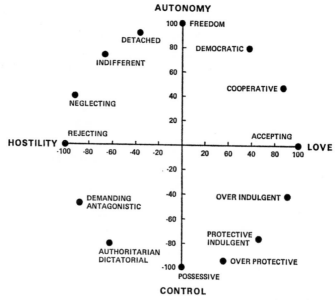

*Figure 2.* A hypothetical circumplex of maternal behavior concepts. (Reprinted by permission of the American Psychological Association from E. S. Schaefer, A circumplex model for maternal behavior, *Journal of Abnormal and Social Psychology*, 1959, 59, 226–235.)

tivation for the development of this method was provided by the earlier studies of Shoben (1949), Mark (1953), and Stogdill (1936) as well as by other research and clinical studies of parent behavior and attitudes. Twenty-three five-item scales were developed to measure specific attitudes toward child rearing. Factor analyses of that method show high replication for three major factors (Schaefer, 1961; Zuckerman, Ribback, Monashkin, & Norton, 1958). Studies that have used this instrument have not found substantial evidence of the validity of parental attitudes for predicting either maternal behavior or child behavior. Research reported since Becker and Krug's (1965) review supports their conclusion that other methods for studying parent behavior probably are more valid.

Despite the low validity of the PARI, the concepts that were developed in it provided a basis for developing a method for rating maternal behavior from extensive recorded observations of maternal behavior from the Berkeley Growth Study (Schaefer, Bell, & Bayley, 1959). Thirty-two trait level concepts such as Ignoring, Expression of Affection, and Intrusiveness were defined by specifying five to seven trait-actions (Furfey, 1926) that were to be rated from observations of mothers' behavior during mental tests of their infants during the first three years of life. Twenty-eight scales were adapted for rating written records of interviews with the mothers in their homes when the children were nine to fourteen years of age. Adequate reliabilities were achieved by combining ratings by three independent judges and relatively high stability or consistency through time was found for a dimension of Loving Acceptance versus Hostile Rejection between the infancy ratings and the adolescent ratings. Correlations of these maternal behavior ratings with the children's social, emotional, and cognitive development suggested that such ratings have relatively good validity for predicting child behavior.

Factor analyses of the maternal behavior ratings revealed two major dimensions of maternal behavior that, when plotted, revealed the circular ordering of maternal behavior concepts that is reproduced in Figure 1 (Schaefer, 1959). The empirical data were generalized by organizing abstract concepts for parental behavior into the circumplex model that is shown in Figure 2 (Schaefer, 1959). Organizations of data on maternal behavior reported by Sanford, Adkins, Miller, & Cobb (1943) and Baldwin, Kalhorn, & Breese (1945) were interpreted as supporting the model. In interpreting these empirical and theoretical organizations of parent be-

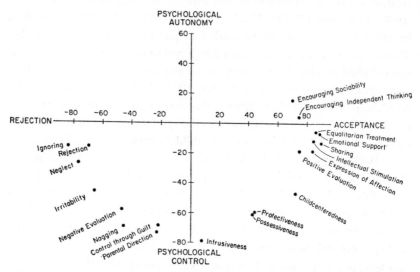

*Figure 3.* Conceptual plane generated by Acceptance versus Rejection and Psychological Autonomy versus Psychological Control. (Reprinted by permission of the American Psychological Association from E. S. Schaefer, A configurational analysis of children's reports of parental behavior, *Journal of Consulting Psychology,* 1965b, 29, 552–557.)

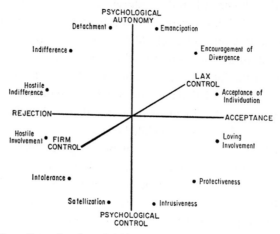

*Figure 4.* A three-dimensional model for parent behavior. (Reprinted by permission of the American Psychological Association from E. S. Schaefer, A configurational analysis of children's reports of parental behavior, *Journal of Consulting Psychology,* 1965b, 29, 552–557.)

havior, emphasis should be given to the ordering of variables within the conceptual space rather than to the reference axes that have been used.

In order to investigate whether this circumplex ordering of parental behavior could be confirmed from another perspective, the Child's Report of Parent Behavior Inventory, consisting of twenty-six ten-item scales, was developed to measure many of the same concepts included in the studies on parent attitudes and maternal behavior ratings. New concepts were developed to measure different sectors of the circumplex model (Schaefer, 1965a). Separate factor analyses of children's and adults' descriptions of maternal and paternal behavior revealed a well-replicated three-dimensional factor structure. The conceptual plane plotted for the concepts that had loadings on Acceptance versus Rejection and Psychological Control is reproduced in Figure 3 (Schaefer, 1965b). A second conceptual plane was plotted for concepts that had high loadings on factors of Psychological Control and Lax Control versus Firm Control; the empirical data were generalized into the three-dimensional model for parent behavior reproduced in Figure 4. Although an attempt was made to select concepts for sectors of the conceptual plane defined by factors of Acceptance versus Rejection and Psychological Autonomy versus Psychological Control, the third dimension of Lax Control versus Firm Control is shown without an attempt to generate concepts for all sectors of a spherical model.

Clear replication of a spherical model for reports of parental behavior by American children and adults was followed by an attempt to replicate the findings for another language/cultural group with a revised version of the Child's Report of Parent Behavior Inventory. Some of the initial scales were combined from the results of factor and item analyses, and new scales were developed. The scales were translated and, if necessary, adapted for a French-speaking Belgian population by Renson (1965). Separate factor analyses for reports of maternal and paternal behavior by boys and girls replicated the three dimensions found for American subjects (Renson, 1965; Renson, Schaefer, & Levy, 1968). A map for the spherical structure of that data was developed by extending scale vectors to unit length, and computing the angular locations of the vectors for the stereographic plot that is shown in Figure 5. All concepts could be plotted in a single hemisphere except Extreme Autonomy, which, when inverted, fell into the sector of Lax Control. Again the plane that moves from Acceptance to Psychological Control to Rejection is more adequately represented than other sectors of the sphere. In order to achieve a more comprehensive description of parental behavior, additional concepts would be required that would be designed to fill the empty sectors and, if possible, the other hemisphere. Additional reported factor analyses of the revised version of the Child's Report of Parent Behavior Inventory for American college students by Cross (1969), for Japanese children by Kojima (1967), and for Canadian children by Patsula (1969), and unpublished factor analyses for subjects from Czechoslovakia, Germany, Iran, and India show high replication of a three-dimensional spherical model for parent behavior across Eastern and Western national and cultural groups. The factor structures of Japanese children reported by Kojima are ex-

*Figure 5.* A map of Walloon children's reports of parent behavior. (Reprinted by permission of the Society for Research in Child Development from G. J. Renson, E. S. Schaefer, & B. I. Levy, Cross-national validity of a spherical conceptual model for parent behavior, *Child Development*, 1968, 39, 1229–1235.)

tremely similar to those for subjects from Western countries, but some differences in rotated factor structures were found for Iranian and Indian samples despite a high degree of similarity. Typically, the structures show highly similar ordering of concepts in conceptual planes or in spherical configurations despite differences in exact angular locations. The configuration or organization of concepts, after allowing for error owing to different samples, can be interpreted as showing topological invariance across cultures for three-dimensional factor structures for this conceptual space. Statistical tests are needed to test the hypothesis of topological invariance of conceptual configuration across sets of data varying in sex of child, sex of parent, age of child, and national and cultural group that were derived from inspection of correlation matrices and plotted configurations.

The two-dimensional model for maternal behavior derived from ratings of observations and interviews by professional psychologists and the three-dimensional spherical model derived from children's reports of parent behavior show similar ordering of parent behavior concepts despite the incompleteness of both sets of data. Moderately high correlations between the Berkeley Growth Study ratings of maternal behavior from interviews when the children were nine to fourteen years of age, and retrospective reports on that period by the children when they were approximately thirty-six years of age suggests that both of the methods can yield valid data (Schaefer & Bayley, 1967). The relatively good replication of a three-dimensional structure for children's reports of parent behavior across diverse groups suggests that other types of data on parental behavior should confirm that structure. Therefore, other research on parental behavior will be reviewed to determine the extent of agreement or convergence in two- and three-dimensional models for parent behavior.

Schaefer's (1961) review of converging conceptual models for maternal behavior and child behavior noted the great similarity of two-dimensional models proposed by Roe (1957), Symonds (1939), and Slater (1962). More recently, Peterson and Migliorino (1967) have reported multi-factor and two-factor analyses of ratings of maternal behavior from interviews with American and Sicilian mothers. They report very poor replication for the multi-factor analyses but adequate replication for the two factors Affection and Control, which they relate to the two orthogonal dimensions of Schaefer's (1959) circumplex model. Peterson and Migliorino's factor of control emphasized variables of strictness, obedience training, and permissiveness about sex and aggression as contrasted with the high involvement emphasized in Schaefer's model. Becker (1964), in developing a three-dimensional model for parent behavior, noted that Schaefer's (1959) Autonomy-Control dimension included elements of both high involvement and strictness and identified dimensions of Warmth versus Hostility, Permissiveness versus Strictness, and Calm Detachment versus Anxious Emotional Involvement. Despite differences in labeling dimensions in Becker's (1964) analysis of parent behavior ratings by psychologists and Schaefer's (1965b) analysis of children's reports of parent behavior, both analyses are identifying the same three-dimensional conceptual space. Earlier Lorr and Jenkins (1953) had identified similar dimensions from a second-order factor analysis of Roff's (1949) factor analysis of the Fels Parent Behavior Rating Scales.

Further confirmation of a three-dimensional conceptualization of parental behavior is found in factor analyses of two additional independent conceptualizations of children's reports of parental behavior. Roe and Siegelman (1963) have reported three factors isolated from the ten scales of the Parent-Child Relations Questionnaire that they have labeled Loving versus Rejecting, Casual versus Demanding, and Overt Attention. Siegelman (1965), from a factor analysis of the fifteen scales of Bronfenbrenner's (1961) Parental Behavior Questionnaire, isolated three dimensions that he labeled Loving, Demanding, and Punishment. Goldin (1969), in his review of this area of research, states a preference for Siegelman's dimensions because Siegelman's "system better explains earlier, intercorrelational studies of children's reports of parent behavior." Although the labels for major dimensions of parent behavior that have been proposed by Schaefer, Becker, Roe and Siegelman, and Siegelman differ, they are sufficiently similar to allow a crude identification of one with another despite the fact that the empirical studies from which they were derived probably yielded different locations in a spherical conceptual space. Perhaps the most fruitful way to integrate these studies would be to give all of the child's report of parent behavior inventories to the same representative sample and determine empirically the interrelationships of the items and scales that have been developed. Mapping the conceptual sphere that the previous three-dimensional factor analyses suggest might be better than attempting to name the factors — a subjective decision by the investigator which is guided by factor rotations determined by earlier unsystematic scale development.

The proposed study would show whether independent investigators are sampling the same or different sectors of a conceptual space and would provide a further test of the adequacy of a spherical model for the parental behavior domain. The study might thus consolidate the development of this research area and provide a basis for the development of new concepts that would sample empty sectors of the conceptual space or would reveal new parental behavior dimensions. The conceptual convergence that has already been achieved provides a basis for systematic sampling of parent behaviors in new studies of parent-child relationships and a conceptual framework for the integration of existing studies.

### DEVELOPMENT OF HIERARCHICAL, CIRCULAR, AND SPHERICAL MODELS FOR CHILD BEHAVIOR

Since Schaefer's (1961) development of a circumplex model for child behavior, a number of factorial studies of ratings of social and emotional behavior or interpersonal behavior have provided support for that scheme. Although the voluminous literature on two-dimensional models for personality research (Eysenck, 1953; Foa, 1962; Leary, 1957; Lorr & McNair, 1965) cannot be reviewed here, evidence of convergence upon two- and three-dimensional models for child behavior ratings is summarized below.

Schaefer (1961) noted that circumplex orderings for behavior ratings of nursery school children reported by Richards and Simons (1941) and of thirteen-year-old children reported by McDonough (1929) were very similar, and generalized those findings into a circumplex model for child behavior. Schaefer labeled the reference dimensions Extroversion versus Introversion and Love versus Hostility and developed labels for sectors of the circular space that fell between those dimensions. Becker and Krug (1964) also developed a two-dimensional circumplex model for ratings of child behavior with reference dimensions of Extroversion versus Introversion and Emotional Stability versus Emotional Instability, labeled the sectors of the circumplex, and related their model to Schaefer's (1961) model. Subsequently, Baumrind and Black (1967) presented a circular ordering of clusters of child behaviors, developed higher-order concepts for the different sectors and dimensions, and plotted Schaefer's (1961), Becker and Krug's (1964), and their own model in a single diagram. The degree of ambiguity of abstract concepts, despite the essential similarity of these three circular orderings of child behavior, is shown by the fact that

147

Baumrind and Black placed their dimension of Stable versus Unstable Behavior at the same sector as Schaefer's and Becker and Krug's dimension of Extroversion versus Introversion. Baumrind and Black also identified Schaefer's dimension of Love versus Hostility and Becker and Krug's dimension of Emotional Stability versus Emotional Instability with their dimension of Conformity versus Non-Conformity. The lack of exact meaning of higher level constructs shows the need to define abstract concepts with more specific behaviors and the need for empirical integration of operationally defined concepts.

Silverstein (1969) has published an analysis that supports Schaefer's (1961) identification of Peterson's (1960) two major replicable factors with two major dimensions of a circumplex of child behavior. Walker (1968) has plotted the two-dimensional space generated by clusters derived from *Q*-sort descriptions of child behavior, and Black (1965) identified two major factors from teachers' ratings of child behavior that he labeled general adjustment and extroversion versus introversion.

Schaefer and Droppleman's (Schaefer, Droppleman, & Kalverboer,

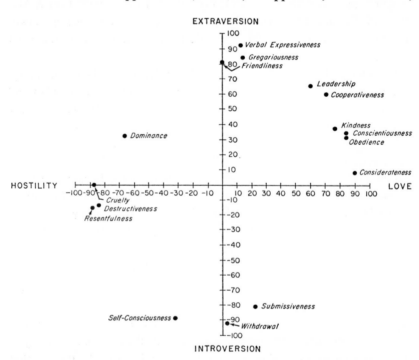

*Figure 6.* A two-dimensional plot of classroom behavior of American children.

1965) Classroom Behavior Checklist was guided by Schaefer's (1961) circumplex model for child behavior. Seventeen scales for trait-level concepts were developed, each consisting of five to nine specific classroom behavior items. Median internal consistency reliabilities for these short scales for a single rater were .86 for boys and .77 for girls; rate-rerate reliability with a four-month interval was .65 for boys and .50 for girls. Mean inter-rater reliability for 172 paired ratings for junior high school boys was .50. Reduced variability of scale scores and skewed distributions resulted from the "like" or "not like" response to each item. Tetrachoric correlations between scale scores were computed, the correlation matrix was factor analyzed, and the loadings on the two factors were plotted, as shown in Figure 6. The two-dimensional plot replicated the two hypothesized dimensions of Love versus Hostility and Extroversion versus Introversion, showed a circular ordering of concepts, but also showed large empty sectors of this two-dimensional space.

The Classroom Behavior Checklist was translated, revised, and extended for use in the Netherlands by Schaefer and Kalverboer (Schaefer, Droppleman, & Kalverboer, 1965). The scales that were added were designed to obtain information on hyperkinetic, distractible behavior. A total of 29 five- to eleven-item scales were developed, and ratings were collected on 113 boys. The median internal consistency reliability for the 89 scales was .81, with a range from .68 to .94.

The first two factors extracted from the Netherlands data (plotted in Fig. 7) showed an interpretable two-dimensional structure, with major dimensions of Extraversion versus Introversion and Adjustment versus Maladjustment. All twenty-nine scales had substantial loadings on one or both of these two factors, thus replicating the circular configuration that was found in the American Classroom Behavior Checklist. Because the third factor extracted from the Netherlands data had substantial loadings for many of the scales that had high loadings on the first factor of Adjustment versus Maladjustment, factors one and three were plotted. This plot revealed an ordering of concepts from a sector of Irritability, Dominance, Cruelty, Resentfulness, and Covert Hostility that might be labeled Hostility to a sector of Distractibility, Work Fluctuation, Inappropriate Talkativeness, Hyperactivity and Low Conscientiousness that might be labeled Low Task-Oriented behavior.

In order to generate a map of a spherical model of classroom behavior, the scale vectors were extended to unit length for the first three factors of

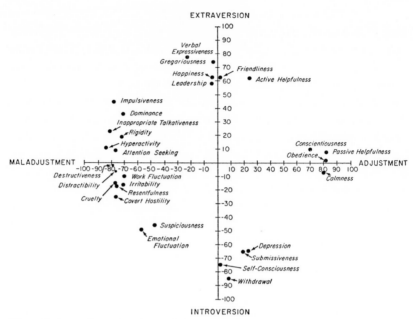

*Figure 7.* A two-dimensional plot of classroom behavior of Dutch children.

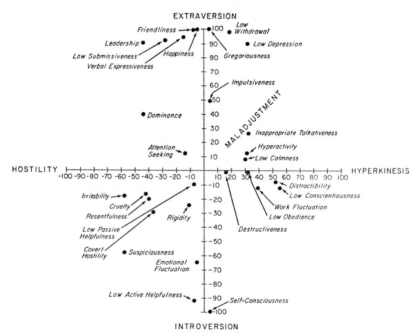

*Figure 8.* An orthographic projection of a three-dimensional analysis of classroom behavior of Dutch children.

150

this Netherlands data, scales that had positive loadings on the factor of Adjustment versus Maladjustment were inverted to allow a plot of a single hemisphere, and an orthographic projection was made by plotting the extended factor loadings. The pole of Maladjustment is located at the center of the polar map that is shown in Figure 8. Sectors of Extraversion, of Hostility, and of Hyperkinetic, Distractible behavior appear as clusters on this polar map. Although some sectors of the spherical space are empty, and other sectors are not adequately sampled, theoretically scales might be developed that would more adequately describe those sectors of this spherical configuration.

In order to determine whether the Netherlands three-dimensional analysis could be replicated and whether additional major dimensions of classroom behavior could be isolated, Schaefer, Aaronson, and Burgoon (1965) developed 64 five-item scales for a broad range of classroom behavior concepts. Scale reliability estimated by Kuder-Richardson formula 20 ranged from .73 to .96 with a median of .86 for ratings on 153 male and female seventh-graders in integrated schools. The first three factors that were extracted from intercorrelations of these scales replicated major dimensions of Extraversion versus Introversion, Task-Oriented behavior, and Hostility and showed a distribution of concepts in sectors of a spherical model. Extraction of additional factors revealed minor poorly defined factors of Independence versus Dependence and Conformity. Rotation of additional factors separated Extraversion versus Introversion into minor factors that were judged to be poorly defined and not replicable. If more detailed analysis is desirable, the relatively reliable, well-defined scales may be more useful than analysis of heterogeneous, poorly defined, unreplicable minor factors.

Schaefer and Aaronson (1967) selected from the 64-scale version 12 scales that were judged to define the three major factors, and adapted them for a preschool and early primary age group. Factor analyses of intercorrelations of the 12 scales for a sample of Head Start kindergarten children replicated the three major dimensions, which were best defined by Gregariousness and Verbal Expressiveness, Irritability and Resentfulness, and Perseverance and Concentration. Factor analyses of the sixty items for 2,500 first-graders and 1,486 second-graders yielded almost identical factor loadings for three major dimensions that replicated the kindergarten data. A factor analysis of data for 287 German children also confirmed the three major dimensions of classroom behavior that were found for American and Dutch children. These replications support a hypothesis that, if appropriate scales are included, these factors can be isolated in different age groups and national groups. The replicated factor structures, with high factor loadings for items as well as scales, show that three major factors that include much of the variance in classroom behavior and adjustment might be measured by three short scales. Scales that have shown substantial loadings on the three factors are listed here as a guide for sampling the dimensions.

*I. Task-Oriented Behavior.* Perseverance, Conscientiousness, Attentiveness, Concentration, Methodicalness, Academic Seriousness, Achievement Orientation. The opposite pole typically shows loadings on Distractibility, Hyperactivity, and Inappropriate Talkativeness although these scales also show loadings on the factor of Hostility.

*II. Hostility.* This factor is well defined by Cruelty, Irritability, Resentfulness, Quarrelsomeness, Hostile Dominance, Covert Hostility, Suspiciousness, and Argumentativeness. Some of the Hostility scales tend to have loadings on Extraversion, and others have loadings on Introversion, which may be related to Ross, Lacey, and Parton's (1965) report of factors of Passive Aggressive Behavior and Aggressive Behavior. The opposite pole has been difficult to define, with the highest loadings for Considerateness. Kindness, as defined, typically has higher loadings on Extraversion (i.e., expressive, outgoing behavior).

*III. Extraversion versus Introversion.* Verbal Expressiveness, Gregariousness, Friendliness to Teacher, Cheerfulness versus Depression, Social Withdrawal, Submissiveness, Emotional Passivity, and Self-Consciousness.

A more differentiated analysis of the conceptual space would be shown by mapping these scales and other scales that fall between the factors identified above. Typically, scales are fairly widely distributed through a configuration, and the location of the factors is a result of the location of the scales that are included.

Ross, Lacey, and Parton's (1965) study illustrates how different factors are isolated from different samples of measures and a rotation of different numbers of factors. These investigators extracted and rotated four factors from a set of classroom behavior items that they labeled Passive Aggressive Behavior, Aggressive Behavior, Withdrawn Behavior, and Pro-Social Behavior. When the spherical configuration that was generated by the first three components of that analysis was plotted, items included in the Pro-Social Behavior factor fell in the center of a sector that included task-oriented behavior, extraverted behavior, and positive loving social behavior. The spherical configuration generated by Ross, Lacey, and Parton's three principal components was very similar to the three-dimensional configurations described above. Also, plotting the first three principal components of teachers' ratings provided by Digman (1965) revealed a similar configuration. These findings suggest that similar three-dimensional configurations can be found for comprehensive studies of classroom behavior despite differences in factors that are produced by different concepts and rotation of different numbers of factors.

Kohn et al. (1970) have reported data that support a hypothesis that independent conceptualizations of classroom behavior would define sectors of a spherical configuration and have demonstrated that problem checklists are highly related to molar behavior dimensions. Kohn et al. (1970) developed a Social Competence Scale and a Problem Checklist, both of which yielded two major factors that were labeled at the negative pole as Anger-Defiance and Apathy-Withdrawal. Factors of the Social Competence Scale correlated highly with factors of the Problem Checklist for kindergarten children. Ratings were collected in first grade on Peterson's Problem Checklist (1961), which yields scores for Personality Problems and Conduct Problems, and with the Schaefer and Aaronson Classroom Behavior Inventory (1967), which yields scores for Extraversion versus Introversion, Hostility, and Task Orientation. Intercorrelations of these scores showed that Peterson's factor of Personality Problems is correlated with Schaefer and Aaronson's factor of Introversion and, to a lesser extent, with both Hostility and Low Task-Orientation, and Peterson's Conduct Problems shows high correlations with Hostility and Low Task-Orientation. Kohn's scores for Apathy-Withdrawal and Anger-Defiance show appropriate correlations with Peterson's and Schaefer and Aaronson's variables, although the year-to-year correlations are relatively low. Kohn's empirical data support a hypothesis that major dimensions typically fall within the same conceptual space. However, Kohn and Silverman's (1966) and Peterson's (1961) methods do not differentiate Low Task-Oriented behavior from Hostile behavior.

This review suggests that a two-dimensional circular model for social and emotional behavior or interpersonal behavior has been replicated in a number of studies. When that domain is extended to include task-oriented behavior in the classroom, three major dimensions of Extraversion versus

Introversion, Low versus High Hostility, and Low versus High Task-Oriented behavior can be found in independent studies, and a three-dimensional configuration can be developed that provides a more differentiated view of the interrelationships of measures.

Several unpublished studies have shown that teachers' ratings of the child's adjustment tend to be correlated with each of the three major dimensions. A plot of this conceptual space shows that Adjustment would fall in the octant of a sphere that is defined by Extraversion, Low Hostility, and Task-Oriented behavior. Since intelligence test scores show low correlations with these behavioral dimensions, such scores would complement behavior ratings as indices of social competence in the classroom.

### THE STRUCTURE OF LANGUAGE, OF PERCEPTION AND DESCRIPTION, OF BEHAVIOR, AND OF PERSONALITY

The analyses of conceptual structures that have been discussed here have been developed from intercorrelations of quantified descriptions or ratings of parents and children. Since all methods reviewed depend upon verbal descriptions of behavior, the structure of personality language must be isomorphic with the structure of interpersonal description. Burt's (1941) proposal that objects, minds, and the experience that minds have of objects are merely Gestalten and that "we are reduced to the study of a changing structure of relations linking two sets of systems; and these systems themselves are simply structures of relation" might be extended to the language with which we describe the experience that minds have of objects. A dictionary or thesaurus gives fragmented relationships between concepts by their definition, by listing supraordinate and subordinate concepts, and by listing antonyms and synonyms of the concepts. In his discussion of the connections between words, Whorf (1956) holds that "In more subtle matters we all, unknowingly, project the linguistic relationships of a particular language upon the universe and see them there." Thus, the structure of language may determine the tendency to give similar ratings for traits that are related in the minds of the raters. Newcomb (1931) has interpreted this tendency as attributable to "logical presuppositions in the minds of the raters." Brunswick's (1955) lens model for perception, which notes the vicarious mediation of cues that are integrated into a focal variable, may also be relevant to the relation between observations of behavior and descriptions of behavior. Hypotheses about focal variables such as hostility or observation of a single specific behavior that is interpreted as hostility may influence many specific behavior ratings.

Several different approaches to the interrelationships of personality concepts have been developed. Osgood, Suci, and Tannenbaum's (1957) Semantic Differential, a technique for the measurement of meaning, has been used to determine the interrelationships of descriptors. Passini and Norman (1966) found that the factor structures in ratings of complete strangers were highly similar to those in ratings of persons that the rater knew well. Schaefer and Plutchik (1966) have studied the extent to which diagnostic constructs imply or are associated with a systematic sample of traits and emotions. A single circular configuration for traits and emotions and a circular organization of diagnostic constructs were found that supported "the hypothesis that emotional, trait, and diagnostic signs form a conceptually differentiated but highly integrated system of interconnected signs." Mischel's (1968) discussion of "traits and states as constructs" reviewed many of the studies of the interrelationships of concepts and of the extent to which those interrelationships determine preceptions of others. The high internal consistency reliability that can be achieved in developing a priori scales also shows the predictability of the structure of a set of descriptions of specific behaviors. The general finding that the structures isolated from judgments of the similarity or relationship of concepts are very similar to the structures found from intercorrelations of ratings of well-known persons reveals a close relation between the structure of interpersonal perception/description and the structure of language.

Although the semantic structure of language, which is apparently similar across language and cultural groups (Miron & Osgood, 1966), must reflect to some degree the structure of behavior, the structure of interpersonal description does not prove the validity of those descriptions. The extent of agreement among observers, across different relationships with the subjects, across situations, and through time does not justify inferring stable personality structures from limited observations of behavior (Mischel, 1968). Despite this conclusion from empirical research, psychotherapists' descriptions of their patients, according to Meehl (1960), typically stabilize after two or three hours of psychotherapy.

### A HIERARCHICAL, CONFIGURATIONAL ANALYSIS OF THE INTERRELATIONSHIPS OF TWO DOMAINS

A combination of the hierarchical and configurational approaches can be used to study the interrelationship of two conceptual domains, one of

155

which might be labeled the predictor (P) domain and the other the criterion (C) domain. Then the set of predictor and criterion items might be labeled Pi and Ci, the predictor and criterion scales Ps and Cs, and the factors that are extracted Pf and Cf. If only two or three major factors are extracted for the predictor space and the criterion space, the factor loadings can be used to plot conceptual configurations, Pc and Cc, in which the items and scales are located in conceptual maps.

Interrelationships of the predictor space and the criterion space can be studied at the several levels of specificity or generality represented by the items, scales, factors, and configurations generated by the factors. To illustrate the economy of statistical analysis and interpretation that is achieved by analysis at the higher levels of abstraction, the number of intercorrelations that would be found through intercorrelation of items, scales, and factors is shown in the accompanying tabulation for a problem that included 260 items, 26 scales, and 3 factors in the predictor set (child report of parental behavior) and 741 items, 18 scales, and 3 factors in the criterion set (self-report of adjustment).

|     | Pi | Ps | Pf | Pc |
|-----|-----|-----|-----|-----|
| Ci .......................... | 192,660[a] | 19,266 | 2,223 | 741 |
| Cs .......................... | 4,680 | 468 | 54 | 18 |
| Cf .......................... | 780 | 72 | 9 | 3 |
| Cc .......................... | 260 | 26 | 3 | |

[a] Number of possible interrelationships for the cell generated by intersection of P and C.

The large number of possible intercorrelations at the level of predictor and criterion items suggests the need to move to higher levels of generality represented by scales or factors. Combinations of different levels of generality for the predictor and criterion sets represented by the intercorrelations of Pf with Cs or Cf with Ps give a more detailed picture of interrelationships than the intercorrelations of factor scores represented by Pf with Cf. The last row and last column in the tabulation represent the possibility of mapping each of the predictor items, scales, and factors into a unique point on a map of the conceptual configuration for the criterion space and of mapping the criterion variables upon the map of the predictor space. Schaefer and Lauterbach (1965) have provided an example of mapping criterion variables upon a predictor space and vice versa with predictor data that consisted of adult retrospective reports of their parents' behavior and criterion data consisting of personality inventory data.

Conceptual configurations can be used to develop an integrated view of a conceptual space and of the relations of antecedents and consequents of that conceptual space. If one were able to collect data that included (a) family variables that might influence maternal behavior such as low income, poor physical health of mother, father absence, and family size; (b) a set of maternal behaviors with a particular child; and (c) a set of child behavior and adjustment variables, a map could be generated for the maternal behaviors with the child, and the family variables and the child behavior and adjustment variables might be correlated and plotted on the maternal behavior map. Of course, each of the family variables and the maternal behavior variables might also be plotted upon the map of the child behavior and adjustment variables. To achieve stable estimates of interrelationships between conceptual domains, more reliable and valid data are needed for more comprehensive conceptual schemes and for more adequate samples of subjects. Existing data might also be reanalyzed with this hierarchical configurational approach.

### POTENTIAL APPLICATIONS OF THE HIERARCHICAL CONFIGURATIONAL APPROACH

In this paper, a hierarchical, configurational approach to the study of conceptual domains has been presented and has been applied to the study of parent behavior and child behavior. Further application of these methods might contribute to advances in conceptualizing those domains and might be used to develop conceptual models for other areas of personality research, particularly for the study of dyadic relationships. Applications of these methods to the study of teacher-pupil, husband-wife, therapist-patient, employer-employee, and peer relationships might lead to the development of a general theory of dyadic relationships. Another interesting direction for future research would be to attempt to conceptualize the child's behavior directed toward the parent as thoroughly as previous research has investigated the parent's behavior directed toward the child. Systematic conceptualization of a person's relationship with himself might also be a fruitful direction for future personality research.

The definition of abstract personality concepts can be greatly improved through hierarchical and configurational methods. By systematically reducing more abstract personality dimensions or traits to more concrete, specific, observable behaviors, the ambiguity of personality language can be significantly reduced. The configurational approach also defines a concept through the entire network of relationships in which it is embedded.

The meaning of a concept can be clearly communicated by the specific behavior items that are used to define it as well as by neighboring concepts, by polar opposite concepts, and by concepts that are 90° removed in a spatial plot.

As indicated above, maps derived from the application of independently developed conceptual schemes to the same sample can integrate different studies more effectively than matching factors by inspection. Maps can also show empty sectors of a conceptual space that have not yet been explored. Attempts to fill empty sectors of a conceptual map would contribute to a more comprehensive conceptualization of that space but would probably not contribute so greatly to prediction as would efforts to develop new dimensions for that domain. Theoretically, a comprehensive mapping of a conceptual sphere would not yield higher predictions of other variables than adequate sampling of factors that provide a conceptual framework for the sphere, but it would lead to a better description of that conceptual space. Conceptual configurations might be used as a guide for selection of scales that would provide a definition of the major dimensions in prediction studies. If possible, the three major dimensions of parent behavior and child behavior that have been discussed here should be represented in future comprehensive studies of parent behavior and child behavior.

It is hoped that the review of methodology for analysis and synthesis, or differentiation and integration, of behavior concepts that has been presented herein will lead to more effective and efficient analyses of psychological domains. The development from circular to spherical conceptual models for parent behavior and child behavior that has been discussed here suggests that major replicable dimensions and configurations can be isolated for these and other domains.

## References

Baldwin, A. L., J. Kalhorn, & F. H. Breese. Patterns of parent behavior. *Psychological Monographs*, 1945, 58 (3, Whole No. 268).

Baumrind, D., & A. E. Black. Socialization practices associated with dimensions of competence in preschool boys and girls. *Child Development*, 1967, 38, 291–327.

Becker, W. C. The matching of behavior rating and questionnaire personality factors. *Psychological Bulletin*, 1960, 57, 201–212.

————. Consequences of different kinds of parental discipline, in M. L. Hoffman & L. W. Hoffman, eds., *Review of child development research*, Vol. 1, pp. 169–208. New York: Russell Sage, 1964.

———— & R. S. Krug. A circumplex model for social behavior in children. *Child Development*, 1964, 35, 371–396.

# EARL S. SCHAEFER

———. Parent Attitude Research Instrument: A research review. *Child Development*, 1965, 36, 329–365.

Black, M. S. The development of personality in children and adolescents. *Educational and Psychological Measurement*, 1965, 25, 767–785.

Bronfenbrenner, U. Some familial antecedents of responsibility and leadership in adolescents, in L. Petrullo & B. M. Bass, eds., *Leadership and interpersonal behavior*, pp. 239–271. New York: Holt, 1961.

Brunswick, E. The conceptual framework of psychology, in O. Neurath, R. Carnap, & C. W. Morris, eds., *International encyclopedia of unified science*, Vol. 1, pt. 2, pp. 655–760. Chicago: University of Chicago Press, 1955.

Burt, C. L. *The factors of the mind: An introduction to factor analysis in psychology*. New York: Macmillan, 1941.

Cattell, R. B., ed. *Handbook of multivariate experimental psychology*. Chicago: Rand McNally, 1966.

Cronbach, L. J., & P. E. Meehl. Construct validity in psychological tests. *Psychological Bulletin*, 1955, 52, 281–302.

Cross, H. J. College students' memories of their parents: A factor analysis of the CRPBI. *Journal of Consulting and Clinical Psychology*, 1969, 33, 275–278.

Digman, J. M. A test of a multiple-factor model of child personality. Unpublished MS., University of Hawaii, 1965.

Eysenck, H. J. *The structure of human personality*. London: Methuen, 1953.

Foa, U. G. The structure of interpersonal behavior in the dyad, in J. Criswell, H. Solomon, & P. Suppes, eds., *Mathematical methods in small group processes*, pp. 166–179. Stanford, Calif.: Stanford University Press, 1962.

Furfey, P. H. An improved rating scale technique. *Journal of Educational Psychology*, 1926, 17, 45–48.

Goldin, P. C. A review of children's reports of parent behaviors. *Psychological Bulletin*, 1969, 71, 222–236.

Guilford, J. P. When not to factor analyze. *Psychological Bulletin*, 1952, 49, 26–37.

Guttman, L. A new approach to factor analysis: The radex, in P. F. Lazarsfeld, ed., *Mathematical thinking in the social sciences*, pp. 258–348. Glencoe, Ill.: Free Press, 1954.

———. Order analysis of correlation matrices, in R. B. Cattell, ed., *Handbook of multivariate experimental psychology*, pp. 439–458. Chicago: Rand McNally, 1966.

———. The development of nonmetric space analysis: A letter to Professor John Ross. *Multivariate Behavioral Research*, 1967, 2, 71–82.

Harman, H. *Modern factor analysis*. Chicago: University of Chicago Press, 1960.

Hundleby, J. D., & R. B. Cattell. Personality structure in middle childhood and the prediction of school achievement and adjustment. *Monographs of the Society for Research in Child Development*, 1968, 33 (3, Serial No. 121).

Kohn, M., B. L. Rosman, & L. A. Jordan. Congruent dimensions of child personality from four independently developed research instruments. Paper presented at the meeting of the Eastern Psychological Association, Atlantic City, N.J., April 1970.

Kohn, M., & H. W. Silverman. The relationship of competence and symptom factors to each other and to teachers' categorical ratings. Paper presented at the meeting of the Eastern Psychological Association, New York City, April 1966.

Kojima, H. Children's reports of parental behavior and attitudes: Semantic differential questionnaire and personality factors. Bulletin of the Faculty of Education, Kanazawa University, Japan. *Humanities and Social and Educational Sciences*, 1967, 16, 47–61.

Leary, T. F. *Interpersonal diagnosis of personality*. New York: Ronald, 1957.

Loevinger, J. Objective tests as instruments of psychological theory. *Psychological Reports*, 1957, 3, 635–694.

Lorr, M., & R. L. Jenkins. Three factors in parent behavior. *Journal of Consulting Psychology*, 1953, 17, 306–308.

Lorr, M., & D. M. McNair. Expansion of the interpersonal behavior circle. *Journal of Personality and Social Psychology*, 1965, 2, 823–830.

McDonough, M. R. *The empirical study of character: Part II. Studies in psychology and psychiatry.* Washington, D.C.: Catholic University Press, 1929.

Mark, J. C. The attitudes of mothers of male schizophrenics toward child behavior. *Journal of Abnormal and Social Psychology*, 1953, 48, 185–189.

Meehl, P. E. The cognitive activity of the clinician. *American Psychologist*, 1960, 15, 19–27.

Miron, M. S., & C. E. Osgood. Language behavior: The multivariate structure of qualification, in R. B. Cattell, ed., *Handbook of multivariate experimental psychology*, pp. 790–819. Chicago: Rand McNally, 1966.

Mischel, W. *Personality and assessment.* New York: Wiley, 1968.

Newcomb, T. An experiment designed to test the validity of a rating technique. *Journal of Educational Psychology*, 1931, 22, 279–289.

Osgood, C. E., G. J. Suci, & P. H. Tannenbaum. *The measurement of meaning.* Urbana: University of Illinois Press, 1957.

Passini, F. T., & W. T. Norman. A universal conception of personality structure? *Journal of Personality and Social Psychology*, 1966, 4, 44–49.

Patsula, P. J. Felt powerlessness as related to perceived parental behavior. Ph.D. thesis, University of Alberta, Canada, 1969.

Peterson, D. R. The age generality of personality factors derived from ratings. *Educational and Psychological Measurement*, 1960, 20, 461–474.

———. Behavior problems of middle childhood. *Journal of Consulting Psychology*, 1961, 25, 205–209.

———. Scope and generality of verbally defined personality factors. *Psychological Review*, 1965, 72, 48–59.

——— & G. Migliorino. Pancultural factors of parental behavior in Sicily and the United States. *Child Development*, 1967, 38, 967–991.

Renson, G. J. Belgian children's perception of parent behavior as measured by Schaefer's technique. M.A. thesis, George Washington University, 1965.

———, E. S. Schaefer, & B. I. Levy. Cross-national validity of a spherical conceptual model for parent behavior. *Child Development*, 1968, 39, 1229–1235.

Richards, T. W., & M. P. Simons. The Fels Child Behavior Scales. *Genetic Psychology Monographs*, 1941, 24, 259–309.

Roe, A. Early determinants of vocational choice. *Journal of Counseling Psychology*, 1957, 4, 212–217.

——— & M. Siegelman. A parent-child relations questionnaire. *Child Development*, 1963, 34, 355–369.

Roff, M. A factorial study of the Fels Parent Behavior Scales. *Child Development*, 1949, 20, 29–45.

Ross, A. O., H. M. Lacey, & D. A. Parton. The development of a behavior checklist for boys. *Child Development*, 1965, 36, 1013–1027.

Sanford, R. N., M. M. Adkins, R. B. Miller, & E. Cobb. Physique, personality, and scholarship. *Monographs of the Society for Research in Child Development*, 1943, 8 (1, Serial No. 34).

Schaefer, E. S. A circumplex model for maternal behavior. *Journal of Abnormal and Social Psychology*, 1959, 59, 226–235.

———. Converging conceptual models for maternal behavior and for child behavior, in J. C. Glidewell, ed., *Parental attitudes and child behavior*, pp. 124–146. Springfield, Ill.: Thomas, 1961.

———. Children's reports of parental behavior: An inventory. *Child Development*, 1965, 36, 413–424. (a)

# EARL S. SCHAEFER

———. A configurational analysis of children's reports of parental behavior. *Journal of Consulting Psychology*, 1965, 29, 552–557. (b)

——— & M. R. Aaronson. Classroom behavior inventory, preschool to primary. Unpublished form, 1965.

——— & B. R. Burgoon. Classroom behavior inventory. Unpublished form, 1965.

Schaefer, E. S., & N. Bayley. Consistency of maternal behavior from infancy to preadolescence. *Journal of Abnormal and Social Psychology*, 1960, 61, 1–6.

———. Maternal behavior, child behavior, and their intercorrelations from infancy through adolescence. *Monographs of the Society for Research in Child Development*, 1963, 28 (3, Serial No. 87).

———. Validity and consistency of mother-infant observations, adolescent maternal interviews, and adult retrospective reports of maternal behavior. *Proceedings of the 75th annual convention of the American Psychological Association*, pp. 147–148. Washington, D.C.: The Association, 1967.

Schaefer, E. S., & R. Q. Bell. Development of a parental attitude research instrument. *Child Development*, 1958, 29, 339–361.

——— & N. Bayley. Development of a maternal behavior research instrument. *Journal of Genetic Psychology*, 1959, 95, 83–104.

Schaefer, E. S., L. F. Droppleman, & A. F. Kalverboer. Development of a classroom behavior checklist and factor analyses of children's school behavior in the United States and the Netherlands. Paper presented at the meeting of the Society for Research in Child Development, Minneapolis, 1965.

Schaefer, E. S., & C. G. Lauterbach. Mapping the projections of child variables upon a spherical parent behavior model and vice versa. Paper presented at the meeting of the American Psychological Association, Chicago, September 1965.

Schaefer, E. S., & R. Plutchik. Interrelationships of emotions, traits and diagnostic constructs. *Psychological Reports*, 1966, 18, 399–410.

Shepard, R. N. Analysis of proximities as a technique for the study of information processing in man. *Human Factors*, 1963, 5, 33–48.

Shoben, E. J., Jr. The assessment of parental attitudes in relation to child adjustment. *Genetic Psychology Monographs*, 1949, 39, 101–148.

Siegelman, M. Evaluation of Bronfenbrenner's questionnaire for children concerning parental behavior. *Child Development*, 1965, 36, 163–174.

Silverstein, A. B. A circumplex derived from personality ratings. *Perceptual and Motor Skills*, 1969, 28, 613–614.

Slater, P. E. Parent behavior and the personality of the child. *Journal of Genetic Psychology*, 1962, 101, 53–68.

Stogdill, R. M. The measurement of attitudes toward parental control and the social adjustment of children. *Journal of Applied Psychology*, 1936, 20, 359–367.

Symonds, P. M. *The psychology of parent-child relationships.* New York: Appleton, 1939.

Thurstone, L. L. *Multiple-factor analysis.* Chicago: University of Chicago Press, 1947.

Tryon, R. C., & D. E. Bailey. The BC TRY computer system of cluster and factor analysis. *Multivariate Behavioral Research*, 1966, 1, 95–111.

Walker, R. N. A scale for parents' ratings: Some ipsative and normative correlations. *Genetic Psychology Monographs*, 1968, 77, 95–133.

———. Some temperament traits in children as viewed by their peers, their teachers, and themselves. *Monographs of the Society for Research in Child Development*, 1967, 32 (6, Serial No. 114).

Whorf, B. L. Language, mind, and reality, in B. J. Carroll, ed., *Language, thought, and reality: Selected writings of Benjamin Lee Whorf*, pp. 246–270. New York: Wiley, 1956.

Zuckerman, M., B. B. Ribbach, I. Monashkin, & J. A. Norton, Jr. Normative data and factor analysis on the Parental Attitude Research Instrument. *Journal of Consulting Psychology*, 1958, 22, 165–171.

◈ SEYMOUR WAPNER, LEONARD CIRILLO, AND A. HARVEY BAKER ◈

# Some Aspects of the Development
# of Space Perception

THIS paper presents some empirical findings and theoretical concepts pertaining to a problem that we and others at Clark University have been working on for a number of years. This is the problem of the development of an essential feature of perception — space perception. In keeping with the approach we have been using for sometime, we shall treat the development of space perception from a particular perspective — the organismic-developmental point of view (Werner, 1957, 1961). We should like to note at the outset that we have severely restricted our treatment of the development of the organism-environment system serving to organize objects and their displacements spatially. Our treatment is restricted because it depends largely on ontogenetic findings from a limited age range, that of 6 to 20 years. Yet — and this is where our approach is distinctive — it derives broader significance from our basic assumption that ontogenesis is only one exemplar of transformation of a system that can be treated effectively by comparative-developmental analysis. Other exemplars of organism-environment system change or differences that can be treated developmentally include comparisons between younger and aged adults, between normal adults and pathological individuals, between individuals under drugged and placebo conditions, and between individuals under stress and optimal conditions.

The essential prerequisite for such a broad treatment of diverse groups

NOTE: The research reported in this paper was conducted at Clark University and supported by Research Grant MH-00348 from the National Institute of Mental Health. We wish to express our appreciation to John Gittins and Lois Douglas, research assistants in this project, and to Dr. Neil Rankin for his critical comments.

and conditions by a circumscribed set of principles is a general assumption of organismic-developmental theory: organisms in their environmental settings constitute systems which may be analyzed and compared with one another in formal, organizational terms. In such a formal, comparative analysis a system is treated as having a characteristic structure which is maintained or transformed by specifiable dynamic processes. Focusing on the characteristic structure of the system entails analysis of the system into more or less differentiated parts, these parts being more or less integrated with one another in specifiable ways. Focusing on the dynamics of the system entails the determination of the means by which a characteristic structure, viewed as an end, is achieved or maintained. These two features, the structural or part-whole analysis of the system and the dynamic or means-ends analysis of the system, are complementary aspects of the formal description of the system.

The comparison and conceptual ordering of formally described systems is regulated by the orthogenetic principle which defines development in terms of the degree of organization attained by the organism-environment system. The more differentiated and hierarchically integrated a system, in the relations among its parts and between means and ends, the more highly developed it is said to be. If one system is more differentiated and hierarchically integrated than another, it is developmentally more advanced than the other. If a single system is increasing in differentiation and hierarchic integration, it is developing. If a single system is dedifferentiating and disintegrating, it is regressing. In this way, the orthogenetic principle is a formal definition of development and, as such, is applicable to the comparison of different systems as well as to the analysis of a single system in transition (Kaplan, 1967).

Of crucial significance for the development of the man-environment system in general and for the development of cognition, including space perception, in particular, is the increased differentiation between the poles of the system — the organism and its environment. Man is not only an organism reacting to physical stimuli or acting upon the environment with the guidance of momentary signals. Rather, he is oriented toward knowing, toward the construction of objects which mediate between him and his physical milieu. Whereas sensorimotor action is marked by a relative lack of differentiation between signal and action, cognition is marked by distance between the organism and its world of objects. This distance characteristic of cognition is manifest both in the perceptual construction

163

of a stable world of things and events and, to an even greater degree, in the conceptual construction of symbols representing such things and events (Werner & Kaplan, 1963). The development of the man-environment system marked by the emergence of cognition does not imply the loss of more primitive modes of operation. These are transformed by their integration in a system newly reorganized and hierarchized into dominant and subordinate subsystems. Action, for instance, is no longer simply a response to momentary signals. It is stabilized by its adjustment to a permanently structured perceptual world and regulated by symbolically posited goals.

It should be evident that the analysis of one state of the organism-environment system and the analysis of the system in transition are related undertakings. What is from a limited perspective a system of determinate structure and dynamics is, when viewed in depth, a way station in a continual reorganization of the system, a product of a development or a regression.

We assume with Bertalanffy (1962) that "the developmental system possesses in each of its temporal slices an exceptional condition . . . towards which the system tends, and towards which it tends to return after disturbance" (p. 185). Such exceptional conditions may characterize different hierarchically organized subsystems in a developed system. An exceptional condition is a preferred condition, a stable state of the system attained by a process of equilibration following perturbation.

Equilibration is a central principle in the organismic-developmental analysis of perception. Perception is assumed to reflect the relation between stimuli from the object and the state of the organism. There is further assumed to be a fundamental biological tendency of the organism toward the stabilization of this relation between psychophysical stimuli and the psychophysiological state of the organism. When a stable state of the system is disturbed, equilibrial processes come into play and serve as a means to the end of restoring a stable organism-environment relation. The process of equilibration may vary in its character, depending upon the level of development of the system or subsystem considered. What is a state of equilibrium for a developed organism with differentiated goals and the capacity to adopt diverse tasks is dependent upon the specific end pursued by the organism in a determinate situation. A balanced body posture, a stable perceptual world, and a coherent representation of reality may all be characterized as reflections of organism-environment equilibria. Only by virtue of its relation to the organism's momentary orientation may one such state be singled out in order to examine the processes responsible for its achievement.

Given these general features of the theory which underlies our experimental analysis, we may now turn to the problem proper — the development of space perception. We shall present findings on two types of localization, objective localization and egocentric localization, followed by findings pertinent to autokinetic motion. In objective localization, both the body and object are located with respect to a unitary spatial framework, as, for example, in orientation with respect to verticality. In the second form of localization, egocentric, the framework for the organismic assessment of location is provided by bodily properties: objects are located in relation to some body part or property which is used as a spatial reference; localization with respect to straight-ahead or eye level is an example. Although egocentric location of an object depends upon its relation to the body, objective location is independent of this relation.

For each section of the paper, there will first be a brief presentation of general propositions drawn from work we have done with adults. After this we shall deal with our central theme, the ontogenesis of spatial organization, by describing our findings on age changes insofar as they bear on these general propositions. When possible, we shall present additional studies dealing with the comparison of individuals and experimental conditions which can be ordered developmentally in terms of formal structural properties. We seek to determine whether these comparative findings parallel the findings for age changes.

## Verticality

Our research on the perception of verticality is far more complete than that on apparent straight-ahead, eye-level, and autokinetic motion because perception of verticality has been worked on more intensively by ourselves and by other investigators for many years. The studies from our own laboratories, and it is these to which the presentation will largely be devoted, were initiated some 20 years ago with adults. Only after accumulation of these findings were systematic studies of ontogenesis undertaken.

The mechanisms formulated to deal with the effects of different classes of stimulation on the perception of verticality in the studies on adults were rooted in a number of basic propositions. Two of these have already been described: the assumption of an organism-environment *field*, according to which perception reflects the relation between the state of the organism and impinging stimulation, and the assumption of *stabilization* tendencies, according to which the organism-environment relation is regulated by equilibrial processes. The other guiding propositions pertinent here are as follows: (a) all stimulation, from any source is essentially the same, *sensory-tonic*, in nature; the interaction of seemingly diverse factors (e.g., organismic and sensory processes) is possible because these factors are the products of differentiation from a common psychophysical matrix; (b) stimuli are differentiated into two classes, extraneous stimuli and object stimuli, this *duality* of stimulation depending not on physical features but on psychological operations of objectification, such as attending versus not attending; extraneous stimuli directly influence the state of the organism, whereas the effects of object stimuli involve an interrelationship between organism and object; (c) diverse stimuli may be *functionally equivalent* in that they may lead to identical perceptual end-products; (d) finally, sensory-tonic processes may be expressed through different channels (e.g., action and perception) which may substitute or act *vicariously* for one another.

For perception of verticality, and for spatial localization in general, the pertinent properties of organismic state and of stimulation are conceived of as vectors having direction and magnitude. A stable state of the system is one in which there is a balance or harmony of forces — a vectorial correspondence between the state of the organism and object stimulation. This stable relation may be disturbed either by varying object stimulation or by varying organismic state through the manipulation of extraneous stimulation. We have studied the effects of such systematic variation upon the perception of verticality by having the subject adjust a luminous rod in the darkroom to a position which appears vertical.

ADULTS

First, we shall consider some of the findings for adults dealing with the effects of variation in organismic state induced by manipulation of extraneous stimulation. It was found that all forms of unilaterally or asymmetrically applied extraneous stimulation operated in a functionally equivalent manner with respect to the end-product, position of apparent vertical: the apparent vertical (the physical position of a rod which appears vertical to the subject) rotates relatively opposite the side to which unilateral stimulation is applied. This holds for head tilt, body tilt (up to

45°), auditory stimulation, electrical stimulation to the sternocleidomastoid muscle, rotary acceleration and deceleration around the longitudinal axis of the body, and danger to one side (Chandler, 1961; Morant, 1959; Wapner, Werner, & Chandler, 1951; Wapner, Werner, & Morant, 1951; Werner, Wapner, & Chandler, 1951).

In a similar fashion, studies were undertaken of the effect of variation of object stimulation on apparent verticality. The position of the rod at the beginning of a trial was varied. This factor had a systematic effect, insofar as the physical position of the apparent vertical was relatively close to the position in which the rod was located at the beginning of the trial. Based on these findings and the principles stated earlier, hypothetical mechanisms describing the perceptual process were formulated for the operation of both extraneous stimulation and object stimulation. All forms of asymmetrical extraneous stimulation are assumed to disturb the sensory-tonic state of the organism; this disturbance is conceptualized as a "pull" in the direction of the stimulation. Equilibrium is re-established under such conditions through counterbalancing vectors to the opposite side. The asymmetrical distribution of gravitational forces on the body under conditions of body tilt, for example, is compensated by counteractive tonic forces. Such counteraction may be represented as a vectorial shift in organismic state in the direction opposite extraneous stimulation. A truly vertical rod will no longer correspond vectorially to organismic state and will appear tilted in the direction of extraneous stimulation. For the rod to appear vertical to the subject, it must be physically rotated opposite extraneous stimulation toward vectorial correspondence with organismic state.

Asymmetrical object stimulation, such as that ensuing from a physically tilted rod, is also conceived of as disturbing the stable relation between organismic state and the object, here by variation in the object pole of the relation. A new equilibrium is established through changes in organismic state which bring it into vectorial correspondence with proximal stimulation from the object. Such a mechanism accounts for the fact that a slightly tilted line viewed in a darkroom gradually comes to appear vertical (Gibson & Radner, 1937). Such adaptation to tilt is viewed, therefore, as akin to the starting position effect; the rod, for example, must be tilted relatively toward its position at the beginning of the trial to appear vertical to the subject (Wapner & Werner, 1957; Werner & Wapner, 1952a&c, 1956). Perceived verticality, then, is a reflection of a stable vectorial relation between the state of the organism and proximal stimulation from the object. It is not a direct function of either stimuli from the object and sensory processes or organismic variables — it is a property of the organism-environment system.

## AGE CHANGES

Given these hypothetical mechanisms based on work with adults, our first approach to the study of ontogenetic development took body tilt and starting position of the rod as representative of extraneous and object stimulation. This work was based upon the proposition that development is characterized by increasing differentiation or distance between organism and environment, and that such a development would be reflected in ontogenetic changes in the effects of extraneous and object stimulation on apparent verticality. We shall first present the empirical results of this work and then consider the details of interpretation.

Two studies dealt with the effect of 30° lateral body tilt on perception of verticality from the ages of 6 to 19 years. The first study (Wapner & Werner, 1957) had 233 subjects, 118 boys and 115 girls, and the second study (Wapner, 1968) 192 subjects, 96 boys and 96 girls. On the basis of these studies, we can confidently state that there is a general shift in the physical position of an apparently vertical rod from the side of body tilt at the younger age levels to the side opposite body tilt in the older age levels.

For the six- and seven-year-olds, the rod must be rotated relatively toward the longitudinal axis of body and eye in order to appear vertical. Spatial values are egocentrically tied to the postural body framework. Were these subjects to operate completely egocentrically — that is, were there total lack of differentiation between body and object — the pattern of proximal stimulation would have to coincide with the longitudinal axis to lead to the perception of verticality.* With increasing age, the formation of equilibrial processes counteractive to postural and other extraneous variations results in a differentiation of spatial values from the position of the body, that is, egocentricity declines. This is reflected in relative constancy in the perceived orientation of objects. In older subjects, there is actually overconstancy — the rod must be rotated off the plumb line opposite the direction of body tilt in order to appear vertical. We believe that such overconstancy is a consequence of the absence in the darkroom sit-

---

* This statement does not imply, as Taylor (1962) believes it does, that we are nativists. It might just as well be assumed that this mode of correspondence develops, perhaps at the time that the child assumes the upright posture.

uation of external cues which normally keep the counteractive mechanism within bounds.

The two studies just described also provide definitive data concerning age changes in the effect of starting position on apparent verticality: the physical position of the apparent vertical is rotated relatively toward the position in which the rod is placed at the beginning of a trial; this starting position effect is greatest at the youngest age level and decreases with increasing age. These findings, too, are in keeping with the proposition of increasing distance between organism and environment in the developing system. Lack of differentiation is reflected not only in the egocentric tie of spatial values to variations in posture, but also in the tie of organismic state to variations in object stimulation. The tendency of organismic state to accommodate to object stimulation is analogous to tropotaxis, which occurs on the level of action in developmentally lower organisms. For example, the insect stimulated asymmetrically by light turns its body so that the distribution of excitation on the periphery is symmetrized (Hinde, 1970). Starting position effects represent a kind of stimulus-boundedness or dependence upon variations in stimulation. Stimulus-boundedness and egocentricity are complementary aspects of fusion between organism and environment. Both decrease with age as differentiation between organism and environment increases.

Complementing these general developmental changes is the development of stable individual modes of operation in the perception of verticality. We have been interested in analyzing individual consistency in the effects of body tilt and starting position and in the formation of individual equilibrium. The term *individual equilibrium* refers to that systematic variation in the physical position of apparent vertical which is associated with differences between individuals rather than with differences between experimental conditions (Wapner et al., 1951).

Wapner and Werner (1957) based their analyses of individual consistency on the correlations between scores for the twelve conditions employed in their ontogenetic study of verticality*: three positions of body tilt (30° left, erect, 30° right) in combination with four starting positions (30° left, 10° left, 10° right, 30° right). When the rod perceived as vertical deviated clockwise from plumb line, the numerical score was designated +; counterclockwise deviations were designated −. One set of six-

---

* Some attempts are also being made to use factor analysis to study ontogenetic changes in individual consistency.

teen correlations was obtained by correlating each of the four scores for the body left conditions with each of the four scores for the body right conditions.

Since susceptibility to body tilt is reflected in opposite physical placements of the apparently vertical rod under opposite body tilts, individual differences in susceptibility to body tilt would be reflected in negative correlations. Consistent physical placements of the apparently vertical rod regardless of direction of body tilt, on the other hand, would be reflected in positive correlations; thus, positive correlations would indicate differences in individual equilibrium. The result of this analysis was a general, steady increase with age in the number of significant negative correlations, indicating a developmental increase in individual consistency in susceptibility to body tilt.

A set of four correlations was obtained by correlating each of the two scores for starting position left with each of the two scores for starting position right under body tilt left; the same procedure was repeated for body erect and for body right, yielding twelve correlations in all. Individual differences in susceptibility to starting position would be reflected in negative correlations, and differences in individual equilibrium would be reflected in positive correlations. There was, in fact, a general increase with age in the number of significant positive correlations indicating the developmental formation of a stable, personal frame of reference — that is, of individual equilibrium. Since there were no significant negative correlations in any age group, there was no evidence here of individual differences in susceptibility to starting position.

These ontogenetic findings on individual differences* complement the

* Development of individual consistency has also been assessed by deriving from the same data (Wapner & Werner, 1957) three scores reflecting body position, starting position, and individual equilibrium: (a) difference scores were computed between left and right body tilt for each of the four starting positions, and these scores were intercorrelated for each age group; the median correlation increased strikingly with age, supporting the conclusion reached in the text; (b) difference scores between left and right 10° and 30° starting positions for each of the three body tilt conditions were intercorrelated; no reliable correlations were found beyond the youngest age group, indicating an earlier and even sharper drop than that obtained by means of the analyses reported in the text; (c) correlations between mean scores for 10° and 30° starting positions — the closest approximation to identical trials in the study — decreased with age; this is not consistent with the conclusions in the text and indicates that further work is necessary to resolve the discrepancy before definitive conclusions regarding individual equilibrium may be reached. It should be noted, however, that Wapner et al. (1951) obtained correlations of .83 for men and .58 for women between identical trials with body erect, indicating considerable consistency in individual equilibrium.

general ontogenetic findings presented earlier. As will be recalled, there is a developmental shift of apparent vertical from the side of body tilt to the side opposite body tilt; that is, there is the development of a compensatory mechanism and correlative increasing differentiation between organism and environment. The increase in individual consistency in response to body tilt shows that individuals, in the course of ontogeny, come to differ reliably from one another in the degree of compensation for body tilt and, thus, the degree of differentiation between organism and environment. It will also be recalled that starting position effects, which operate counter to the maintenance of a stable perceptual world insofar as the organism changes in keeping with any new input, decrease with age. The establishment of individual equilibrium independent of starting position may also be regarded as an expression of the increasing trend toward stabilization of the outside world, since it reflects the tendency of the individual to form a personal frame of reference.

### COMPARATIVE FINDINGS

The mechanisms formulated to analyze the general effects of extraneous and object stimuli partly depend upon the observations of pathologically dedifferentiated organisms made by Goldstein (1942, 1960). He described two modes of adjustment in patients with unilateral cerebellar lesions. Because of hypersensitivity to stimulation on the side of the lesion, symmetrical stimulation has asymmetrical effects in such patients, who experience a pull toward the side of the lesion. Patients with less severe damage adjust by *yielding* to the stimulation, that is, by tilting head and body toward the side of the lesion. In this new preferred position, the patient feels more comfortable, does not experience a pull, and performs better than when erect. Patients with more severe damage cannot adjust by yielding because they are unable to maintain postural equilibrium (when they attempt to do so, they fall down). They adjust by *counteracting* the felt pull. Continual voluntary effort is required to maintain the posture tilted opposite the side of lesion.

From the clinical picture of patients with lability of body balance, we see that body tonus is changed asymmetrically through sensory stimulation, as it is through muscular action. When yielding does not interfere with the attainment of organismic goals, it is the preferred mode of adjustment. Analogously, on the perceptual level, when the organism is related to an artificially reduced environment in the darkroom (i.e., the rod) organismic state changes to conform to object stimulation. When yielding interferes with the attainment of organismic goals, stability is attained through compensatory or counteractive forces. This corresponds to the darkroom situation in which the subject is prohibited by his adopted task from turning away from object stimulation toward extraneous stimulation; the pull of the extraneous stimulation is compensated by counteractive forces.*

Our findings on age changes are also complemented by comparative data on a variety of other groups and conditions which are ordered developmentally according to the orthogenetic principle. Thus, the findings for older people parallel those obtained with younger children, so that the whole picture on change in spatial organization that occurs from 6 to 90 years of age is as follows: For younger children from 6 years to adolescence, the apparent vertical is located toward the side of body tilt; from adolescence until 50 to 60 years of age, the opposite effect occurs — namely, the apparent vertical is located opposite the side of body tilt; and finally, with people 65 years of age or more, apparent vertical is again located toward the side of body tilt (Comalli, 1965, 1970; Comalli, Wapner, & Werner, 1959). In the study by Comalli et al. (1959), the starting position effect was greatest at the youngest age level and decreased markedly until the 19-year level. There was no consistent change through the 65- to 80-year group. Comalli, working with a large number of subjects in the 80- to 90-year-old group began to find evidence of a further increase in starting position effects. Comalli's (1965) 80-year-old subjects showed greater starting position effects than his 70-year-old group.

In addition to these findings on older people, some early work using schizophrenics was in keeping with expectations from developmental theory. A group diagnosed as catatonic-hebephrenic, another group diagnosed as paranoid schizophrenics, and a control group of normal adults (Carini, 1955) were compared on effect of body tilt on perception of verticality. In normal adults, as found in previous studies, the position of the apparent vertical is relatively opposite the side of body tilt; in contrast, for the most regressed group, the catatonic-hebephrenics, the position of apparent vertical is located toward the side of body tilt, with the paranoids falling in between these extremes. In this study, there were no significant

---

* Since we are restricting ourselves to work done in our own laboratories, we are not presenting important related studies of neurological patients performed by other investigators (e.g., Halpern, 1949, 1951; Halpern & Kidron, 1954; Halpern & Landau, 1953).

differences between groups with regard to the effect of starting position on apparent verticality. In another study (Liebert, Wapner, & Werner, 1957) this effect of body tilt on perception was replicated. Moreover, there were greater starting position effects in schizophrenics compared with normals, which, however, were not significant. In a third study by Wapner and Krus (1960), the effect of body tilt was again replicated, and there were greater starting position effects in schizophrenics, which again were not significant.

The study of neuropathology in interaction with age differences also yields findings which fit expectations. Blane (1962) studied two groups of post-poliomyelitic subjects — those with residual paralysis of left and of right leg; within each group were two subgroups differing in terms of age (9- to 12-year-olds and 15- to 19-year-olds). Blane expected that enduring asymmetrical muscular imbalance of the organism would influence spatial organization and that such an effect would vary with developmental status. The adolescent group (15 to 19 years) located the apparent vertical opposite the side of paralysis; the younger paralytic children (9 to 12 years) located apparent vertical toward the side of paralysis. These findings are in keeping with the general proposition that ongoing asymmetrical muscular imbalance is reflected in space localization. The age changes are in keeping with developmental expectations insofar as there are shifts of apparent vertical to the side of muscular paralysis in the younger children and to the side opposite the muscular paralysis in the older group.

In mentally retarded individuals, the shift in location of apparent vertical from toward to opposite the side of body tilt first occurred in a 19- to 21-year-old group, whereas it occurs earlier in individuals of normal intelligence (Guyette, Wapner, Werner, & Davidson, 1964). In contrast to expectations, however, there was an increase in the effect of starting position with increasing age. Furthermore, when older subjects were ordered into groups of higher and lower developmental status based on performance on the Similarities Subtest of the WAIS, the relatively mature group, again, paradoxically showed larger effects of starting position. This study is one factor which has led to a more complex analysis of the starting position effect in which the latter is viewed as a possible end-product of a number of different processes (Baker, 1968).

Although these findings from comparative studies largely fit in with the general propositions of developmental theory, there was one study with

LSD-25, by Liebert et al. (1957) which produced contradictory findings. LSD-25 was of interest to our programatic approach on the assumption that it induces "regressed states of behavior" so that the individual who has ingested it, in comparison with controls, should show less differentiation and hierarchic integration in behavioral processes. This regression should be reflected in the location of apparent vertical. In keeping with expectation, under LSD-25, normal adults as well as schizophrenics showed greater starting position effects than under placebo conditions. But the results on the effect of body tilt on position of apparent vertical under LSD-25 were not in keeping with expectation: the displacement of apparent vertical opposite the side of body tilt was enhanced rather than minimized (Liebert et al., 1957). Failure to verify the hypothesis poses an important problem which requires exploration. One approach to the problem involved the question whether the inverse findings were a function of the low dosage level (25-40 $\mu$g) of the drug. One of two unpublished studies using a higher dosage level, 75 $\mu$g, produced findings in keeping with the regression hypothesis; the second study showed no effects.

## APPARENT BODY POSITION

The organism-environment system notion implies that the appropriate unit for analysis is the reciprocal relation between the organism and objects, that there can be no perception of objects without a bodily frame of reference and no perception of the body as object without an environmental frame of reference, and that variation or stability in the organism-environment unity is reflected in body as well as object perception (Wapner & Werner, 1965). This formulation suggests that the analysis of spatiality cannot be complete without considering the interconnections between localization of the object and localization of the body under similar conditions. Accordingly, studies were undertaken dealing with effect of variation of body state — lateral body tilt — on perceived location of a main dimension of the body reference system, the longitudinal axis of the body, in a manner analogous to our treatment of perceived location of the main dimension of the external reference system, verticality.

The apparent position of the body in space under varying conditions of lateral body tilt was first measured in adults through the adjustment of a luminous rod in the darkroom to that physical position in which the subject experiences the longitudinal axis of his body to be located. With increasing body tilt, apparent body position is increasingly rotated beyond physical body position in the direction of tilt (Bauermeister, 1964; Mc-Farland, Wapner, & Werner, 1962). Bauermeister (1962, 1964) has treated these findings in terms of a body reference system distinct from the external reference system formulated for the analysis of apparent verticality (Bauermeister, Wapner, & Werner, 1963). The experience of the rod as parallel to the body is assumed to reflect correspondence between proximal stimulation and a system of organismic processes referred to as "body schema," a system involved in the maintenance of a bilaterally balanced part-whole organization in a field of varying internal and external stimulation.* The bilateral balance of the body schema is believed to be disturbed by asymmetrical stimulation and maintained by counteractive processes.

This general treatment assumes that the external reference system and the body reference system are products of a developmental process of differentiation which takes place in the course of ontogenesis. In keeping with this assumption, a study was initiated a few years ago (Wapner, 1968) in which 96 boys and 96 girls between the ages of 6 and 18 were tested in a verticality and body position situation under 30° left and right body tilt. As presented earlier, the rod was perceived as vertical when located toward the side of body tilt in younger subjects and opposite body tilt in older subjects. There were also striking age changes with respect to body position: with age there is a slight decrease in deviation of apparent beyond true location of the body axis followed by an accelerated increase between 13 and 15 years of age; the adults show a greater overestimation than young children. Body tilt also interacted significantly with sex independent of age, the females showing a greater shift of the apparent body axis than the males. The relation between apparent vertical and apparent body position is of great significance for the development of spatial location because it bears on the differentiation between body and object space which, it can be assumed, is reflected in the angular discrepancy between apparent vertical and apparent body position. The angular separation be-

---

* For details, consult Bauermeister (1962). An earlier attempt at a theoretical explanation was made by McFarland et al. (1962). An important issue bearing on the formulation of a specific theoretical model for body perception is whether adjustment of the rod parallel to the body is based upon a reference system involving the gravitational field and related to the perception of verticality or a reference system independent of the gravitational field as provisionally assumed, with Bauermeister, in this paper. For further pertinent data, see Baker, Cirillo, & Wapner (1969).

tween apparent vertical and apparent body position is markedly less in children than in adults, and this holds for both left and right body tilts. It may be noted that the angular discrepancy does not change gradually, but there is a sudden increase in this disparity around the 13- to 15-year age levels. Thus, what may be considered as an objective indicator of the degree of differentiation between the two spatial systems, body and objective, increases in the course of ontogenesis.

Though little comparative data using groups which may be ordered developmentally is available, some preliminary data with a few schizophrenic subjects are in keeping with expectation. For eight schizophrenics, the findings are similar to those of young children; that is, apparent body position is overestimated to a lesser degree than it is in normal adults, and apparent vertical is located to the side of body tilt; thus, the angle of separation of apparent verticality from apparent body position under body tilt is less for schizophrenics than for normal adults. Although these findings are limited, they do suggest a decreased differentiation between external and body reference systems in schizophrenics which is similar to that in young children.

## Straight-Ahead

Despite our recognition that the straight-ahead differs from verticality, we assumed that the general principles characterizing our analysis of an objectively defined spatial dimension should also hold for any egocentrically defined dimension, but that the specific nature of the mechanisms might vary. Accordingly, our studies on egocentric localization, and in particular those dealing with the straight-ahead, involve the analysis of the effects of extraneous and object stimulation, already known to affect perception of verticality. Apparent straight-ahead is measured by the adjustment of a luminous stimulus in the darkroom until the subject experiences it as straight ahead of him, that is, coincident with the median sagittal plane of the body. Asymmetrical stimulation from sources other than this luminous stimulus object are referred to as extraneous, whereas asymmetrical modifications of the stimulus to be adjusted are referred to as object stimulation. Apparent straight-ahead may also be measured by the tactual-kinesthetic adjustment of an indicator to coincide with the median plane.

### ADULTS

The effects of a number of forms of extraneous stimulation upon visual and kinesthetic straight-ahead have been studied. These include: (a) labyrinthian stimulation, that is, rotary acceleration around the vertical body axis and deceleration in the opposite direction, in relation to kinesthetic and visual (Morant, 1952, 1959) straight-ahead; (b) monocular light stimulation in relation to kinesthetic straight-ahead (Werner & Wapner, 1952b); (c) head and eye turning in relation to kinesthetic straight-ahead (Werner, Wapner, & Bruell, 1953); (d) prismatically induced uniocular convergence in relation to visual straight-ahead (Bruell, 1953; Bruell & Albee, 1955; McFarland et al., 1960; Meisel & Wapner, 1969); (e) danger — a precipitous drop — to right or left in relation to visual straight-ahead (Wapner et al., 1956).

With one exception, all of these forms of stimulation yield findings which are in accordance with the hypothetical model: extraneous asymmetrical stimulation results in a shift in the physical position of apparent straight-ahead opposite the direction of stimulation. The one exception is that kinesthetic straight-ahead shifts in the same direction as that of rotary acceleration around the vertical axis and opposite to that of deceleration. Further studies, however, showed that this effect is attributable to the change in the pattern of physical forces involved when the arms are outstretched, as in the kinesthetic situation. When the arms are brought closer to the body, the effects are attenuated (Morant, 1952).

Other studies have introduced the following forms of asymmetrical object stimulation: (a) stimulus figures extending asymmetrically from the point of visual fixation (Bruell, 1953; Bruell & Albee, 1955; Wapner et al., 1953; Wapner et al., 1956); (b) amount of asymmetrical extent (Bruell, 1953); (c) asymmetrical brightness gradient of a luminous figure (Giannitrapani, 1953); (d) asymmetry of striped patterns in three symmetrically located squares (Wapner & Werner, 1955). In accordance with the hypothetical model for object stimulation, all these conditions result in a shift of location of the apparent straight-ahead in the same direction as that of asymmetrical object stimulation. Contrary to an earlier hypothesis of Roelofs (1936), the influence of asymmetrical extent is independent of the intensity of light from the surface of the figure (Werner & Wapner, 1952b).

We must now introduce a third category of stimulation — dynamic object stimulation. Unlike the static qualities we have dealt with up to now, dynamic properties refer to inherent directional qualities, such as those in a picture of a bird in flight or a triangle facing left or right. We assume that such forms exert a "pull" on the organism in the direction of dynamics

177

which is counteracted by an organismic vector in the opposite direction. The stimulus must be shifted opposite the direction of its dynamics to correspond to organismic state and appear straight-ahead. It is expected, therefore, that dynamic object stimulation will shift the location of apparent straight-ahead opposite the direction of dynamics.

In one study based on this line of reasoning (Werner & Wapner, 1954), the stimulus object used was ambiguous as to directional dynamics — it could be seen as two ducks flying in one direction or two planes flying in the opposite direction. In a darkroom, the subject had to tell the experimenter how to move the pattern until it was straight ahead. One group of subjects were told they would see pictures of ducks, and the other that they would see planes. When the pattern was interpreted as ducks flying left, it was physically placed relatively to the right in order to be seen straight-ahead; when interpreted as planes flying right, it was physically placed relatively to the left. The opposite localization held when the pattern was reversed in the left-right dimension.

Consonant with this finding are those using such figures as a triangle or a profile of the face of a man. The findings with these stimuli and those of the previous experiments all can be summarized as follows: the physical position of the apparent straight-ahead shifts in a direction opposite to the direction of dynamics of the object (Werner & Wapner, 1954).

### AGE CHANGES AND COMPARATIVE FINDINGS

In contrast to the situation which obtained with respect to localization of verticality — that is, a clear-cut, replicable, ontogenetic pattern complementary to the general perceptual mechanisms delineated in research with adults — the findings on age changes in localization of the apparent straight-ahead are relatively incomplete and neither clear-cut nor coherent. For convenience of presentation we shall present findings on age changes in the effects, first, of dynamics and static object stimulation and, second, of extraneous stimulation.

On the basis of organismic-developmental theory (Werner, 1961), it was assumed that dynamic properties of objects involve "empathic" response, which is based, developmentally, upon a relative fusion or undifferentiatedness between object and organism. From the developmental principle of increasing differentiation between organism and object, it was hypothesized that the potency of dynamic object stimulation would decrease with age. Investigation of the effects of the dynamics of pictured objects (hands pointing right versus left) upon localization of the apparent straight-ahead, however, revealed no reliable change in the potency of dynamics (Wapner & Werner, 1957).

The age changes expected for effect of static object stimulation also depend on the principle of increasing differentiation between organism and external objects, which would be reflected as a decrease in stimulus-boundedness — that is, less responsivity to variations in the properties of the object. Wapner and Werner (1957) hypothesized that the younger child would show the maximal symmetrization tendency (the apparent straight-ahead would shift maximally in the direction to which the figure extends from the point of fixation); with increase in age, this effect is expected to decrease. In keeping with expectation it was found that the apparent straight-ahead shifts in the direction of extent at all age levels, that this effect is constant and very large for age levels 6–17, and that it decreases abruptly at the 18- to 19-year level.

More recently, the same task was included as one small part of an extensive developmental study (Wapner, 1966a). The results from this unpublished study showed a significant interaction between age and asymmetrical extent, with an overall erratic pattern which might be described as follows: at the youngest ages (6–9 years), an effect opposite to that found in previous studies occurred (shift of apparent median plane *opposite* extent); at ages 10–12 years, a moderate effect consistent with previous studies occurred (shift *toward* extent); and in the oldest groups a minimal shift occurred opposite extent in 16-year-olds and toward extent in 17- to 18-year-olds.

Clearly, the pattern of age changes in direction of shift of apparent straight-ahead obtained here is widely discrepant with that found earlier (Wapner & Werner, 1957). The more recent findings, however, were consistent with others which emerged concurrently in comparing developmentally ordered conditions and groups.

In a series of interrelated experiments, Glick (1964, 1966) explored the hypothesis that experimental instructions might induce in normal adult subjects a transient attitude of greater or lesser differentiation between organism and object. One of his situations involved adjustment to apparent straight-ahead of an asymmetrically extending object. He found that apparent straight-ahead shifted *toward* the side of asymmetrical extent under differentiated set (which, of course, had been found for adults with no instructional sets in all prior studies with this task). Under nondifferentiated instructional set, the apparent straight-ahead was found to shift in the direction *opposite* the side of asymmetrical extent, a finding not obtained with any previously studied sample from any population of subjects, save for the discrepant findings on age changes just discussed.

Follow-up work was undertaken to determine whether other variables assumed to reflect different degrees of differentiation between organism and object would affect the relation between asymmetrical extent and straight-ahead in the same direction as did instructional sets. It was hypothesized that variations in physical proximity between the subject and the stimulus object might similarly induce variations in degree of differentiation. Findings from two experiments — one with retinal size constant (Glick & Wapner, 1966) and the other with physical size of the stimulus constant — were highly consistent with this expectation: under close (2 ft.) subject-stimulus distance, the apparent straight-ahead shifted *opposite* asymmetrical extent, whereas under greater (8 ft.) subject-stimulus distance, the apparent straight-ahead shifted toward asymmetrical extent. Barton (1964, 1966) extended this line of research in a study of neuropathology. He took into account the dual characteristics of right hemiplegic subjects — neuromuscular asymmetry and cortical injury — in comparing a hemiplegic with a non-hemiplegic but otherwise brain-injured group of subjects. He assumed, on the basis of signs other than neuromuscular asymmetry (such as increased bodily concern and language disturbances), that the hemiplegic group would be characterized by less differentiation between organism and object than the non-hemiplegic brain-damaged group. Consistent with this expectation, the hemiplegic group localized the apparent straight-ahead *opposite* the direction of asymmetrical extent, whereas the non-hemiplegic group localized the apparent straight-ahead *toward* asymmetrical extent.

In sum, there were four sets of data (child versus adult; instructionally induced attitude of nondifferentiation versus differentiation; near versus far subject-stimulus distance; and hemiplegic versus non-hemiplegic patients) in which: (a) the condition or group presumed to involve lesser differentiation showed localization of apparent straight-ahead *opposite* the direction of asymmetrical extent, and (b) the condition or group presumed to involve greater differentiation showed localization of apparent straight-ahead *toward* asymmetrical extent. Although these four sets of findings are quite coherent with respect to one another, they are clearly discrepant with the earlier (Wapner & Werner, 1957) ontogenetic finding that the youngest group of children studied (ages 6–7) showed maximal displacement of apparent straight-ahead *toward* asymmetrical extent.

Our efforts to resolve this discrepancy have taken two main directions. First, we have studied the effects of instructional set upon apparent straight-ahead under asymmetrical extent in adults. In one study we used the sets devised by Glick (1964). In two others, we devised two other variants of instructional sets, each attempting in a somewhat different way to induce attitudes of greater versus lesser differentiation between organism and object. In none of these three studies has there been reliable evidence of any change in the effect of asymmetrical object extent upon location of apparent straight-ahead owing to variation in instructional set. Glick's finding regarding an interaction between asymmetrical extent and instructional set has thus far proved unreplicable.

Since no attempt has been made by us to replicate another group of Glick's (1964) findings — that variation in instructional set similarly results in opposite shifts in localization of straight-ahead under conditions of dynamic object and extraneous stimulation — it would be premature to conclude that such sets do not have observable effects upon perceived object location. In this context, it should be noted that there are other data indicating that instructional set can be effective: Porzemsky, Wapner, and Glick (1965) found in one study and its replication that apparent fingertip and apparent target location shift relatively toward each other under an experimentally induced attitude of fusion between self and object, as compared with a separated set. Baker (1968), also working with separated-fused instructional sets, found that such sets resulted in markedly different patterns of change in anticipation-habituation errors over repeated trials. It would, therefore, seem that further work is necessary, first, to determine the range of situations and types of specific instructional sets which are efficacious, and second, to ascertain why sets produce reliable effects in one situation and not in another.

The second direction taken in attempting to resolve discrepant findings on apparent straight-ahead directly concerns the two ontogenetic studies in question. A very detailed and careful re-examination of the methods and procedures followed in these studies revealed that the later study was not an exact replication of the earlier one in at least two respects. First, in the intervening years, the psychophysical procedures commonly used in our laboratory shifted from one in which the stimulus was moved in discrete and small steps with the subject making a judgment after each step, to one in which the stimulus was moved continuously from the start of the trial until the subject told the experimenter to stop. Since other subsequent research regarding localization showed that seemingly minor variations in psychophysical procedure can have measurable effects upon space localization which are of substantive importance (e.g., Bauermeister et al., 1967), it is possible that the difference in psychophysical procedure contributed to the divergent results. Second, the way the task was defined to the subject in the earlier study included the specific statement that he should indicate when the fixated edge of the stimulus was "straight ahead of your nose." In the later study, the subject was simply told to adjust the stimulus till it was straight-ahead. Although in both cases, pre-experimental demonstrations were employed to ensure that the subject understood the task, it is possible that by specifically making reference to a body part, one might be suggesting to the subject some particular strategy to adopt in carrying out the localization task.

It was decided to explore the possibility that these apparently minor variations in experimental procedure contributed to the differences in findings. The particular patterning of the findings from these two studies indicated that only if the following age pattern obtained could the discrepancy be resolved: (a) in the youngest age groups straight-ahead would have to be localized opposite extent, and this would occur in children younger than those used in the earlier study; (b) in the intermediate age groups, under both sets of procedures, apparent straight-ahead is localized maximally toward extent; and (c) in the oldest age group, apparent straight-ahead is localized moderately toward extent. Such a pattern of findings, if observed, would be consistent with the directional findings from the later ontogenetic study (Wapner, 1966a) and would indicate that the discrepancy with the earlier study (Wapner & Werner, 1957) occurred simply because the shift opposite extent occurred for the particular experimental procedures used in this earlier study at a younger age than had been sampled in the most recent ontogenetic study.

In a new study, four groups of 16 subjects — 5½, 8, 12, and 19 years of age — adjusted the stimulus object extending asymmetrically from fixation under conditions of stepwise motion of the stimulus and body-referent instructions ("straight ahead of your nose"), thus replicating the 1957 procedures. A second set of four independent groups of 16 subjects operated under conditions of continuous motion of the stimulus and non–body-referent instructions (straight-ahead defined with no mention of body part), thus replicating the 1966 procedures.* The results for the replication of the earlier study showed a small shift of apparent straight-ahead toward extent in the 5½-year-old group and an increase in the shift of apparent straight-ahead toward extent which was relatively constant in the other three age groups. The main developmental finding of the earlier study, a sharp decrease in the magnitude of the shift toward extent in the oldest group, was not replicated. The results of the replication of the more recent ontogenetic study showed a modest shift toward extent in each of the three younger groups, and maximal shift toward extent in the oldest age group. None of the ontogenetic findings of the recent study (Wapner, 1966a) were replicated.

It may be observed that the general effect of shift in apparent straight-ahead toward extent in adults is fully supported by these studies, but none of our studies with respect to age changes in this effect has produced replicable findings. No reliable age changes in the effect of asymmetrical object stimulation on the location of straight-ahead have been found.

We may now turn to developmental differences in the effect of extraneous stimulation on straight-ahead. Unilateral or monaural auditory stimulation was used by Glick (1964, 1966) in a study using a post-test interview to separate his sample into those subjects with a relatively nondifferentiated and those with a relatively differentiated ongoing organism-object relation. In the nondifferentiated group, apparent straight-ahead was located relatively toward sound; in the differentiated group, it was located relatively opposite sound. Clate (1965) replicated this aspect of Glick's findings in three further experiments. However, both Glick's (1964) and Clate's (1965) studies suffered from a methodological limitation: the criteria for classifying subjects into differentiated and non-differentiated classes used by their judges, who worked blind with respect to the darkroom data, were not made sufficiently explicit. We have recently, therefore, re-explored this experimental situation in some detail and have found that one can reproduce these effects when those subjects who report an experience of autokinesis during the localization trials are classified as differentiated and those who give no evidence of ever experiencing auto-

---

* In order to explore possible interaction effects of type of motion and type of instruction, groups of 5½-, 7-, and 19-year-olds were also run under stepwise presentation of the stimulus in conjunction with non-body-referent instructions, and under continuous motion of the stimulus in conjunction with body-referent instructions. The findings from these latter conditions do not in any way clarify the results reported in the text.

kinesis during these trials are classified as nondifferentiated.* With this criterion for classifying subjects, Downes (1970) replicated Glick's (1964) and Clate's (1965) results.

We have not yet conducted studies regarding age changes in the effects of extraneous stimulation upon the localization of the straight-ahead, but one such study from the literature has come to our attention. Toshima (1967) explored the effects of unilateral auditory stimulation upon the apparent straight-ahead in eight 4-year-olds and eight 22-year-olds. Toshima varied both direction of sound (to right versus left ear) and intensity of the sound (10 versus 50 db). In our view, three features of his method would tend to induce a relative lack of differentiation between organism and object, that is, a relative lack of objectification of the test pattern: a stimulus of minimal structure — a pinpoint of light, with two adjacent pinpoints to minimize autokinetic motion (Baker, 1968); stimulus relatively close (60 cm) to the subject (Baker, Wapner, & Vaughn, 1968; Glick & Wapner, 1966); and the subject's directly adjusting the stimulus by turning a knob himself.

Toshima found that apparent straight-ahead shifts toward monaural stimulation and that this effect is greater for the tone of higher intensity. The general shift toward sound is consistent with the findings for individuals classified as nondifferentiated: with relative lack of differentiation, apparent straight-ahead is shifted toward the side of extraneous stimulation. This is further supported by the age changes revealed in this study — children localize straight-ahead more toward sound than adults, and this tendency is greatly magnified with the high intensity sound. Again, the presumably less differentiated subjects (here, the children) locate straight-ahead more toward the side of asymmetrical extraneous stimulation than do subjects with greater differentiation between organism and object.

To briefly summarize this work: (a) the mechanisms formulated for the effects, in adults, of dynamic object stimulation, static object stimulation, and extraneous stimulation upon apparent verticality seem to hold as well for apparent straight-ahead; (b) the theoretically grounded expectations regarding developmental differences in the effect of extraneous stimulation on apparent straight-ahead are so far supported by the data, but further studies of this relation are necessary; (c) the single ontogenetic

* That a report (lack of report) of autokinesis is an indicator of differentiation (nondifferentiation) dovetails well with the description which Voth (1962) has given of subjects in an autokinetic motion task who report versus those who do not report the experience of autokinetic motion.

study of the relation between dynamics and apparent straight-ahead revealed no age changes; and (d) no reliable developmental differences in the effect of asymmetrical static object stimulation on apparent straight-ahead have been obtained.

## Eye Level

Egocentric localization in the up-down dimension of body space has been studied by measuring the location of apparent eye level. An object at apparent eye level is perceived as being in the plane bisecting the eye sockets. To assess apparent eye level, the subject is required to adjust a luminous stimulus in a darkroom to a position in space which appears at (neither above nor below) eye level. Apparent eye level has been measured under static and dynamic extraneous and object stimulation.

### ADULTS

With regard to extraneous stimulation in adults, apparent eye level is: (a) displaced relatively toward the feet under conditions involving greater as compared with lesser tension of the antigravity musculature — wearing versus not wearing a weighted vest when erect, erect versus tilted backward and supine, and supine while pushing versus not pushing against an external force with the feet (Comalli, 1963; Sziklai, Wapner, McFarland, & Werner, 1964); (b) displaced in the direction of the vectorial qualities of emotional states — success and failure induced moods of joy and depression (Wapner et al., 1957) and manic and depressed phases of manic-depressive psychosis (Rosenblatt, 1956).

Apparent eye level is located relatively toward the direction of static object stimulation, including such exemplars as asymmetrical extension (Jaffee, 1952), asymmetry of configuration of dual test pattern (Wapner & Werner, 1955), and starting position (Jaffee, 1952; Wapner & Werner, 1955).

Apparent eye level has been studied under extraneous dynamic stimulation as well as dynamic stimulation from the object. Dynamic stimulation from an extraneous source — a gliding tone changing in pitch from low to high or high to low — shifts apparent eye level in the direction of dynamics (Glick et al., 1965). Dynamic object stimulation, including such stimuli as pointing hands, shifts apparent eye level opposite the direction of dynamics (Kaden, Wapner, & Werner, 1955). Jaffee (1952) obtained less conclusive results with other forms of dynamic object stimulation.

185

## AGE CHANGES

An ontogenetic study of apparent eye level (Wapner & Werner, 1957) was originally undertaken to assess the interaction of dynamic object stimulation with age. A total of 237 subjects, 6 to 20 years old, were required to adjust test patterns consisting of silhouettes of hands pointing upward and of those pointing downward so that the fingertip in the center of the test pattern was located at eye level. The position of the apparent eye level significantly shifted opposite the direction of dynamics; there was a nonsignificant developmental trend with dynamics having no effect until the 10- to 11-year group, following which it decreased in efficacy with increase in age. Of interest was an unexpected ontogenetic trend which, although not significant, was evident in a number of different situations; this consisted of a general shift of apparent eye level, independent of the particular stimulus, from higher to lower positions with increase in age. In the same study words having dynamic properties (e.g., climbing versus falling) showed no overall significant effects of dynamics; however, again there was an ontogenetic trend — this time significant — such that at the youngest age levels apparent eye level was located above objective eye level and apparent eye level shifted downward below objective eye level with increase in age. Two other kinds of object stimulation (silhouette of a pair of eyeglasses and a line) were studied in a more recent investigation involving 240 subjects between 7 and 19 years of age (Wapner, 1966a). It was expected that the glasses were presumably more psychologically tied to the body, and that an abstract line indicator would therefore be adjusted differently depending on age level. Although the eye-glass indicator was adjusted to a position significantly lower than the line, there was no interaction with age. However, once again the apparent eye level shifted from above to below objective eye level with increase in age, with a significant ontogenetic change for both stimuli. Furthermore, the influence of starting position upon apparent eye level was significant, and its effect decreased significantly with age. There is, then, a reliable shift in apparent eye level to a position below objective eye level during the course of ontogenesis.

## COMPARATIVE FINDINGS

Further effects have been found with groups of subjects and transient states which are orderable developmentally. The apparent eye level is located highest in catatonic-hebephrenic schizophrenics, lowest in normal adults, with paranoids falling in between (Carini, 1955; Wapner & Krus, 1960). Furthermore, in normal adults the apparent eye level is located significantly higher under LSD-25 than under placebo conditions and the same relation holds for schizophrenics under LSD-25 but is less potent (Krus, Wapner, Bergen, & Freeman, 1961; Wapner & Krus, 1959, 1960).

The studies of apparent eye level, using words with dynamic properties and pointing hands, were extended ontogenetically from the original 6- to 20-year-olds to 80-year-olds. Pictures of hands had overall effects, with apparent eye level located opposite the direction of dynamics; words did not. There were no significant interactions involving age and conditions, but through the life span beginning at 7 years, apparent eye level shifted downward until middle age, when it shifts, moving steadily upward until 80 years of age (Comalli, 1970).

The studies of apparent eye level we have reported indicate that variables theoretically identified as important for up-down localization do indeed influence the adjustment of a stimulus to apparent eye level. The specific directional effects, however, cannot yet be accounted for in terms of a unitary model. As a first step, it may be necessary to separate the variables used into two broad classes parallel to those distinguished for other dimensions of space. One class of variables, including object stimulation, extraneous stimulation, and mood, might furnish an adequate basis for an equilibrial model for perception of eye level. The second class of variables, including age, schizophrenics versus normals, and LSD-25 versus placebo may represent, in an as yet unspecified manner, variations in the degree of differentiation between the organism and the environment.

A second step will involve the formulation of one or more equilibrial models for the effects of the first class of variables — those introducing up-down vectors. The influence of the variations in differentiation presumed to account for the second class of variables — which now are grouped on the basis of the empirical equivalence of their effects on eye level — will have to be conceptualized in terms of its influence on the inferred processes of equilibration. This enterprise requires empirical investigation of the interaction between the two classes of variables, those involving asymmetry and those reflecting variations in organism-object differentiation. Such studies have not yet been undertaken.

We may, finally, briefly consider alternative explanations in this area. Howard and Templeton (1966) review some of the evidence on apparent eye level and criticize the present approach strongly. Some of their criti-

187

cisms are based on incorrect readings of findings.* They offer an alternative explanation of the downward shift in apparent eye level with age. The interpretation assumes that subjects judge the height of objects with ground level as a norm, that objects above ground level appear suspended, and that this quality intrudes on judgments of eye level. Thus, an object at eye level will appear to be higher and will have to be adjusted lower than true eye level in order to appear to be at eye level. That is, apparent eye level will be depressed relative to true eye level. Since height increases with age, objects at real eye level will be closer to the ground for younger than older children, and younger children will, therefore, have a less depressed apparent eye level than older subjects. It should be noted that this explanation does not account for apparent eye level's being higher than true eye level in young children. It also does not account for the parallel between the observed age changes and the effects of drugs or schizophrenia on apparent eye level. Nevertheless, we are presently reanalyzing our ontogenetic data to explore the possibility that age changes in apparent eye level are fully attributable to increasing height.

## Autokinetic Motion

Up to this point we have restricted ourselves to reporting work on perceived location. We now turn to perceived motion. It is not unreasonable to expect that factors which are known to affect perceived location might

* Howard and Templeton say that Rosenblatt (1956) "predicts that elated psychotics have an 'upward organismic vector,' which causes an apparent elevation of the real eye level and a depression of apparent eye level" (p. 189), and point out that this would be inconsistent with other theoretical expectations. Rosenblatt, however, did not make this prediction, and his findings are the opposite of those implied in this statement. His findings were consistent with the others reported in the text: elevated mood is significantly associated with relatively high apparent eye level and depressed mood with relatively low apparent eye level.

Some critical remarks are based on the following reading of Glick (1959). Howard and Templeton (1966) say he "found that when the subject pressed down with his hands to force his head up against a spring, the apparent eye-level was displaced upwards, and when the subject pressed up to force his chin down against a spring, the apparent eye-level was displaced downward" (p. 187). Subjects, however, actually were instructed to press up with the head or down with the chin against a pressure plate and there was no involvement of the hands. This does not, however, refute their general point that actual tonus would be symmetrical here. More important, the direction of results was again opposite to that reported in this quotation: under instructions to push *up*, apparent eye level was displaced *downward*; under instructions to push *down*, apparent eye level was displaced *upward*. As with other sources of extraneous stimulation and other spatial referents, adjustment of the stimulus was opposite to the direction of extraneous stimulation.

also affect perceived motion, and that those principles of our approach applicable to location might also apply to perceived motion.

Our focus is on one form of illusory movement — the autokinetic phenomenon. The perceived movement of a stimulus which is physically constant in position is our initial concern for a number of reasons. Autokinetic motion is sometimes reported by subjects during our work in spatial location, so that the relation between perceived motion and location is of concern on empirical and methodological grounds. Also, we use variations in the direction of autokinetic movement as a natural way of objectively demonstrating the dynamic properties of objects. Finally, it is more convenient to study the effects of asymmetrical stimuli on autokinetic motion than on real motion because the latter involves variations in the relation between observer and stimulus which necessitate complicated techniques for introducing asymmetry.

Because we have as yet done relatively little empirical work on autokinetic motion, we shall rely more heavily upon work of other investigators in treating autokinetic motion from our own point of view. In doing so, we shall provisionally adopt the working hypothesis that autokinetic motion in a given direction is influenced by asymmetrical conditions in the same way as is apparent location: for example, under conditions making for autokinetic motion to the left, the perceived location of the object shifts to the left, and, in order for it to coincide with apparent straight-ahead, it must be shifted to the right. If this hypothesis were true, the mechanisms formulated for the analysis of perceived location would hold as well for autokinetic motion.

### ADULTS

There is some evidence to support the hypothesis that asymmetrical extraneous stimulation leads to a predominance of autokinetic motion toward stimulation, parallel to the findings on localization. Such a generalization holds for sound (Corso & Soloyanis, 1962) and for monocular stimulation (Carr, 1910; Crovitz, 1962). Again, evidence in keeping with the generalization was found by Gregory and Zangwill (1963) and Nagatsuka (1960) for muscular involvement induced by weighting one side of the body, but Kline (1951) found evidence neither to support nor to contradict it.

The findings on effects of asymmetrical muscular involvement induced by rotating eyes, head, or trunk do not readily fit this generalization; at best, they suggest that although such muscular involvement clearly plays a significant role in autokinetic motion, this role cannot be characterized in terms of a specific directional relation between side of application of stimulation and direction of autokinetic motion. For example, although autokinetic motion has been reported in the same direction as the direction of eye gaze for a smaller "inner" zone, for an "outer" zone autokinetic motion is reported first in a direction opposite eye gaze, followed by autokinetic motion in the same direction as eye gaze (Carr, 1910). When the subject gazes to one side and then returns his eyes to straight-ahead and observes a light, it appears to move opposite gaze according to Glick (1968). According to Gregory and Zangwill (1963), however, the findings are more complicated: the initial movement is opposite the direction of eye turning, and there is then a reversal, with movement in the direction of eye turning.

There are even greater complexities involved with head turning. Nagatsuka (1960) reports autokinetic motion in the direction of head rotation, but other studies make it clear that more sophisticated analysis of the effective conditions of muscular strain will be necessary. In this connection, Battersby, Kahn, Pollack, and Bender (1956) found that trunk and head turning alone had no effect on autokinetic motion, but that when head and body were rotated in the same direction, autokinetic motion was in the opposite direction — that is, in the direction of eye strain. However, it should be noted that when head and trunk are rotated, the effective stimulus conditions are complicated by the fact that the eyes must be rotated in a direction opposite that of head and trunk. Kochendorfer (1968) found that with rotation of trunk away from the stimulus and with head and eyes centered on the stimulus, autokinetic motion was in the direction of trunk rotation and opposite the direction of head strain. Kochendorfer found that such left-right muscular involvement has different effects from up-down strain of head and body, insofar as there is greater predominance of autokinetic motion in the left-right dimension of space with left-right strain. The complexity of such rotational conditions of eye, head, and trunk systems, at this stage of analysis, perhaps most appropriately warrants statements of their influence on autokinetic motion in terms of spatial dimensions rather than specific directions (see Marshall, 1966).

Because of the complexity of the conditions of muscular innervation in these studies, and because of our interest in parallels in effect of conditions on localization and autokinetic motion, we are presently conducting experiments designed to assess effects on autokinetic motion of somewhat simpler, but better controlled and defined asymmetrical muscular involvement. For this purpose, a pinpoint of light in an otherwise dark room is observed under conditions of uniocular-muscular involvement. Asymmetry of convergence is introduced by having the subjects wear a prism with its base placed temporally in front of one eye. The prism displaces the light temporally so that it does not fall on corresponding points in the two eyes. For fusion to occur, the eye must rotate nasally — greater ocular-muscular strain to the left with prism in front of the right eye, and greater ocular-muscular strain to the right with prism in front of the left eye. With 4° prisms, preliminary results indicate that autokinetic motion tends to predominate — but not to a significant degree — in the direction of greater muscular strain. The data are being further analyzed while additional work is being conducted with 8° prisms.

Should the complete findings prove significant in the indicated direction, they would be clearly consonant with our studies on the effect of these ocular-muscular conditions on location with respect to the apparent straight-ahead. As demonstrated by Bruell (1953) and Meisel and Wapner (1969) in adults, the apparent straight-ahead shifts opposite to the direction of greater convergences or, stated another way, the perceived location of the object shifts in the direction of greater ocular-muscular strain. Such findings would be bolstered by others concerning ongoing neuromuscular asymmetries, such as those obtained for people differing in handedness. Wishner and Shipley (1954), for example, found that there is more autokinetic motion to the right in right-handed than in left-handed subjects.

A number of studies demonstrate the effect of asymmetrical static object stimulation upon autokinetic motion. Adams (1912) cites a study by Bourdon (1904) in which the subject fixated one edge of a bar of light extending to the left of point of fixation. There was autokinetic movement to the right, that is, opposite asymmetry. Glick (1964) had subjects fixate one edge of a luminescent square; he, too, found that there was significantly more autokinetic motion in the direction opposite asymmetrical extent. Bruell and Albee (1956), building on the findings concerning the relation between asymmetrical extent and apparent straight-ahead, reasoned that a fixated line becoming the edge of a rectangle by gradual exposure of a luminous area to one side would result in autokinetic motion in the opposite direction. This is precisely what they found. Finally, Sadler, Mefferd, and Wieland (1966) found, among other results, that introduction of a second, nonfixated stimulus results in greater initial autokinetic motion of the fixated light in the same dimension as that marked by the relation between the two lights. The direction of initial movement is not specified.

The work on effect of dynamic object stimulation on autokinetic motion described below is largely confined to that conducted in the Clark laboratories. Previous studies demonstrated that directional dynamics of objects significantly affect their spatial location. The perceived location of silhouettes of hands, triangles, and face profiles, for example, shifts in the direction of dynamics. In order to appear straight-ahead, they are adjusted opposite to the direction of dynamics. We have assumed that directional dynamics exert a pull on the organism in the direction of the dynamics and that this is counteracted by an organismic pull in the opposite direction. Just as the vectorial quality exerts itself in a shift in location in the direction of dynamics, so the vectorial quality was expected to become manifest in autokinetic motion such that the stimulus object apparently moves in the direction of the dynamics.

Comalli, Werner, and Wapner (1957) carried out three experiments on this issue. In the first experiment, silhouettes of a running horse, a running boy, and an arrow were employed, each facing left under one condition and facing right under another. Using a measure of duration of reported movement in a given direction over a 30-second trial, it was found that autokinetic motion is predominantly in the direction of dynamics. This finding was replicated in a further study by Comalli (1960) using chemists and artists. Both groups showed more autokinetic motion in the direction of dynamics, and the effect was greater for artists than for chemists.

In the remaining two experiments (Comalli et al., 1957), the effects of set upon the relation between a directionally ambiguous pattern and autokinetic motion were measured. In one experiment, a stimulus pattern that could be interpreted as a bird flying in one direction or a plane flying in the opposite direction was employed. Autokinetic motion was predominantly in the direction of the dynamics induced by naming the stimulus *bird* or *plane*. In the final experiment, similar results were obtained for the up-down dimension using an ambiguous *rising balloon* or *falling parachute* figure. Toch (1962, 1963) has also found that meaningful pictures move autokinetically in the direction depicted. The particular virtue of the experiments with directionally ambiguous pictures is to show that the effects of dynamics do not depend upon the retinal distribution of stimulation.

Some experimentation has also been conducted (Miller, Werner, & Wapner, 1958) using what has been tentatively classified as extraneous dynamic stimulation — a gliding tone shifting from high to low or low to high pitch is assumed to induce organismic changes in terms of up-down vectors. When a stationary pinpoint of light is observed by the subject while exposed to the gliding tones, duration of autokinetic motion in the direction of dynamics increases.

This situation was also used in two studies reported by Glick et al. (1965) dealing with the relation between duration of perceived movement and perceived location of an object in the up-down dimension. In this study, too, a luminous horizontal line exhibited significantly more autokinetic motion in the upward direction for ascending than for descending tone. In the localization experiment, the luminous line appeared relatively higher for the descending than for the ascending tone. There is, therefore, a paradoxical, inverse relation between the direction of autokinetic motion and of change in apparent location of the visual object under gliding tone conditions. A similar paradox is apparent in phenomenal reports in some studies, in that movement is experienced without apparent change in location or displacement (Graybiel & Hupp, 1946; Gregory & Zangwill, 1963; Moustgaard, 1963). Some observations suggest that, at least with gliding tones, apparent body displacement or motion is induced, which indicates that it would be worthwhile to consider body-object relations when dealing with the relation between autokinetic motion and space localization (Brosgole, 1967; Glick & Wapner, 1967; Glick et al., 1965).

AGE CHANGES

Before the studies to be reported here, little research on age changes in autokinetic motion had been undertaken (Blane, 1962; Fisher, 1962; Hamm & Hoving, 1969). We began by studying age changes in autokinetic motion under conditions known to affect space localization differently in children as compared with adults (Baker & Wapner, 1969; Wapner, 1966a). Two such variables are object asymmetry — that is, asymmetry in the extension of the stimulus with respect to the point of fixation — and ocular-muscular asymmetry introduced by turning the eyes left or right. A total of 228 subjects, 19 boys and 19 girls in each of six age groups, ranging from 7 to 19 years old were tested. The subject was told that the stimulus (a luminous square) would be moved in the darkroom, though it was in fact stationary; he was to report its motion. He was pretrained in verbally reporting motion with a physically moving square. Each subject was given six trials — two conditions of object asymmetry (fixate left versus right edge of square) combined with three conditions of eye turning (fixated edge left of, right of, and at objective median plane). Each trial lasted 60 seconds from the first report of autokinetic movement. The dependent variable was duration of autokinetic motion in a given direction.

The major findings were as follows: (a) There is little or no effect of eye turning at the earliest age level, but with increasing age there is a marked increase in predominance of motion opposite the direction of eye turning. (b) There is little or no effect of asymmetrical extent from 8 to 14 years of age, but for the two oldest age groups, motion opposite the side of extent clearly predominates.*

Thus, with both object asymmetry and oculomotor asymmetry, there is a significant increase with age in the predominance of motion opposite the direction of asymmetry. These findings are consonant with previous findings regarding localization of the straight-ahead in adults — apparent straight-ahead is located toward the side of asymmetry of the object, indicating that the apparent location of the object shifts opposite to extent. In the present study, the object appears to move opposite to extent in older subjects. Similarly, pervious work indicates that apparent straight-ahead, measured kinesthetically, is displaced in the direction of gaze toward a visual stimulus — that is, the apparent location of an object shifts opposite to the direction of gaze; in the present study, the object appears to move opposite to the direction of gaze in older subjects.

Another study of autokinetic motion, currently being conducted by Reif, deals with the interaction of age and dynamic object stimulation. Our expectations were guided by the same theoretical proposition discussed earlier in connection with space localization. First, considering the inverse relation between motion and localization, independent of age, autokinetic motion is expected to be influenced in the direction of dynamics; second, the increasing differentiation between object and organism in the course of ontogenesis should be manifest in decreasing potency of dy-

---

* Other findings show that the predominance of motion opposite asymmetry decreases systematically over the course of the 60-second trial. This holds for all age groups, indicating that even the youngest responded systematically to the task. The data further suggest that even the youngest subjects show more motion opposite asymmetry of the object and of eye turning early in the trial.

namic object stimulation with increasing age. A total of 80 subjects, 8 boys and 8 girls each at ages 6–7, 9–10, 12–13, 15–16, and 18–19 were tested in the autokinetic situation. Four luminous stimulus patterns with dynamics were used — pictures of an arrow, pointing fingers, a running boy, and a running horse. Using as a dependent variable the amount of motion in left, right, up, and down directions in a 30-second period, we found that, first, there is a powerful general effect of dynamics on autokinetic motion, with autokinetic motion in the direction of dynamics, and second, all age groups show this effect to a similar degree except for the middle age group (12–13 years), which shows little effect of dynamics on autokinetic motion. Although the hypothesis of a decrease over this age range in the effects of dynamics is not supported by these data, they do show a potent effect of dynamic object stimulation on autokinetic motion in the youngest age groups. This contrasts with object stimulation and eye turning, which, as the earlier study showed, increase in potency of effect with increasing age.

The findings of the studies just reported bear on a theory of autokinetic motion in a number of ways. Both the character of the effective independent variables and the observed ontogenetic changes in autokinetic motion appear difficult to handle in terms of a peripheral mechanism such as the eye movement theory of autokinesis offered, in modern form, by Matin and MacKinnon (1964). They showed that stabilization of the retinal image in the horizontal dimension markedly reduced autokinetic motion in that dimension, and argued that "these results strongly support the view that autokinesis is due to the occurrence of involuntary eye movements which continually shift the target image across the retina, and are consistent with the notion that local sign is involved in the perception of visual direction" (p. 147). This theory implies that all variables influencing autokinesis are mediated by their effects on involuntary eye movements. The task of such a theory, then, is to show that eye movements are in fact influenced in the hypothesized manner by the range of variables, including those reported here, that are known to influence autokinesis. The study actually performed by Matin and MacKinnon (1964) does not at all demonstrate that involuntary eye movements are the necessary and sufficient condition for autokinetic motion.

A number of other investigators, whose theoretical position seems much closer to our own, have provided additional evidence that the eye movement explanation is insufficient. Brosgole (1968), for example, showed that autokinesis of an afterimage was in the same direction as that of a fixated target continually located in its center, ruling out an eye movement explanation. On the basis of other work, Jordan (1968) as well as Brosgole and his associates (Brosgole, 1966, 1967, 1968; Brosgole & Cristal, 1967; Brosgole, Cristal, & Carpenter, 1968; Brosgole & Hansen, 1969) have argued that autokinesis is egocentrically determined. To contrast this view with the eye movement theory, one might say that it is not shifts of the target in relation to fixed local signs which account for autokinesis, but shifts in the values of local signs in relation to a target that may, in fact, be stationary. This view is similar to our own working hypothesis: autokinesis as well as shifts in localization — here, apparent straight-ahead — is based upon changes in organismic state to which proximal stimulation from the object is related. These changes may be reflected in experienced body position (see Jordan [1968] on felt eye position) and body motion (Glick et al., 1965) as well as in shift of object location and movement.

As previously mentioned, a major argument against this approach is based on the phenomenon of paradoxical motion — that is, motion without apparent displacement or opposite the direction of apparent displacement (Adams, 1912; Bourdon, 1904; Glick & Wapner, 1967; Glick et al., 1965; Graybiel, Clark, MacCorquodale, & Hupp, 1956; Moustgaard, 1963). Gregory and Zangwill (1963) found autokinetic motion to be systematically related to conditions of muscular fatigue without any phenomenal shift in the locus of the object. They argue that autokinesis is "due to fluctuating efficiency of the oculomotor system. Fluctuations in motor efficiency must be corrected by varying command signals in order to maintain fixation. These are wrongly taken to represent movement of the external light" (p. 260). Glick (1968) has measured both apparent movement and shift in the locus of the target under the conditions used by Gregory and Zangwill (1963) to produce autokinetic motion. The measures of motion and of shift in location were clearly and unparadoxically related. Glick (1968) also measured the apparent straight-ahead kinesthetically with eyes closed after the same conditions of eye muscle fatigue. The results of this nonvisual determination were parallel in direction to those of the visual determination, providing evidence of a general organismic change rather than the purely local change in the visuo-motor subsystem posited by Gregory and Zangwill (1963).

Although we reject both Matin and MacKinnon's (1964) eye movement theory and Gregory and Zangwill's (1963) cybernetic model as *general* explanations of autokinesis, we agree with Glick (1968) that autokinetic motion may not reflect a single underlying process and may, therefore, not be amenable to any single explanation, including ours in terms of organism-object relations. One of the heuristic values of our approach in this area has been to show the involvement of the organism as a total system in the formation of the perceptual world and, thus, to counter the tendency to overextend models which are based on purely local mechanisms, whether sensory or visuo-motor.

## General Comments

We have reviewed some general and developmental findings on objective localization, egocentric localization, and autokinetic motion. These findings were generated from two theoretical approaches: The first is the organismic approach, as represented by sensory-tonic field theory (Werner & Wapner, 1949) in which perception is characterized as a reflection of equilibratory relations between the two poles of the organism-environment system. The second approach is the developmental one, as embodied in the orthogenetic principle; here, this principle is specified in terms of comparison between systems differing in the degree of distance between the organism and its environment.

In evaluating the theory underlying our work on space perception to date, we distinguish between two criteria: heuristic fruitfulness and explanatory value. It should be evident from the findings presented here and elsewhere (Wapner, 1964a&b, 1966b, 1969; Wapner & Werner, 1965) that our approach has had marked heuristic value in uncovering extensive and varied empirical relations to which one would not have been so readily directed from other viewpoints. The organismic approach, for example, has led to the discovery of relations between different forms of stimulation which are not considered when space perception is dealt with only in terms of isolated sensory subsystems. Likewise, the formal parallels demonstrated between diverse groups and conditions, such as ontogeny, psychopathology, and drugs — especially with respect to perception of verticality — will have to be taken into account by any attempt at a general theory of space perception.

There is little doubt that the organismic-developmental approach has been heuristically fruitful, but there is some question about the value of the explanatory models which have thus far been formulated in this approach. These limitations in explanatory value point to some directions that may be taken to increase the power of the theory.

Some of the limitations of our explanatory models demonstrated in the present review and others mentioned elsewhere (Wapner et al., 1969) may be noted. Our failure to find a replicable ontogenetic pattern in the effect of asymmetrical object stimulation upon localization of straight-ahead, when contrasted with the findings for verticality, indicates that there *may* be differences between egocentrically and objectively defined dimensions of space which are not adequately accounted for by the parallel models formulated to deal with both. Although this exemplifies the empirical limitations on already formulated models, there are other domains in which no model has as yet been sufficiently formulated. For example, we have not explicitly formulated a general equilibratory model to account for the specific directional effects observed in the up-down dimension of space (the apparent eye level task). Finally, the relations between certain constructs have not yet been fully worked out. For example, a more systematic treatment of the relation between the external reference system and the body reference system is required.

The preceding comments regarding the limitations of our theoretical work suggest new undertakings which would be obvious extensions of lines of research we have long pursued. In another place (Wapner et al., 1969) we have begun a more extensive theoretical reformulation in terms of the relations between different levels of organization. In particular, we have specified two different levels of equilibration between the organism and impinging stimulation: the sensorimotor level and the perceptual level. This line of thought is not completely new to us, since we have previously taken some initial empirical steps to assess the effects of asymmetrical stimulation on changes of postural orientation in different age groups (Wapner & Werner, 1957). Now, however, technical advances in information pick-up and data analysis permit us to turn this theoretical interest into more extensive concrete research.

This planned research is based on the proposition that the sensory-tonic state of the organism may be expressed in action as well as perception. Symmetrization of excitation by taxes in lower organisms is an example. In adult humans, adaptation to asymmetrical stimulation may be achieved by various means, including shifts in postural orientation as well as covert changes in state when a stable postural orientation is maintained. The influence of the diverse forms of asymmetrical stimulation on the organization of perceptual space should itself vary systematically with actively adopted or externally imposed constraints on sensorimotor action. It should be noted, in this regard, that almost all our studies of space perception include as a constant condition the imposition of postural constraints both in the form of body supports and headrests and in the form of instructions to maintain a certain orientation toward one stimulus (e.g., fixating a light source). The generality of the principles derived from the exclusive use of such traditional methods is always questionable, on at least two counts. First, think how restricted a picture of visual and auditory localization of a source would be if it were derived solely from observations of subjects whose eye and head movements were experimentally restrained. Second, such methods assume that the effects of other conditions upon localization of a source of stimulation is independent of variations in postural orientation. In other words, perception is treated in artificial isolation from the acting organism. Our attempt to study the relations between asymmetrical stimulation, space perception, *and* postural orientation is a logical extension of the organismic approach, according to which the functional significance of a part process is not a fixed property but is derivative of relations between the part process and its organismic context.

This new direction of research also derives from the developmental perspective, insofar as the equilibratory process involving internal shifts in the sensory-tonic state of the organisms are viewed as differentiating from the overt shifts in postural orientation which are involved in the maintenance of sensorimotor equilibrium. In this sense, then, the equilibratory models formulated for perceptual location and motion are descriptions of a system of "virtual" action which find their counterpart in the literal actions of postural adaptation. The study of ontogenesis in this domain serves to test and to sharpen our conception of the differentiation and establishment of hierarchical relations between perception and action. Finally, this proposed work should enable us to formulate a more adequate and general theoretical account of space perception as the product of a developmental process of formation by an active organism.

## References

Adams, H. F. Autokinetic sensations. *Psychological Monographs*, 1912, 14 (2, Whole No. 59).

Baker, A. H. Perception under active and passive attitudes of self in relationship to world. Ph.D. thesis, Clark University, 1968.

———, L. Cirillo, & S. Wapner. Perceived body position under lateral body tilt.

*Proceedings of the 76th Annual Convention of the American Psychological Association*, 1969, 4 (pt. 1), 41–42.

Baker, A. H., & S. Wapner. Age changes in autokinetic motion. Paper presented at the meeting of the Society for Research in Child Development, Santa Monica, March 1969.

––––––– & O. Vaughn. Subject-stimulus distance and localization. Paper presented at the meeting of the Psychonomic Society, St. Louis, October 1968.

Barton, M. I. Aspects of object and body perception in hemiplegics: An organismic-developmental approach. Ph.D. thesis, Clark University, 1964. (Microfilm No. 64-12, 153.)

–––––––. An organismic-developmental approach to perception in individuals with ongoing neuromuscular asymmetries, in S. Wapner & B. Kaplan, eds., *Heinz Werner 1890–1964*. Worcester, Mass.: Clark University Press, 1966.

Battersby, W. S., R. L. Kahn, M. Pollack, & M. B. Bender. Effects of visual vestibular, somatosensori-motor deficit on autokinetic perception. *Journal of Experimental Psychology*, 1956, 52, 398–410.

Bauermeister, M. The relation between subjective body space and objective external space under conditions of body tilt. Ph.D. thesis, Clark University, 1962. (Microfilm No. 62-6451.)

–––––––. The effect of body tilt on apparent verticality, apparent body position, and their relation. *Journal of Experimental Psychology*, 1964, 67, 142–147.

–––––––, S. Wapner, & H. Werner. Sex differences in the perception of apparent verticality and apparent body position under conditions of body tilt. *Journal of Personality*, 1963, 31, 394–407.

–––––––. Method of stimulus presentation and apparent body position under lateral body tilt. *Perceptual and Motor Skills*, 1967, 24, 43–50.

Bertalanffy, L. V. *Modern theories of development*, Oxford University Press, London, 1933; New York: Harper Torchbooks, 1962.

Blane, T. Space perception among unilaterally paralyzed children and adolescents. *Journal of Experimental Psychology*, 1962, 63, 244–247.

Bourdon, B. *La perception visuelle de l'espace*. Paris: Reinwald, 1904.

Brosgole, L. Change in phenomenal location and perception of motion. *Perceptual and Motor Skills*, 1966, 23, 999–1001.

–––––––. Induced autokinesis. *Perception and Psychophysics*, 1967, 2, 69–73.

–––––––. The autokinesis of an after-image. *Psychonomic Science*, 1968, 12, 233–234.

––––––– & R. M. Cristal. Vertically induced autokinesis. *Psychonomic Science*, 1967, 7, 337–338.

––––––– & O. Carpenter. The role of eye movements in the perception of visually induced autokinesis. *Perception and Psychophysics*, 1968, 4, 123–124.

Brosgole, L., & K. H. Hansen. The effect of change in body orientation upon the perceived direction of autokinesis. *Psychonomic Science*, 1969, 15, 204.

Bruell, J. H. Visual egocentric localizations: An experimental study. Ph.D. thesis, Clark University, 1953. (Microfilm No. 5836.)

––––––– & G. W. Albee. Effect of asymmetrical retinal stimulation on the perception of the median plane. *Perceptual and Motor Skills*, 1955, 5, 133–139.

–––––––. A new illusion of apparent movement and the concept of retinal local signs. *Journal of Psychology*, 1956, 41, 55–59.

Carini, L. P. An experimental investigation of perceptual behavior in schizophrenics. Ph.D. thesis, Clark University, 1955. (Microfilm No. 13009.)

Carr, H. H. The autokinetic sensation. *Psychological Review*, 1910, 17, 42–75.

Chandler, K. The effect of monaural and binaural tones of different intensities on the visual perception of verticality. *American Journal of Psychology*, 1961, 76, 260–265.

Clate, S. B. Effects of articulation of body on object perception. M.A. thesis, Clark University, 1965.

Comalli, P. E., Jr. Studies in physiognomic perception: VI. Differential effects of directional dynamics of pictured objects on real and apparent motion in artists and chemists. *Journal of Psychology*, 1960, 49, 99–109.

————. Body position and localization of a visual object. *Perceptual and Motor Skills*, 1963, 16, 86.

————. Cognitive functioning in a group of 80–90 year old men. *Journal of Gerontology*, 1965, 20, 14–17.

————. Life-span changes in visual perception. Unpublished MS., Temple University, 1970.

————, S. Wapner, & H. Werner. Perception of verticality in middle and old age. *Journal of Psychology*, 1959, 47, 259–266.

Comalli, P. E., Jr., H. Werner, & S. Wapner. Studies in physiognomic perception: III. Effect of directional dynamics and meaning-induced sets on autokinetic motions. *Journal of Psychology*, 1957, 43, 289–299.

Corso, J. F., & G. Soloyanis. Auditory stimulation and induced changes in autokinetic movement. *Proceedings of the Pennsylvania Academy of Science*, 1962, 36, 140–144.

Crovitz, H. F. Directional differences in autokinesis based on stimulation of the left versus the right eye. *Perceptual and Motor Skills*, 1962, 15, 631–634.

Downes, R. The relationship of autokinetic motion to object and body perception under varied body environment arrangements. M.A. thesis, Clark University, 1970.

Fisher, S. Developmental sex differences in right-left perceptual directionality. *Child Development*, 1962, 33, 463–468.

Giannitrapani, D. Effect of brightness gradients on the position of the apparent median plane. M.A. thesis, Clark University, 1953.

Gibson, J. J., & M. Radner. Adaptation, after-effect and contrast in the perception of tilted lines. I. Quantitative studies. *Journal of Experimental Psychology*, 1937, 20, 453–467.

Glick, J. A. The effect of static and dynamic extraneous stimulation on the apparent horizon. M.A. thesis, Clark University, 1959.

————. An experimental analysis of subject-object relationships in perception. Ph.D. thesis, Clark University, 1964. (Microfilm No. 64-12, 60.)

————. An experimental analysis of subject-object relationships in perception, in R. N. Haber, ed., *Contemporary theory and research in visual perception*, pp. 458–461. New York: Holt, 1968.

————. An experimental analysis of subject-object relationships in perception, in S. Wapner & B. Kaplan, eds., *Heinz Werner 1890–1964*. Worcester, Mass.: Clark University Press, 1966.

————. Relationships between autokinetic motion and spatial displacement. Paper presented at the meeting of the Eastern Psychological Association, Washington, D.C., April 1968.

———— & S. Wapner. Effect of variation in distance between subject and object on space localization. *Perceptual and Motor Skills*, 1966, 23, 438.

————. The relationship between perceived movement and apparent displacement: A reply to Brosgole. *Acta Psychologica*, 1967, 26, 236–240.

———— & H. Werner. Some relations between autokinetic motion and space localization. *Acta Psychologica*, 1965, 24, 41–48.

Goldstein, K. The two ways of adjustment of the organisms to cerebral defects. *Journal of Mount Sinai Hospital*, 1942, 9, 504–513.

————. Sensory-tonic theory and the concept of self-realization, in B. Kaplan & S. Wapner, eds., *Perspectives in psychological theory*, pp. 115–123. New York: International Universities Press, 1960.

Graybiel, A., B. Clark, K. MacCorquodale, & D. Hupp. Role of vestibular nystagmus in visual perception of a moving target in the dark. *American Journal of Psychology*, 1956, 59, 259–266.

Graybiel, A., & D. Hupp. The oculo-gyral illusion: A form of apparent motion which may be observed following stimulation of the semicircular canals. *Journal of Aviation Medicine*, 1946, 17, 3–27.

Gregory, R. L., & O. L. Zangwill. The origin of the autokinetic effect. *Quarterly Journal of Experimental Psychology*, 1963, 15, 252–261.

Guyette, A., S. Wapner, H. Werner, & J. Davidson. Some aspects of space perception in mental retardates. *American Journal of Mental Deficiency*, 1964, 69, 90–100.

Halpern, L. The syndrome of sensorimotor induction in disturbed equilibrium. *Archives of Neurology and Psychiatry*, 1949, 62, 330–354.

————. The syndrome of sensorimotor induction in combined cerebellar and labyrinthine injury. *Journal of Nervous and Mental Disease*, 1951, 114, 114–141.

———— & D. P. Kidron. Sensorimotor induction syndrome in unilateral disequilibrium. *Neurology*, 1954, 4, 233–240.

Halpern, L., & J. Landau. Head posture and visual functions. *Monthly Review of Psychiatry and Neurology*, 1953, 125, 148–163.

Hamm, N., & K. Hoving. Age and sex differences in perception of autokinesis in children. *Perceptual and Motor Skills*, 1969, 28, 317–318.

Harmon, H. *Modern factor analysis.* Chicago: University of Chicago Press, 1960.

Hinde, R. A. *Animal behavior: A synthesis of ethology and comparative psychology* (2nd ed.). New York: McGraw-Hill, 1970.

Howard, I. P., & W. B. Templeton. *Human spatial orientation.* New York: Wiley, 1966.

Jaffe, K. Effect of asymmetrical position and directional dynamics of configurations on the visual perception of the horizon. M.A. thesis, Clark University, 1952.

Jordan, S. Autokinesis and felt eye-position. *American Journal of Psychology*, 1968, 81, 497–512.

Kaden, S. E., S. Wapner, & H. Werner. Studies in physiognomic perception: II. Effect of directional dynamics of pictures, objects and of words on the position of the apparent horizon. *Journal of Psychology*, 1955, 39, 61–70.

Kaplan, B. Meditations on genesis. *Human Development*, 1967, 10, 65–87.

Kline, N. S. The effect of tonus-inducing stimuli on the perceived movement of a stationary and of a moving point of light. M.A. thesis, Clark University, 1951.

Kochendorfer, R. Autokinetic motion and body position. M.A. thesis, Clark University, 1968.

Krus, D., S. Wapner, J. Bergen, & H. Freeman. The influence of progesterone on behavioral changes induced by lysergic acid diethylamide (LSD-25) in normal males. *Psychopharmacologia*, 1961, 2, 177–184.

Liebert, R. S., S. Wapner, & H. Werner. Studies in the effect of lysergic acid diethylamide (LSD-25): Visual perception of verticality in schizophrenic and normal adults. *Archives of Neurology and Psychiatry*, 1957, 77, 193–201.

Marshall, J. E. Eye movements and the visual autokinetic phenomenon. *Perceptual and Motor Skills*, 1966, 22, 319–326.

Matin, L., & G. E. MacKinnon. Autokinetic movement: Selective manipulation of directional components by image stabilization. *Science*, 1964, 143, 146–148.

McFarland, J. H., S. Wapner, & H. Werner. The relation between perceived location of objects and perceived location of one's own body. *Perceptual and Motor Skills*, 1962, 15, 331–341.

McFarland, J. H., H. Werner, & S. Wapner. The effect of muscular involvement on sensitivity: Asymmetrical convergence on the distribution of visual sensitivity. *American Journal of Psychology*, 1960, 73, 523–534.

Meisel, P., & S. Wapner. Interaction of factors affecting space location. *Journal of Experimental Psychology*, 1969, 79, 430–437.

Miller, A., H. Werner, & S. Wapner. Studies in physiognomic perception: V. Effect of ascending and descending gliding tones on autokinetic motion. *Journal of Psychology*, 1958, 46, 101–105.

Morant, R. B. Factors influencing the apparent median plane under conditions of labyrinthian stimulation. Ph.D. thesis, Clark University, 1952.

———. The visual perception of the median plane as influenced by labyrinthian stimulation. *Journal of Psychology*, 1959, 47, 25–35.

Moustgaard, I. K. A phenomenological approach to autokinesis. *Scandinavian Journal of Psychology*, 1963, 4, 101–105.

Nagatsuka, Y. [On the effect of observing body condition upon apparent movement and autokinetic movement.] *Tohoku Journal of Experimental Psychology*, 1960, 2, 173–182. (Abstract)

Porzemsky, J., S. Wapner, & J. A. Glick. Effect of experimentally induced self-object cognitive attitudes on body and object perception. *Perceptual and Motor Skills*, 1965, 21, 187–195.

Roelofs, C. O. Optische Lokalisation. *Archiv fur Augenheilkunde*, 1936, 109, 212–224.

Rosenblatt, B. P. The influence of affective states upon the body image and upon the perceptual organization of external space. Ph.D. thesis, Clark University, 1956. (Microfilm No. 18076.)

Sadler, T. G., R. B. Mefferd, Jr., & B. A. Wieland. Extent, direction, and latency of autokinetic movement as a function of placement of an adjacent light. *Perceptual and Motor Skills*, 1966, 23, 1087–1096.

Sziklai, C., S. Wapner, J. H. McFarland, & H. Werner. Effect of tonus changes on perceived location of visual stimuli. *Aerospace Medicine*, 1964, 35, 519–523.

Taylor, J. G. The behavioral basis of perception. New Haven, Conn.: Yale University Press, 1962.

Toch, H. H. The effect of "meaning" on the autokinetic illusion. *American Journal of Psychology*, 1962, 75, 605–611.

———. Interaction of determinants of perceived movement direction. *Perceptual and Motor Skills*, 1963, 16, 621–628.

Toshima, T. The effects of auditory stimuli on visual perception of apparent median plane. *Psychologia — An International Journal of Psychology in the Orient*, 1967, 10, 213–216.

Voth, H. M. Ego autonomy, autokinesis and recovery from psychosis. *Archives of General Psychology*, 1962, 6, 288–293.

Wapner, S. An organismic-developmental approach to the study of perceptual and other cognitive operations, in C. Scheerer, ed., *Cognition: Theory, research, promise*, pp. 6–44. New York: Harper, 1964. (a)

———. Some aspects of a research program based on an organismic-developmental approach to cognition: Experiments and theory. *Journal of the American Academy of Child Psychiatry*, 1964, 3, 193–230. (b)

———. Mechanisms of perception-personality relationships. Progress Report, USPHS Grant No. MH00348, 1966. (a)

———. An organismic-developmental approach to perceived body-object relations, in N. Jenkin & R. H. Pollack, eds., *Proceedings of a conference on perceptual development: Its relation to theories of intelligence and cognition*, pp. 250–288. Chicago: Institute for Juvenile Research, 1966. (b)

———. Age changes in perception of verticality and of the longitudinal body axis under body tilt. *Journal of Experimental Child Psychology*, 1968, 6, 543–555.

———. Organismic-developmental theory: Some application to cognition, in L. Langer, P. H. Mussen, & M. Covington, eds., *Trends and issues in developmental psychology*, pp. 38–67. New York: Holt, 1969.

———, L. Cirillo, & A. H. Baker. Sensory tonic theory: Toward a reformulation. *Archivio di Psicologia, Neurologia e Psichiatria*, 1969, 30, 493–512.

Wapner, S., & D. M. Krus. Behavioral effects of lysergic acid diethylamide (LSD-25): Space localization in normal adults as measured by the apparent horizon. *Archives of General Psychiatry*, 1959, 1, 417–419.

———. Behavioral effects of lysergic acid diethylamide (LSD-25). Progress Report, Grant No. MH-2262, 1960.

Wapner, S., J. Weinberg, J. A. Glick, & G. Rand. Effect of speed of movement on tactual-kinesthetic perception of extent. *American Journal of Psychology*, 1967, 80, 608–613.

Wapner, S., & H. Werner. Gestalt laws of organization and organismic theory of perception: Effect of asymmetry induced by the factor of similarity on the position of the apparent median plane and apparent horizon. *American Journal of Psychology*, 1955, 68, 258–265.

———. *Perceptual development*. Worcester, Mass.: Clark University Press, 1957.

———. An experimental approach to body perception from the organismic-developmental point of view, in S. Wapner & H. Werner, eds., *The body percept*, pp. 9–25. New York: Random House, 1965.

———, J. H. Bruell, & A. G. Goldstein. Experiments on sensory-tonic field theory of perception: VII. Effect of asymmetrical extent and starting position of figures on the visual apparent median plane. *Journal of Experimental Psychology*, 1953, 46, 300–307.

Wapner, S., H. Werner, & K. A. Chandler. Experiments on sensory-tonic field theory of perception: I. Effect of extraneous stimulation on the visual perception of verticality. *Journal of Experimental Psychology*, 1951, 42, 341–345.

Wapner, S., H. Werner, & P. E. Comalli, Jr. Space localization under conditions of danger. *Journal of Psychology*, 1956, 41, 335–346.

Wapner, S., H. Werner, & D. M. Krus. The effect of success and failure on space localization. *Journal of Personality*, 1957, 25, 752–756.

Wapner, S., H. Werner, & R. B. Morant. Experiments on sensory-tonic field theory of perception: III. Effect of body rotation on the visual perception of verticality. *Journal of Experimental Psychology*, 1951, 42, 351–357.

Werner, H. The concept of development from a comparative and organismic point of view, in D. Harris, ed., *The concept of development*. Minneapolis: University of Minnesota Press, 1957.

———. *Comparative psychology of mental development*. New York: Science Editions, 1961.

——— & B. Kaplan. *Symbol formation*. New York: Wiley, 1963.

Werner, H., & S. Wapner. Sensory-tonic theory of perception. *Journal of Personality*, 1949, 18, 88–107.

———. Experiments on sensory-tonic field theory of perception: IV. Effect of initial position of a rod on apparent verticality. *Journal of Experimental Psychology*, 1952, 43, 68–74. (a)

———. A program for the study of the basic mechanisms underlying perception-personality relationships. Progress Report No. 2, Grant MH-348, 1952. (b)

———. Toward a general theory of perception. *Psychological Review*, 1952, 59, 324–338. (c)

———. Studies in physiognomic perception: I. Effect of configurational dynamics and meaning-induced sets on the position of the apparent median plane. *Journal of Psychology*, 1954, 38, 51–65.

———. Sensory-tonic field theory of perception: Basic concepts and experiments. *Revista di Psicologia*, 1956, 50, 315–337.

——— & J. H. Bruell. Experiments on sensory-tonic field theory of perception: VI. Effect of position of head, eyes, and of object on position of the apparent median plane. *Journal of Experimental Psychology*, 1953, 46, 293–299.

Werner, H., S. Wapner, & K. A. Chandler. Experiments on sensory-tonic field theory of perception: II. Effect of supported and unsupported tilt of the body on the visual perception of verticality. *Journal of Experimental Psychology*, 1951, 42, 346.

Wishner, J., & T. E. Shipley. Direction of autokinetic movement as a test of the "sensory-tonic field" theory of perception. *Journal of Personality*, 1954, 23, 99.

*LIST OF CONTRIBUTORS*

# List of Contributors

JACQUELINE GOODNOW, originally from the University of Sydney, is professor of psychology at George Washington University and member of a program emphasizing perceptual and cognitive development. Her Ph.D., in clinical psychology, is from Radcliffe. A long-term interest in cognition, and a more recent interest in problems common to perception and cognition, underlie the work reported in this volume and her current work on the way children deal with two-dimensional representations of their three-dimensional world. Since 1967, she has held a Research Career Development Award from the National Institute of Child Health and Human Development.

ERNEST R. HILGARD, emeritus professor of psychology and education at Stanford University, received his Ph.D. at Yale University and remained there as an instructor until moving to Stanford in 1933, where he has been ever since, except for wartime service in Washington. His interests have ranged widely over problems of human and animal learning, motivation, social behavior, and, more recently, the study of hypnotic phenomena, as reflected in this volume. He spent a year studying child development on sabbatical at the University of Chicago in 1940, and is at present president of the Board of Trustees of a private experimental elementary school specifically devoted to the encouragement of creativity. Although formally retired, he continues to teach and to conduct research at Stanford.

JANE V. HUNT received her Ph.D. in child development from the University of California at Berkeley. Following three years of clinical diagnostic work with handicapped infants and young children, she joined the staff of

207

the Institute of Human Development at the University of California, Berkeley, where she is an assistant research psychologist. Her research interests include prediction of adult mental abilities from early infant and preschool measures derived from longitudinal studies and early cognitive patterns in mental retardation. NANCY BAYLEY, now retired, was formerly research psychologist at the Institute of Human Development, University of California at Berkeley. She received her Ph.D. from the State University of Iowa and came to the University of California in 1928 as a research associate at the Institute of Child Welfare. For a nine-year interim period, starting in 1954, she was chief of the Section on Early Development in the Laboratory of Psychology of the National Institute of Mental Health, Bethesda, Maryland. Her professional career has included terms as president of the Society for Research in Child Development, of the Western Psychological Association, and of the American Psychological Association's Divisions on Developmental Psychology and Maturity and Old Age. In 1966 she received the Distinguished Scientific Contribution Award from the American Psychological Association.

GERALD R. PATTERSON is a research associate at Oregon Research Institute, Eugene, where he directs a project studying the families of hyperaggressive children; he is a research professor in the College of Education, University of Oregon, has held a Research Scientist Development Award since 1968, and is a consultant to the Review Committee for the Center for Studies in Crime and Delinquency, in the National Institute of Mental Health. He has published widely in professional journals and other publications, primarily in the areas of social learning, behavior modification, and child clinical psychology. JOSEPH A. COBB is a research associate at Oregon Research Institute, Eugene, where he is part of a team working with families of hyperaggressive children under an NIMH grant. He is also an assistant professor in the Special Education Department, College of Education, University of Oregon, and is developing an academic survival skill program for preschool and primary school children at the Center for Research and Demonstration in the Early Education of Handicapped Children.

EARL S. SCHAEFER, who received a Ph.D. in psychology from the Catholic University of America, has been on the staff of the National Institute of Mental Health since 1953. Conceptualization and measurement of parent behavior and child behavior at the Laboratory of Psychology, NIMH, with

Richard Q. Bell and Nancy Bayley, led to the development of circular and spherical models for those domains. His findings at the conclusion of the Infant Education Research Project suggested the need for intervention research on early child care and education by the family, which in turn led to his present position as Chief of the Section on Early Child Care Research, Center for Studies of Child and Family Mental Health, National Institute of Mental Health.

SEYMOUR WAPNER is G. Stanley Hall Professor of Genetic Psychology and chairman of the Department of Psychology at Clark University. A Michigan Ph.D., he taught at the University of Rochester and Brooklyn College before coming to Clark. His programmatic researches in perception, cognition, and the relations between perception and personality have been informed by and instrumental in the development of organismic-developmental theory. LEONARD CIRILLO received his Ph.D. in clinical psychology from Clark University. After holding positions at the University of Denver and Yeshiva University, he returned to Clark, where he is currently associate professor of psychology. A. HARVEY BAKER received his Ph.D. in developmental and experimental psychology from Clark University in 1968. After spending a further year at Clark as a research associate, he joined the Human Developmental Group of Educational Testing Service as a research psychologist.

*INDEX*

# Index